The Force of Truth

The Force of Truth

CRITIQUE, GENEALOGY, AND TRUTH-TELLING IN MICHEL FOUCAULT

Daniele Lorenzini

The University of Chicago Press   CHICAGO AND LONDON

The University of Chicago Press, Chicago 60637
The University of Chicago Press, Ltd., London
© 2023 by The University of Chicago
Published 2023
Printed in the United States of America

32 31 30 29 28 27 26 25 24 23   1 2 3 4 5

ISBN-13: 978-0-226-82743-8 (cloth)
ISBN-13: 978-0-226-82745-2 (paper)
ISBN-13: 978-0-226-82744-5 (e-book)
DOI: https://doi.org/10.7208/chicago/9780226827445.001.0001

© Le Bord de l'eau éditions, July 2017
Original title: *La force du vrai: De Foucault à Austin*
Translated, revised, and expanded by the author.

Library of Congress Cataloging-in-Publication Data

Names: Lorenzini, Daniele, author, translator.
Title: The force of truth : critique, genealogy, and truth-telling
  in Michel Foucault / Daniele Lorenzini.
Other titles: Force du vrai. English | Critique, genealogy, and
  truth-telling in Michel Foucault
Description: Chicago : The University of Chicago Press, 2023. |
  Originally published as La force du vrai : de Foucault à
  Austin. | Includes bibliographical references and index.
Identifiers: LCCN 2022056832 | ISBN 9780226827438 (cloth) |
  ISBN 9780226827452 (paperback) | ISBN 9780226827445
  (ebook)
Subjects: LCSH: Foucault, Michel, 1926–1984. | Truth.
Classification: LCC B2430.F724 L6613 2023 | DDC 194—dc23/
  eng/20230206
LC record available at https://lccn.loc.gov/2022056832

♾ This paper meets the requirements of ANSI/NISO Z39.48-1992
(Permanence of Paper).

Contents

INTRODUCTION

Writing the History of Truth

Does truth have a history? This question still occupies a central place in contemporary philosophical and political debate. Those who give it a negative answer routinely argue that—alongside Friedrich Nietzsche, the American pragmatists, French historical epistemologists such as Gaston Bachelard and Georges Canguilhem, Ludwig Wittgenstein, or Thomas Kuhn—it is clearly the "postmodern" thinkers, and among them in particular Michel Foucault, who deserve the most blame for reducing truth to a mere historical accident. Foucault is indeed commonly considered to be one of the main champions of relativism about truth;[1] and because of his enormous influence in virtually all fields of the humanities and social sciences, he is regularly accused of being the tutelary father of the contemporary devaluation of truth and "facts"—in other words, of the current "post-truth era." For instance, in *Post-Truth*, Lee McIntyre writes:

> Even if right-wing politicians and other science deniers were not reading Derrida and Foucault, the germ of the idea made its way to them: science does not have a monopoly on the truth. It is therefore not unreasonable to think that right-wingers are using some of the same arguments and techniques of postmodernism to attack the truth of other scientific claims that clash with their conservative ideology.[2]

We must criticize Foucault, we are told, because we must resist the idea that truth is a mere historical epiphenomenon and, what is more, nothing else than a side effect of power relations.

This influential, almost unquestioned way of interpreting Foucault mostly derives from a (mis)reading of his arguments in *The Order of Things* and *Discipline and Punish*, his debate with Noam Chomsky, or his short text "The Political Function of the Intellectual."[3] It dates back to—at least—the 1980s, when prominent philosophers and political theorists such as Nancy Fraser, Jürgen Habermas, and Charles Taylor started criticizing Foucault for claiming that "there is no truth that can be espoused, defended, or rescued against systems of power," because "each such system defines its own variant of truth."[4] Hilary Putnam, too, blames Foucault for "attacking our present notion of rationality from within" by suggesting that "the beliefs we hold right now are no more rational than the medieval belief in the Divine Right of Kings," and that "our present ideology is the product of forces that are irrational *by its own lights*."[5]

Forty years later, the charge has become even more damning: by disqualifying all claims to objectivity and thereby reducing truth to a historically situated epiphenomenon of power dynamics in a given society, Foucault and the other postmodern thinkers effectively removed out from under us all stable ground for drawing a distinction between "what we have a reason to think and what mere relations of power are doing to our thinking"[6]—or between, say, a serious scientific study about the effects of climate change and a tweet by Donald Trump claiming there is no such thing as climate change. As Daniel Dennett concisely puts it in an interview with *The Guardian*,

> I think what the postmodernists did was truly evil. They are responsible for the intellectual fad that made it respectable to be cynical about truth and facts.[7]

A History of Truth That Does Not Rely on "the Truth"

Leaving aside the most sensationalist claims, this line of criticism warrants serious consideration. To do so, I will briefly address one of the most systematic recent attacks on Foucault's views about truth: Jacques Bouveresse's book, *Nietzsche contre Foucault*.[8] Indeed, I take Bouveresse's main arguments to constitute a paradigmatic example of a traditional and still very influential way of conceiving the relation between truth and history that this book aims to call into question, in order to offer the first comprehensive interpretation of Foucault's "history of truth."

Drawing from some of the ideas that Bernard Williams defends in *Truth and Truthfulness*, Bouveresse argues that it is one thing to say that there can be a history of "different ways of distinguishing between truth and falsity, and of formulating or establishing the truth," but it is an entirely different thing to say that "truth itself has a history."[9] Thus, for him, there is, on the one hand, "the Truth"—a timeless and suprahistorical concept, minimally defined by (but, importantly, *not* reducible to) Alfred Tarski's material adequacy condition according to which "'Snow is white' is true if and only if snow is white"—and, on the other hand, "the knowledge we have of the truth, the criteria we rely on to decide whether a proposition is true or not, the greater or lesser importance we give to truth and falsehood respectively," which "unquestionably" have a history.[10] In all fairness, Bouveresse does voice some reservations about the "assurance" with which Williams maintains that "the concept of truth itself—that is to say, the quite basic role that truth plays in relation to language, meaning, and belief—is not culturally various, but always and everywhere the same," that "everybody everywhere" has "the same concept of truth," and that "the fact that they may have very different theories of truth just shows how much people's theories of truth misrepresent their grasp of the concept."[11] However, Bouveresse ultimately admits that he agrees with Williams's claims, thus distancing himself from a minimalist conception of truth.[12]

One of the postulates on which Bouveresse's approach implicitly relies is therefore what I would call a certain Platonism about truth: to say that truth has a history would entail for him contradicting or negating the very concept of truth, thereby reducing it to a mere illusion. In his book, Bouveresse refers to Nietzsche's essay "On Truth and Lie in an Extra-Moral Sense" (1873), in which Nietzsche famously claims that truths are but illusions whose nature has been forgotten.[13] But while, according to Bouveresse, Nietzsche's later writings show that he eventually changed his mind on this subject, Foucault somehow remained a "prisoner" of this idea throughout his entire life. It is this idea, Bouveresse concludes, that animates Foucault's project of writing a history of truth, thereby rendering it simply untenable.[14]

It is worth emphasizing that, in order to substantiate his conclusion, Bouveresse exclusively addresses Foucault's inaugural lecture and first lecture course at the Collège de France, in 1970–71,[15] and takes virtually no interest in the later lectures and writings in which Foucault—as this book will show—significantly developed, clarified, and in part transformed his way of conceiving of a history of truth.[16] It should also be stressed that, in these texts and lectures, Foucault never claims that truth is but an illusion. On the contrary, Foucault's work is perfectly compatible with a minimalist conception of truth, even though he never explicitly defended it, because ultimately he was not interested in elaborating any specific theory of truth.[17] What *is* an illusion, in Foucault's view, is rather "the Truth" understood in a Platonic fashion as a timeless and suprahistorical Idea.[18]

Therefore, when Bouveresse polemically asks how the history of something that does not exist, that is, the truth, can be written, he is actually tilting at windmills, since he *equates* the claim that "the Truth" does not exist with the claim that truth does not exist. "The history of truth," he writes, "cannot be the history of truth," but "must necessarily be the history of something other than what it presents itself to be the history of."[19] Thus, when Foucault speaks of a history of truth, he is "actually speaking of a history of things that are related in various ways to the truth and that are likely, for their part, to really have a history."[20] Foucault would in fact agree with this conclusion, if the "truth" Bouveresse describes were to be understood in minimalist terms—that is, without assuming it possesses any sort of underlying essence or suprahistorical nature.[21] Yet, even though Bouveresse does not deny the existence of different, historically situated "games of truth" (to use a Foucauldian terminology that he would likely reject), he explicitly postulates, *outside* of these games, a suprahistorical concept of Truth that constitutes their raison d'être and in light of which their claim to distinguish truth from falsity can (and must) be assessed:

> A clear distinction must be drawn between, on the one hand, the means and procedures we have at our disposal at any given time to decide whether a statement is true or false, and which are historically situated, contingent, modifiable, imperfect, and fallible, and on the other hand, the truth or falsity of the statement, which can very well be ascertained without us having anything to do with it.[22]

Drawing from Foucault, I shall argue that, on the contrary, we *always* have something to do with it, and that there is no *vérité du dehors*, that is, no Truth external to a series of historically situated games of truth that establish the rules for obtaining it—and thereby, as we will see, no Truth external to a given regime of truth that determines "the obligations of individuals with regard to procedures of manifestation of truth."[23] Indeed, one of the main claims of this book will be that, as soon as we depart from a minimalist understanding of the word "truth" and start analyzing the concept or the nature of truth, or the conditions necessary and sufficient for something to count as true or for someone to count as a teller of the truth, we necessarily enter the realm of history—as well as of ethics and politics. Foucault's project of writing a "history of truth," correctly understood, is thus perfectly tenable, and very far from merely a naive postmodern attack on the existence of truth or facts.

In light of these considerations, it is also possible to make better sense of the title that Foucault gave to a lecture on Nietzsche he delivered at McGill University in 1971: "How to Think the History of Truth with Nietzsche without Relying on Truth."[24] What constitutes a contradiction in terms in Bouveresse's eyes becomes perfectly intelligible as soon as we realize that, for Foucault, to think the history of truth without relying on truth (or better, on "the Truth") does not mean, as he explicitly argues, to think such a history "in an element where truth does not exist."[25] It rather means, *without* calling our minimalist understanding of the word "truth" into question, to show that there is no such thing as a suprahistorical concept or underlying essence that defines "the Truth"—and that, *in this sense*, "truth itself has a history."[26] This history, as we will see, ends up taking in Foucault's work the form of a *genealogy* of some of the principal "regimes of truth" that characterize our contemporary society (what I call the scientific, confessional, and critical regimes of truth, respectively); a genealogy, or a historical narrative, that "refuses the certainty of absolutes" and "rejects the metahistorical deployment of ideal significations and indefinite teleologies" in order to "dispel the chimeras of the origin" conceived as the "site of truth."[27]

Therefore, Foucault's project of writing a history of truth—by which he means a history (or better, a genealogy) of regimes of truth—far from entailing the claim that truth does not exist, draws from Nietzsche in that it aims to problematize the *value* of truth. There is an intuitive connection between the revelation of the historicity of a given belief, concept, or practice and its (at least potential) devaluation. This is what Amia Srinivasan aptly calls "genealogical anxiety": the worry that historical contingency could undermine the (epistemic, political, ethical) value of our beliefs, concepts, and practices.[28] Unsurprisingly, this worry is particularly acute when it comes to the concept of truth, because knowing the truth—about the world, about others, and about oneself—is normally construed as *intrinsically* valuable. Why is that? This, I argue, is the fundamental question that Foucault's history of truth ultimately raises and aims to examine— a question that is not exactly inspired by Nietzsche's claims in "On Truth and Lie in an Extra-Moral Sense," as Bouveresse suggests, but rather by some of the most famous passages of the third essay of his *Genealogy*:

From the very moment that faith in the God of the ascetic ideal is denied, *there is a new problem as well*: that of the *value* of truth.—The will to truth needs a critique—let us define our own task with this—the value of truth must for once be experimentally *called into question*.[29]

What value does truth possess? Far from claiming that it does not possess any, and that we must simply do away with it, Nietzsche and Foucault both question the "unconditional" nature of our will to truth, that is, the idea that it needs no justification, since truth must be conceived as intrinsically valuable.[30] Following Nietzsche and Canguilhem, Foucault argues that this idea is deeply rooted in the modern, scientific regime of truth, but importantly, for him, it also characterizes the confessional and critical regimes of truth in our contemporary society.[31] As I will show, writing a history of truth therefore means, for Foucault, tracing a genealogy of these regimes of truth in order to open up the conceptual and political space that allows us to ask after their effects and value: to problematize the effects and to revalue the value of truth. When, throughout this book, I refer to Foucault's project of a history of truth, this is therefore what I take the expression "history of truth" to mean.

Toward an Ethics and Politics of Truth-Telling

In the lecture on March 11, 1981, of his course at the Collège de France, *Subjectivity and Truth*, Foucault argues that "the reality to which a discourse refers, whatever it may be, cannot be the raison d'être of that discourse itself," because "the existence of a true discourse, of a veridical discourse, of a discourse with the function of veridiction . . . is never entailed by the reality of the things of which it speaks."[32] Indeed, according to Foucault, "the game of truth is always a singular historical event, an ultimately improbable event in relation to that of which it speaks."[33] It is precisely this *singular historical event* that we must strive to reconstruct:

> To do the history of the truth, of games of truth, of practices, economies, and politics of veridiction, [presupposes that one cannot in any way] be content with saying: If such a truth has been said, it is because that truth was real. One must say rather: Reality being what it is, what were the improbable conditions, the insular conditions that meant that a game of truth could appear in relation to that reality, certainly a game of truth with its reasons, its necessities, but reasons and necessities that are not simply the fact that the things in question existed?[34]

The above-cited passages should discourage any attempt at characterizing Foucault as an "irrealist," that is, as someone who denies the existence of an extralinguistic reality and maintains that reality is but a function of discourse.[35] They also spell out a further insight that is crucial for his project of a history of truth: the *existence* of a given true discourse or a given game of truth can never be explained solely on the basis of its reference to or correspondence with reality. Of course, within many of our most ordinary and common games of truth, correspondence with reality does make it possible to establish the truth value of a statement: "It is because the sky is blue that it is true to say: the sky is blue."[36] Foucault's point is not to deny the epistemic legitimacy of these games of truth, but to problematize the idea that their historical emergence can be accounted for solely by referring to the existence of a given reality. In short, any analysis that refers "the game of truth to reality by saying: 'The game of truth is explained because the real is such'" is, according to Foucault, "absolutely untenable and insufficient," because "reality will never account for that particular, singular, and improbable reality of the game of truth in reality."[37] If that were the case, there would be no point in writing a (genealogical) history of truth. Indeed, it seems that *any* kind of genealogical project must be somehow committed to this claim—not only "subversive" genealogies such as Nietzsche's or Foucault's, but also the "vindicatory" state of nature genealogies elaborated by Edward Craig, Bernard Williams, and Miranda Fricker.[38] The latter too, by relying on the definition of a series of basic needs that aim to explain why it was necessary for the survival of human beings to elaborate shared games of truth centered on testimonial practices and information pooling, clearly emphasize the *instrumental* origins of such games,[39] and thus (implicitly) substantiate Foucault's insight that reality alone is not enough to account for their historical emergence and their continuing existence.

This explains why Foucault's history of truth is also, at the same time, a history of truth-*telling*: its aim is to genealogically trace the emergence of true discourses, not in the abstract, nor by considering them simply entailed by the reality of which they speak, but by construing them as singular events in human history. Thus, it is clear that a history of truth must also ask the question of *who* can and actually does utter them, in what circumstances, and at what cost. In recent years, Foucault's analyses of different historical forms of truth-telling—from ancient *parrhesia* and Christian confession to juridical avowal and psychoanalytic discourse—have attracted growing attention in the Anglophone scholarly literature.[40] What is still lacking, however, is an account that situates them systematically within the broader context of his project of a history of truth, while addressing the latter's philosophical, ethical, and political implications in detail. This gap is striking, but it can no doubt be explained by reference to the fact that—even though his work is compatible with a minimalist conception of truth—Foucault was not interested in *defining* what truth is, nor in elaborating or defending a specific *theory* of truth.[41] Foucault's project of a history of truth aims to examine some of the principal games and regimes of truth that have emerged throughout human history; more precisely, it aims to trace the genealogy of the regimes of truth that he considers most relevant for us today. Instead of reducing the question of truth to a purely logical or epistemological question, or to the philosophical task of elaborating a suprahistorical definition or theory of truth, Foucault incessantly asks us to be *surprised* by the proliferation of true discourses and never to take their emergence and existence for granted.

I believe this is why Foucault's project of a history of truth has so far never received sustained attention in the Anglophone scholarly literature, with most scholars finding his (apparently) scattered remarks on truth confusing at best, confused or contradictory at worst. Foucault's history of truth has never been considered rigorous: how can we write the history of truth without first defining what truth is? And, if Foucault had defined truth, he would obviously have realized that the history he wanted to write was not the history of truth, but the history of something else. As I argued above, however, this line of criticism misses the point, and it has prevented scholars from devoting attention to one of the most relevant aspects of Foucault's work[42] — the common thread that connects his 1980s-era analyses of truth-telling, techniques of the self, and subjectivation to his interest, throughout the 1970s, in Nietzschean genealogy, power/knowledge mechanisms, and the "politics of truth."[43]

It is through a close confrontation with Nietzsche that Foucault, in 1970 and 1971, initially elaborates his project of a history of truth, and at the same time manifests his interest in the genealogical method—albeit still only as an object of study.[44] However, this project does not take a full-fledged form until his 1973–74 lecture course at the Collège de France *Psychiatric Power*. There, and more specifically in the lecture on January 23, 1974, not only does Foucault sketch "a little history of truth in general" centered on the distinction between "truth-event" and "truth-demonstration" (one that, albeit modified, will prove crucial going forward), but he also uses the term "genealogy" to describe *his own* approach for the first time.[45] Consequently, the focus of this book will be on Foucault's project of a history of truth from 1974 to 1984. One of its main aims will be to show that this project is nourished, not only by a confrontation with Nietzsche, but also by a—mostly implicit, but no less crucial—dialogue with early analytic philosophy of language, and in particular with ordinary language philosophers such as Ludwig Wittgenstein and J. L. Austin.

The upshot will be to newly understand Foucault's history of truth as part and parcel of—or perhaps the necessary correlate to—an ethics and politics of truth-telling whose contemporary relevance this book sets out to establish. To do so, first, I rely on the theoretical and methodological tools elaborated by Foucault in *Psychiatric Power* and *On the Government of the Living* to argue for the need to question a purely logical or epistemological conception of truth, and examine instead the complex ethical and political dimensions of the practice of truth-telling. Drawing from

Foucault's analysis of ancient *parrhesia*, I then define it as a speech act whose effects pertain to a domain that has so far been widely neglected by the philosophy of language: the perlocutionary domain. More precisely, through a close engagement with J. L. Austin's work on performative utterance and illocutionary force, and with Stanley Cavell's writings on passionate utterance, I argue that the main function of *parrhesia* is to manifest the ethical and political relation of human beings to truth. Hence, far from being limited to its pragmatic force, the performativity of language requires analysis of its "dramatic" dimensions, that is, its contribution to the shaping of the subject herself. With words, we do not only do *things*; we also create and transform *ourselves* as subjects. Finally, I argue that Foucault's genealogy of some of the principal regimes of truth that characterize contemporary society, including the "critical" one, allows us to examine what I call the possibilizing dimension of his genealogical method, along with its specific normativity. I thus provide a rebuttal to a major criticism raised against Foucauldian genealogy, most famously by Nancy Fraser and Jürgen Habermas: that it lacks normative force and is therefore incapable of telling us why we should resist the mechanisms of power it reveals. This charge, however, misses the point: it conceives Foucauldian genealogy exclusively as a subversive or problematizing method, whereas I show that Foucault's genealogical project also aims to reveal that each power/knowledge apparatus, or better, each specific regime of truth, has already been contested by multiple forms of counter-conduct that are *normatively significant* for us because they concretely embody "the possibility of no longer being, doing, or thinking what we are, do, or think."[46]

By advancing a new reading of Foucault's project of a history of truth as a genealogy of the most relevant contemporary regimes of truth, and deriving an ethics and politics of truth-telling from it, this book also aims to reevaluate Foucault's critical project as a whole, to shed light on its (implicit) normative commitments, and to defend its current ethico-political relevance.

The Force of Words and the Force of Truth

Rethinking the role of critique today, especially in its relation to truth and truth-telling, is indeed a particularly delicate and urgent task.[47] Under what conditions is "telling the truth" an effective critical activity? And does the critical aspect of the practice of truth-telling exclusively depend on the revelation of "truths"? If we understand "truth" as synonymous with evidence or "facts," the answer to the last question is clearly negative. Indeed, contemporary examples such as the migrant crisis in the Mediterranean show that the accumulation of evidence and facts about the violence perpetrated on migrants, in the attempt to expose the deadly effects of EU policies of migration containment, is certainly enough to *prove* the point. Yet it is not enough to *disrupt* these policies, nor the rise of racism and xenophobia in Europe.[48] Unfortunately, truth and facts *alone* are not enough to sustain an effective critical practice—and they are not enough because they have no force *in and of themselves*.[49] This, of course, does not mean that we should ignore facts, nor merely avoid talking about truth in the political and ethical spheres.[50] It instead means—or so I argue—that one of the most important questions to raise in elaborating an ethics and politics of truth-telling is the question of the *force of truth*, or of "truth as a force."[51]

The mounting chorus of objections is already making itself heard:[52] the truth is certainly not a force among other forces, and if it does have a "force," it is a sui generis (an exclusively "rational") one. After all, once the truth is established, far from "forcing" us in any way, it "frees" us from previous prejudices or false opinions. In other words, truth and force (or power) must be radically pulled apart: where there is one, there is no room for the other, and vice versa. However, the idea that "truth does not belong to the order of power, but shares an original affinity with freedom" is precisely the kind of philosophical myth that Foucault's "political history of truth" aims to question—not in order to naively *reduce* truth to power, but to open up the conceptual space that allows us to examine the complex issue of their *relations* anew.[53] Foucault's genealogy of some of the most relevant contemporary regimes of truth, and his analysis of the practice of *parrhesia* (which I suggest interpreting in light of the notion of perlocutionary effect), are crucial aspects of this critical endeavor, which—as we shall see—ultimately aims to transform the specific truth-power-subject nexus on which contemporary governmental strategies rely.[54]

The question of the force of truth is thus closely connected with the question of the force of words, that is, of the capacity that words have to *do* things—or, as Oswald Ducrot puts it, to transform reality.[55] As I will argue, however, to raise this question in relation to *parrhesia* means to cast doubt on the idea that the performativity of language relies exclusively on the execution of a certain conventional or institutional procedure—the idea, in other words, that in order to produce effects on reality, language must follow and, in a way, *reproduce* already established norms. By contrast, the perlocutionary analysis of parrhesiastic utterance bears witness to the capacity that words have to *subvert* established norms, thus transforming reality in unforeseen and unforeseeable ways—as the recent examples of BLM and the #MeToo movement clearly show.

In *How to Do Things with Words*, Austin famously argues that, in order to be "happy" or "felicitous"—that is, to exert (illocutionary) force
and, hence, to do what it says—a performative utterance must satisfy six
conditions. The first condition (A.1) stipulates that "there must exist an
accepted conventional procedure having a certain conventional effect, that
procedure to include the uttering of certain words by certain persons in
certain circumstances"; the second condition (A.2) establishes that "the
particular persons and circumstances in a given case must be appropriate
for the invocation of the particular procedure invoked."[56] In *Language and
Symbolic Power*, Pierre Bourdieu aptly remarks that these conditions are
not linguistic, but sociological:

> The question of performative utterances becomes clearer if one sees it as
> a particular case of the effects of symbolic domination, which occurs in
> all linguistic exchanges. The linguistic relation of forces is never defined
> solely by the relation between the linguistic competences present. And
> the weight of different agents depends on their symbolic capital, that
> is, on the *recognition*, institutionalized or not, that they receive from a
> group. Symbolic imposition—that kind of magical efficacy which not
> only the command and the password, but also ritual discourse or a simple
> injunction, or even threats or insults, purport to exert—can function only
> if there is a convergence of social conditions which are altogether distinct
> from the strictly linguistic logic of discourse.[57]

In other words, according to Bourdieu, "the whole social structure
is present in each interaction (and thereby in the discourse uttered)."[58]
Consequently, "the performative utterance, as an act of institution, cannot socio-logically exist independently of the institution which gives it
its raison d'être": its claim "to act on the social world through words, i.e.
magically, is more or less crazy or reasonable depending on whether it
is more or less based on the objectivity of the social world."[59] However,
as we shall see, a surprising shift occurs in Bourdieu's argument when
these conclusions, which definitely hit the mark as far as Austin's definition of performative utterance goes, are applied to *all* forms of linguistic
exchange.[60] Indeed, in order to criticize linguistic reductionism and the
idea that the force of words lies in the words themselves, Bourdieu risks
falling into a radical sociological reductionism. Specifically, he risks denying that words can *ever* "break" with socially established conventions and
norms, thereby maintaining that their effects on reality are *always* socially
determined—a conclusion that Judith Butler rightly rejects, referring to
it as a "conservative account of the speech act."[61]

While I agree with Bourdieu's critique of linguistic reductionism, since the force words have clearly does not lie exclusively in the words themselves—just as the force that true discourses have does not lie exclusively in their being true—I will argue that Austin's insights also open up the possibility of addressing this force *beyond* its conventionally or institutionally determined effects. Two main paths can be followed to explore this possibility further.

The first path was inaugurated by Jacques Derrida in "Signature Event Context" and developed by Judith Butler in *Excitable Speech*.[62] The point here is to reinterpret Austin's notions of performative utterance and illocutionary force such that performative "infelicities"—or, at least, some of them—are considered to be forms that illocutionary force itself can take, and more precisely ways for speech to *resist* the norms that regulate it and to *break* with its context. The "insurrectionary potential" of speech is thus sought on the side of the functioning, or rather the *dysfunctioning*, of performative utterances: according to Butler, language is not "a static and closed system whose utterances are functionally secured in advance by the 'social positions' to which they are mimetically related."[63] On the contrary, "an utterance may gain its force precisely by virtue of the break with context that it performs," and *this* is what is crucial for the "political operation of the performative."[64]

Building on Derrida's reading of *How to Do Things with Words*, Butler thus argues—against Bourdieu—that performative force can also be exerted by rehearsing "conventional formulae in non-conventional ways": false or wrong invocations should be understood as *reiterations* that are capable (at least potentially) of "challenging existing forms of legitimacy," of breaking with them and introducing "the possibility of future forms," thus opening the performative onto an "unpredictable future."[65] In short, according to Derrida and Butler, it is from its *iterability*, that is, its capacity to break with preestablished contexts and "to assume new contexts," that the performative derives its force—one that Butler, drawing from the work of Shoshana Felman, examines specifically in relation to "the status of speech as a bodily act" and the "rhetorical effects of the body which speaks."[66]

While recognizing the interest and political relevance of these analyses, this book takes a different path, one pioneered by Cavell in his seminal work on passionate utterance. Thus, instead of reinterpreting the notions of performative utterance and illocutionary force in a way that significantly departs from the meaning Austin originally ascribed to them, I draw from his succinct analysis of the perlocutionary effect, as well as from Foucault's lectures and writings on *parrhesia*, in analyzing the issue of the force that words—or better, *some* words, in *certain* circumstances—hold in relation to socially established conventions and norms. The perlocutionary analysis of *parrhesia* remains of course sensitive to social context and to the specific situation in which the parrhesiastic discourse is uttered. It also remains faithful to one of the main intuitions of Foucault's *Archaeology of Knowledge*,[67] which Jocelyn Benoist effectively summarizes as follows:

> Whatever one does with language (including "speech acts"), one never does it except by borrowing possible statements, that is, statements which are already formed and available, or by inventing them, that is, by uttering statements which are not yet formed but nevertheless possible at that moment given the actual discursive configuration in which one finds oneself.[68]

However, I argue that this does not condemn us to merely *reproducing* socially established conventions and norms. On the contrary, as so many historical and contemporary examples show, a statement uttered in a given context and in a certain way by a subject who decides to "speak out" *can* introduce a break with those conventions and norms.[69] Examining this possibility in light of the notion of perlocutionary effect, instead of redefining illocutionary force, allows us to better grasp its precarious and fragile nature, and to show more clearly that some of the most relevant consequences of our words are, at the time that we utter them, essentially *indeterminate*—they will only take on a given form "as we go along."[70]

At the same time, as I pointed out above, in addressing *parrhesia* it is impossible to separate the force of words from the force of truth—which is why, as we shall see, *parrhesia* should not be reduced to mere rhetoric. In Austin, Bourdieu, Derrida, Butler, and Cavell, the issue of the force of words is always carefully isolated from any discussion of questions of meaning and truth. By contrast, the perlocutionary analysis of *parrhesia* shows that truth plays a crucial role when it comes to the *critical force* that speech can exert within and upon a given network of power relations. As we shall see, however, this entails redefining truth-telling as an *ethos*, that is, as a way of living and being, and thus conceiving of truth—at least in this context—as an ethico-political force.

While this redefinition of truth as *ethos* and perlocutionary force is in keeping with Austin's and Cavell's respective attempts to bring the philosophical concern with (constative, logical, or epistemological) truth "down to size," I will show that it does not entail a naive reduction of truth to mere force.[71] Indeed, to examine the link between the force of words and the force of truth, and to maintain that truth can play—under certain conditions—the role of an ethico-political force, does not entail following Derrida in arguing that Austin simply got rid of the "truth/ falsehood fetish" by replacing it, in a supposedly Nietzschean move, with the sole reality of "force" understood in a naturalist and voluntarist sense.[72] As Cavell rightly argues,

> Austin's introduction of an idea of force, his "substitution" of something about force for something about truth is meant not as a revelation of truth as illusion or as will to power (if something of the sort is what Derrida signals as "Nietzschean"), but rather as specifying the extent to which what may be called the value of truth—call it an adequation of language and reality, or a discovering of reality—is on the contrary as essential to performative as to constative utterances.[73]

Building on this intuition, and through the discussion of Foucault's history of truth and the perlocutionary analysis of *parrhesia*, this book ultimately aims to investigate the conditions and principal features of critical discourse and attitude within the context of an ethics and politics of truth-telling—that is, in their complex relations with power, subjectivity, and truth.[74]

Truth-Event

One of the most distinctive features of Foucault's work in the 1970s and 1980s is his relentless examination of the multiple historical forms taken by the connection between knowledge, power, and individualization — or better, as he begins to put it around 1978, between the ways in which truth is produced or manifested, the procedures through which human beings are governed, and the processes by which their subjectivity is constituted (in terms of both "subjection" and "subjectivation").[1] It is notably in the first half of his 1980 lecture course at the Collège de France, *On the Government of the Living,* that Foucault forges a set of methodological and conceptual tools that prove essential in addressing the following questions: Why does the reference to truth play such a constant and crucial role in the procedures through which human beings are governed and constituted as subjects? How can we make sense and characterize this role? Foucault's history of truth sets out to respond precisely to these questions.

"A Little History of Truth in General"

To write a history of truth we must, first and foremost, dislodge a certain conception of truth from the dominant position it occupies in modern and contemporary society, as well as in our philosophical discourse — a conception of truth, that is, which presents truth as a universal and suprahistorical concept. In his 1973–74 lecture course, *Psychiatric Power,* Foucault makes clear that metaphysical and epistemological conceptions of truth constitute privileged objects of genealogical *problematization* for him,[2] while his main aim consists in systematically widening and pluralizing the ways in which we think about truth — encompassing, most notably, the political and ethical domains. Therefore, as he puts it in the lecture on January 23, 1974, his history of truth is predicated on a conceptual shift from the limited, policed concept of "truth-demonstration" to the broader, pro-

tean concept of "truth-event."[3] This shift is analogous to the one Foucault
already called for in his first series of lectures at the Collège de France, *The
Will to Know*—from knowledge as *connaissance* to knowledge as *savoir*:

> The undertaking then is this. Is it possible to do a history whose reference
> would not be a system of subject and object—a theory of knowledge-
> *connaissance*—but that would be addressed to the events of knowledge-
> *savoir* and to the effect of knowledge-*connaissance* internal to these events?
> The problem is one of gauging the possibility of reversing the traditional
> configuration that posits knowledge-*connaissance*—as form or faculty—as
> precondition and then the events of knowledge-*savoir* as singular acts that
> actualize this faculty and may in some cases modify its form.[4]

It is to this undertaking that Foucault devotes most of his work in the
1970s and 1980s. The distinction he draws in the above-cited passage between knowledge-*connaissance* and knowledge-*savoir* is examined (and
reworked) in more detail in 1974, within the context of a striking "paren-
thesis" in which Foucault sketches "a little history of truth in general."
There, Foucault establishes a distinction between two types, or rather two
"series" of truths—a distinction that, as it turns out, should not be interpreted as a straightforward opposition.

On the one hand, there is what Foucault calls the scientific (or logico-
scientific, or epistemological) conception of truth, which he claims is
characterized by two main features. First, it posits that "there is truth
everywhere, in every place, and all the time."[5] This is the *principle of the
omnipresence of the truth*: it is always possible to pose the question of truth,
and to pose it about everything. Of course, as Foucault remarks, there are
moments "when the truth is grasped more easily, points of view that allow
it to be perceived more easily or certainly, and instruments for discovering
it where it is hidden, remote, or buried."[6] Indeed, the fact that the truth is
supposed to be everywhere does not entail that it is always easy to grasp;
on the contrary, to attain the truth may require the implementation of
very complex and difficult operations. However, this difficulty remains
a function of the circumstances in which one finds oneself, as well as of
one's own limitations. In other words, it depends on the individual or
her society, and not on truth itself, which is always there waiting to be
"discovered":

> For scientific practice in general, there is always the truth; the truth is
> always present, in or under every thing, and the question of truth can be

posed about anything and everything. . . . This means that for a scientific type of knowledge nothing is too small, trivial, ephemeral, or occasional for the question of truth, nothing too distant or close to hand for us to put the question: what are you in truth [*en vérité*]?[7]

As we shall see, this same question—"What are you in truth?"—also characterizes the confessional regime of truth that Foucault begins to examine in 1975, thus acquiring a more explicit ethico-political dimension.[8] Indeed, according to Foucault, the subject in contemporary society is constantly required to answer the question, Who are you in truth?

Second, the scientific conception of truth postulates that there is no one who is "exclusively qualified to state the truth," just as there is no one (or better, *almost* no one) who is disqualified from grasping it from the start.[9] This is the *principle of the (potentially) universal access to the truth*: the individual's capacity to attain the truth exclusively depends on the use she makes of "the instruments required to discover it, the categories necessary to think it, and an adequate language for formulating it in propositions."[10] Thus, this capacity does not depend on the subject's mode of being; in other words, the scientific conception of truth is not part of what Foucault would later call spirituality.

In the first lecture of his 1982 course at the Collège de France, *The Hermeneutics of the Subject*, Foucault addresses the conditions of the subject's access to the truth and famously distinguishes "philosophy" (or, to use the language of *Psychiatric Power*, the "philosophico-scientific standpoint of truth") from "spirituality" by claiming that, in the latter case, the subject must operate a series of transformations on herself in order to attain the truth.[11] In fact, spirituality postulates that "the truth is never given to the subject by right," and therefore that the subject "must be changed, transformed, shifted, and become, to some extent and up to a certain point, other than herself" to have the right to access it.[12] Now, according to Foucault, the question of the subject's access to the truth was indissolubly linked to spirituality throughout Greek, Hellenistic, and Roman antiquity. By contrast, "the history of truth enter[ed] its modern period" when it was established that "what gives access to the truth, the condition for the subject's access to the truth, is knowledge-*connaissance* and knowledge-*connaissance* alone."[13] This does not mean, of course, that the truth could henceforth be obtained, as it were, automatically, without conditions. On the contrary, both *internal* conditions (formal or objective conditions, rules of method) and *external* conditions (sociopolitical or cultural conditions, moral conditions) govern the act of knowledge, and yet these conditions no longer concern "the subject in her being" or "the structure of the subject as such."[14] Instead, the philosophico-scientific standpoint of truth is connected with a technology of demonstration, that is, "a technology for the construction or the finding of truth *as a universal right* [*en droit universel*]."[15]

On the other hand, in *Psychiatric Power* Foucault refers to a different, more archaic "standpoint of truth" that, he claims, was gradually obscured and colonized by truth-demonstration. It is a truth that is not waiting for us "everywhere and at all times," but a "dispersed, discontinuous, inter-rupted truth which will only speak or appear from time to time, where it wishes to, in certain places."[16] In other words, far from being everywhere and accessible to everyone, in this conception the truth has "its favorable moments, its propitious places, its privileged agents and bearers": it has its own *geography*, its own *calendar* (or better, its own *chronology*), and its "privileged and exclusive" *messengers* or *operators*.[17] Some of the examples that Foucault mentions are the oracle who speaks the truth at Delphi, the god who heals at Epidaurus, the old medicine of crises, and alchemical practice. So, who exactly are the "operators" of this discontinuous truth? Those "who undergo tests of qualification," those "who have uttered the required words or performed ritual actions," those "whom truth has cho-sen to sweep down on"—"prophets, seers, innocents, the blind, the mad, the wise, etc."[18] It is worth noting that several of these figures (notably the prophet and the sage), as well as the idea of a "test" (*épreuve*) of truth and of a ritual dimension of truth-telling, will be developed in more detail by Foucault in his lectures at the Collège de France from the 1980s.[19] But ultimately, the point is that, as opposed to truth-demonstration, which is omnipresent and universally accessible, this *other* truth occurs instead "as an event."[20]

What Foucault's "little history of truth in general" seems to rely on, then, is a clear-cut opposition between "two series in the Western history of truth": on the one hand, a more recent series, that of truth-demonstration, which is "constant, constituted, demonstrated, discovered"; on the other hand, an older series, that of truth-event, which is discontinuous, aroused, hunted down, produced, and which belongs to "the order of what hap-pens."[21] In the former case, Foucault argues, the relation between truth-demonstration and its subjects is one of knowledge-*connaissance*, which means that it is governed by a set of formal rules that establish the condi-tions under which a subject can know an object. By contrast, the relation between truth-event and "the person who is seized by it, who grasps it or is struck by it," is a relation of *shock* or *clash*, a "risky, reversible, warlike" relation, one of "domination and victory"—in short, a relation of power.[22]

Truth-demonstration	Truth-event
omnipresent	dispersed and discontinuous
universally accessible	accessible only in certain times and places, and by specific people
defined in terms of knowledge-*connaissance* (subject-object relation)	defined in terms of knowledge-*savoir* (power relation)

The upshot of this distinction is that a history of truth written within the framework of knowledge-*connaissance*, thereby assuming the point of view of the subject-object relation, would be at best merely the history of one of the two above-mentioned series of truth. This is what Foucault, in 1973, calls an "internal history of truth," one that "is constructed in or on the basis of the history of science" and that "rectifies itself in terms of its own principles of regulation."[23] And he opposes it to another history of truth, an "external, exterior" one, which would focus instead on the "other places where truth is formed" in our society, that is, on the emergence of "games" (*règles de jeu*) through which "one sees certain forms of subjectivity, certain object domains, certain types of knowledge come into being."[24]

However, it is clear that one year later Foucault no longer agrees with this distinction between an internal and an external history of truth—the former being a history of truth written from the standpoint of knowledge-*connaissance*, the latter a history of truth that addresses "the events of knowledge-*savoir*."[25] Indeed, the internal history of truth would not even be a history *of truth*, because—as I argued in the introduction—defending an epistemological (or metaphysical) conception of truth entails defending the idea that the truth has no history, and that the only history that could be written is actually the history of our (more or less successful) attempts to grasp the truth. From this standpoint, the different forms of what Foucault calls truth-event would exclusively play the role of naive, inadequate, or failed attempts to have access to the truth.

In *Psychiatric Power*, then, Foucault (implicitly) redefines his project of a history of truth. In 1970 and 1971, as I mentioned above, he suggested that we should reverse "the traditional configuration that posits knowledge-*connaissance*—as form or faculty—as precondition and then the events of knowledge-*savoir* as singular acts that actualize this faculty and may in some cases modify its form."[26] In 1973, this reversal took the form of a Nietzschean critique of the subject of knowledge-*connaissance* aiming to show how "the political and economic conditions of existence are not a veil or an obstacle for the subject of knowledge-*connaissance* but the means by which subjects of knowledge-*connaissance* are formed, and hence are truth relations."[27] However, this insight still relied on the distinction between *two* histories of truth—a distinction that Foucault eventually rejects. Indeed, in 1974, the upshot of Foucault's "little history of truth" is that, actually, truth-event and truth-demonstration are not to be opposed to one another, because truth-demonstration is but a specific historical form taken by truth-event—one that, nevertheless, attempts to deny or erase this fact, instead presenting itself as universal and suprahistorical. In short, Foucault no longer argues that there are *two* histories of truth: it is only possible to write the history of truth from the standpoint of truth-event, and from this standpoint, "truth-discovery, truth-method, truth as knowledge-*connaissance* relation," will appear as what it really is—namely, one of the multiple forms that the truth-event has taken during the history of humankind.[28]

The opposition between truth-event and truth-demonstration on which Foucault's history of truth seemed to rely is thus ultimately rejected. In *Psychiatric Power*, Foucault explicitly argues that the scientific technology of truth, "the present day extent, force, and power of which there is absolutely no point in denying," is but a form of truth-event: "Truth as knowledge-*connaissance* is basically only a region and an aspect, albeit one that has become superabundant and assumed gigantic dimensions, but still an aspect or a modality of truth as event and of the technology of this truth-event."[29] Indeed, even in terms of truth-demonstration, to be able to grasp the truth, the subject must be qualified by a series of specific (and very demanding) pedagogical procedures and mechanisms of institutional selection:

> Universities, learned societies, canonical teaching, schools, laboratories, the interplay of specialization and professional qualification, are all ways of organizing the rarity of those who can have access to a truth that science posits as universal. It will be the abstract right of every individual to be a universal subject, if you like, but to be one in fact, concretely, will necessarily entail rare individuals being qualified to perform the function of universal subject. In the history of the West since the eighteenth century, the appearance of philosophers, men of science, intellectuals, professors, laboratories, etc., is directly correlated with this extension of the standpoint of scientific truth and corresponds precisely to the rarefaction of those who can know a truth that is now present everywhere and at every moment.[30]

In other words, the scientific standpoint of truth also relies—as does any other form of truth-event—on the rarity or rarefaction of those who can actually discover the truth. The supposedly universal subject of this supposedly universal truth thus turns out to be but an "abstract subject" because, in reality, only a few people are qualified (and authorized) to have access to scientific truth.[31] And truth-demonstration is but a specific historical form of truth-event—one that, at least in Western societies, became dominant at a certain moment in time and is still prevalent today, in part also because it attempts to conceal its historicity behind the alleged universality of the subject of knowledge-*connaissance*.[32] Ten years later, Foucault would argue that a pivotal (albeit paradoxical) role in this history was played by Descartes, who employed the resources of spirituality—that is, of the truth-event technology—to constitute a subject of knowledge-*connaissance* henceforth freed (but only apparently) from all ascetic obligations.[33]

The important point here is that Foucault's history of truth does not rely on a clear-cut opposition between truth-event and truth-demonstration, as if they were two different and incompatible forms of truth, or as if they corresponded to two equally valid standpoints from which to write respective external and internal histories of truth. Instead, by assuming the standpoint of truth-event (the only one from which, properly speaking, it is possible to write a history of truth), Foucault aims to show that the relation between these two historical series is one of inclusion/exclusion[34]—that is, a power relation—which, on the one hand, calls for the elaboration of an archaeology of knowledge-*savoir* and, on the other, requires the development of a genealogy of knowledge-*connaissance*.[35] The former will argue that "scientific demonstration is basically only a ritual," that "the supposedly universal subject of knowledge-*connaissance* is really only an individual historically qualified according to certain modalities," and that "the discovery of truth is really a certain modality of the production of truth."[36] In short, it will argue that truth-demonstration is itself only an aspect or a form of truth-event—one, however, whose "regime" is characterized by the *exclusion* of the series of other truth-events (of which it nevertheless is a part) from the field of truth. But this is not enough for Foucault, who now also explicitly acknowledges the need to write a *genealogy* of truth-demonstration. Such a genealogy will trace the historical emergence of the scientific regime of truth (and, as we shall see, of at least two other regimes of truth that characterize our contemporary society) in order to show how "truth as knowledge-*connaissance* assumed its present, familiar, and observable dimensions"; to show, in other words, how "it colonized and took over the truth-event and ended up exercising a relation of power over it" that has so far been "dominant";[37] and to show how a significant part of its success is attributable to the scientific standpoint of truth presenting itself as the *only* legitimate standpoint, thus concealing the fact that it actually is but a regime of truth among many others.

Foucault introduces the concept of "regime of truth" in *Discipline and Punish*, where it is used to address the formation of "a corpus of knowledge, techniques, 'scientific' discourses" that, within the new penal system of the eighteenth and nineteenth centuries, "becomes entangled with the practice of the power to punish."[38] Initially, through the concept of regime of truth—a somewhat scandalous concept, since it connects the supposedly "pure" notion of truth with the notion of regime (soiled by all the impurities of power and politics)—Foucault aims to eschew the metaphysical-epistemological question of truth as knowledge-*connaissance* relation, and to redefine the question of truth from the standpoint of truth-event.[39] As he argues in a much-debated interview from 1976, despite what a certain philosophical myth would have us believe, "truth isn't outside power, or deprived of power": on the contrary, truth is of this world—not only is it "produced by virtue of multiple constraints," but in turn it "induces regulated effects of power."[40] Therefore, Foucault concludes, "each society has its regime of truth, its 'general politics' of truth," and by these expressions he simultaneously points to

> the types of discourse [society] harbors and causes to function as true; the mechanisms and instances which enable one to distinguish true from false statements, the way in which each is sanctioned; the techniques and procedures which are valorized for obtaining truth; the status of those who are charged with saying what counts as true.[41]

In this interview, Foucault seems to suggest that the scientific regime of truth defines the "political economy" of truth in contemporary Western societies. Such a political economy is characterized by five main features: (1) truth is modeled on "the form of scientific discourse and the institutions which produce it"; (2) truth is "subject to a constant economic and political incitation" (there is an economic and political "demand for truth"); (3) truth is the object of "an immense diffusion and consumption"; (4) truth is "produced and transmitted under the control . . . of a few great political and economic apparatuses," such as the university, the army, the media industry; (5) truth is at stake in "a whole political debate and social confrontation," in a series of "ideological" struggles within society.[42] Now, as we shall see, this is only part of the story that Foucault wants to tell us. Indeed, as he makes clear in his later lectures and writings, there are *multiple* regimes of truth that coexist in our societies and define their political economy of truth—the most relevant of which, alongside the scientific one, are what I call the confessional and the critical regimes of truth.

However, Foucault's initial focus on the scientific regime of truth does make sense insofar as this regime plays a decisive role in the widespread assumption that the project of writing a history of truth is simply untenable. Hence, Foucault needs to do some "unmasking" here to show that the scientific standpoint of truth actively conceals the status of truth as knowledge-*connaissance* as only one of the multiple forms or moments of the history of truth-event. This moment is characterized by knowledge-*connaissance*'s attempt to mask its "impure" origins and "shameful" connection with mechanisms of power: "*O pudenda origo!*"[43] This Nietzschean move is typical of all subversive genealogies, that is, of every genealogical project that focuses on a belief, concept, or practice that is presented to us as universal and suprahistorical in order to unveil its impure and contingent historical origins.[44] By showing that the scientific standpoint of truth, far from being "pure," is itself a regime of truth among others, that is, "a system of ordered procedures for the production, regulation, distribution, circulation, and functioning of statements" that is linked "by a circular relation to systems of power which produce it and sustain it, and to effects of power which it induces and which redirect it," Foucault is thus not only writing a piece of his own history of truth, but also withdrawing the grounds on which the most common objections to the very project of a history of truth rely.[45]

Foucault's conclusion, in 1976, is that the crucial task of the intellectual (or should we say the subversive genealogist?) does not consist in unmasking ideologies and replacing them with the true picture of human beings and society in people's "heads," but in changing "the political, economic, institutional regime of the production of truth" in order to inaugurate "a new politics of truth."[46] But how exactly should we change the regime of truth? And what kind of politics of truth should we strive to obtain? Can Foucault's history of truth tell us something more concrete about this task? I shall engage with these delicate questions in chapter 5.

The Emergence of the Alethurgic Subject

In the first lectures of *On the Government of the Living*, Foucault insists once more on the need to broaden or modify the way in which we think about truth, arguing that truth-demonstration, or truth as knowledge-*connaissance*, is but one of the possible ways in which the truth can be manifested—one of the possible forms of what Foucault now calls "alethurgy," that is, the "manifestation of truth."[47] However, if we compare

Foucault's analyses in *On the Government of the Living* with his lectures and writings from the 1970s, we immediately realize that something has changed: in his discussion of truth and power (now redefined, as we will see, in terms of government), a third dimension has explicitly emerged— the dimension of subjectivity.[48] Of course, this dimension was far from absent from Foucault's work prior to 1980: as we saw, already in 1973 and 1974, Foucault talks about the simultaneous emergence of forms of subjectivity and sets of rules for the establishment of truth, while also addressing the issue of the ways in which the subject can (or should) be qualified or disqualified to have access to the truth; a few years later, in 1978, he explicitly addresses the relations that link truth, power, and subjectivity to each other—and the examples could be multiplied.[49] Yet it is fair to say that it is only in 1980 that Foucault entirely recenters his history of truth on the role that the subject plays in relation to the procedures for the manifestation of truth. Indeed, Foucault's aim is no longer exclusively that of writing an archaeology of knowledge-*savoir* and a genealogy of knowledge-*connaissance*: his history of truth now also functions as a genealogy of the modern subject.[50] Together, these three complementary aspects define one and the same project—a project that, during the 1970s, Foucault repeatedly describes in terms of a "politics of truth" or a "political history of truth" that aims to overturn a series of traditional themes in philosophy ("confession frees," "power reduces one to silence," "truth does not belong to the order of power, but shares an original affinity with freedom"), but that, in 1980, he also characterizes in terms of a "politics of ourselves."[51]

The year 1980, for Foucault, is thus characterized both by significant elements of continuity with his project of a history of truth and by important methodological and conceptual shifts with regard to his previous analyses.

By implicitly referring back to the little history of truth sketched in *Psychiatric Power*, in *On the Government of the Living* Foucault again poses the problem of truth in such a way as to short-circuit the standpoint of truth as knowledge-*connaissance*. In arguing that it would be "very difficult to find an example of a power that is exercised without being accompanied, in one way or another, by a manifestation of truth," Foucault claims that the latter cannot be explained solely on the basis of the "economic" or "utilitarian" need to know what one governs, those one governs, and the means of governing these things and people.[52] Indeed, on the one hand, this truth whose manifestation turns out to be necessary for the exercise of power "goes far beyond knowledge [*connaissances*] useful for government": it is a "somewhat luxurious, supplementary, excessive, useless truth"—excessive and useless, we should add, in terms of truth-demonstration, because of course, in terms of truth-event, the manifestation of truth that accompanies the exercise of power is never "excessive" or "useless."[53] On the other hand, the way in which this truth is manifested does not pertain to the field of knowledge-*connaissance*, for it is not a question of demonstrating or proving anything—of refuting the false while establishing the accuracy of the true—but of "making truth itself appear against the background of the unknown, hidden, invisible, and unpredictable."[54] Therefore, it is clear that the framework of Foucault's analyses in 1980 is still defined by the notion of truth-event, and by the idea that truth as knowledge-*connaissance* is only one aspect or form of alethurgy among many others—only one of the multiple "ritual[s] of manifestation of the truth" that accompany and sustain the exercise of power.[55]

Indeed, what does Foucault have in mind when, in *On the Government of the Living*, he claims that he is no longer concerned with the notion of knowledge-*savoir* and wants to focus on the problem of truth instead? Foucault's main point here seems to be that the procedures through which truth is obtained and manifested—what he now calls alethurgy—are far more numerous and multifaceted than we usually think. Thus, the notion of alethurgy plays a role analogous to the role played by the notion of truth-event in *Psychiatric Power*: much broader than truth conceived as knowledge-*connaissance* (alethurgy, Foucault claims, "is much more than making known [*donner à connaître*]"), the notion of alethurgy indicates the "set of possible verbal or non-verbal procedures by which one brings to light what is laid down as true as opposed to false, hidden, inexpressible, unforeseeable, or forgotten."[56] Truth as knowledge-*connaissance* is clearly included in this definition, but far from exhausts it: "the production of truth in the consciousness of individuals by logico-experimental procedures," Foucault claims, is "only one of the possible forms of alethurgy"— and science is "only one of the possible cases of all these forms by which truth may be manifested."[57] Thus, the shift that Foucault announces in 1980 from the notion of knowledge-*savoir* to the problem of truth, far from marking a radical break with his previous analyses, is just a way of clarifying them. Here, more explicitly than ever before, Foucault indicates that his history of truth does not rely on any alleged opposition— between knowledge-*connaissance* and knowledge-*savoir*, or between truth-demonstration and truth-event—but focuses on a notion that encompasses all of the above: the notion of alethurgy.

Something very similar can be said about the second methodological shift that Foucault mentions in *On the Government of the Living*: the shift from the notion of power to the concept of government. Actually, Foucault argues that this was already carried out in *Security, Territory, Popula-*

tion and *The Birth of Biopolitics*, where he elaborates the notion of power as "government," understood "in the broad sense . . . of mechanisms and procedures intended to conduct human beings, to direct their conduct, to conduct their conduct."[58] Once more, however, far from marking a rupture with his previous analyses of disciplinary and biopolitical power, for Foucault the concept of government constitutes a way of clarifying and developing them.[59] Indeed, the analytic of power relations elaborated in *Discipline and Punish* and the first volume of the *History of Sexuality* now appears to Foucault to be too narrowly focused on (disciplinary and biopolitical) techniques through which one conducts the conduct *of others*. This risks suggesting that power is but "pure violence or strict coercion," whereas Foucault conceives of it as a network of "complex relations" that "involve a set of rational techniques" whose efficiency "is due to a subtle integration of coercion-technologies and self-technologies."[60] The concept of government is redefined by Foucault precisely in order to encompass *both* techniques of power (including disciplinary and biopolitical power) and techniques of the self, thus emphasizing their point of contact and the specific ways in which techniques aimed at conducting others and techniques aimed at conducting oneself *interact*.[61] Consequently, the question for Foucault is no longer exactly "how to resist power," but "how to be governed *otherwise*," that is, how to transform the interplay between— and the respective strategic importance of—techniques of coercion and techniques of the self in any given situation, in order to counteract the effects of domination as much as possible.[62]

Thus, the notion of power/knowledge that Foucault elaborated in his lectures and writings from the 1970s is now bracketed, replaced by the problem of the "government of human beings by the truth."[63] The point is that, according to Foucault, there is a "ring of truth" or an "alethurgic circle" that revolves around the exercise of government, because to conduct the conduct of others (and of oneself), one must always carry out "operations in the domain of truth"—operations that, however, "are always in excess of what is useful and necessary to govern in any effective way."[64] No government, then, without alethurgy.[65] This is the crucial methodological principle that Foucault formulates in *On the Government of the Living*—one that underpins most of his work from the 1980s, which still takes on a genealogical form in order to show that the relation between government and truth has assumed many different guises throughout the history of humankind before its elaboration in terms of the (modern) connection between "an art of government and, let's say, political, economic, and social rationality."[66]

More importantly, however, this methodological principle is used by

Foucault to recenter his analysis on the role that *the subject* plays in relation to the government of human beings by the truth. Indeed, he immediately rephrases the latter in terms of the problem of the *autos*, the first person, when he offers a new, "alethurgic" reading of Sophocles's *Oedipus Rex*— a reading, that is, "not in terms of desire and the unconscious, but in terms of truth and power."[67] The aspect of Sophocles's tragedy that captures Foucault's interest in 1980 is the alethurgy of those who were themselves present—the servants and slaves—"seeing with their own eyes and acting with their own hands."[68] Their alethurgy therefore has the structure of *testimony*: the Corinthian slave and the Theban shepherd witnessed and took part in the decisive events that should be brought to light; they can speak the truth precisely because they can say "I," "myself," *autos*—it is I who did this, it is I who saw that, and it is I who is speaking to you now.[69]

This testimonial (or "judicial") alethurgy completes and, in a sense, authenticates the uncertain alethurgy of the gods, thus transforming the enigmatic truth that was said at the beginning of the tragedy into an "inevitable truth to which Oedipus is forced to submit and the spectators themselves have to recognize."[70] In other words, without this "point of subjectivation" in the "general procedure and overall cycle of alethurgy," the manifestation of truth would have remained incomplete.[71] And Foucault makes it very clear that it is precisely this element of the first person, this point of subjectivation in the alethurgic procedures, that interests him first and foremost:

> The problem is how and for what reasons truth-telling came to authenticate its truth, be asserted as manifestation of truth, precisely to the extent that the person speaking can say: It is me who holds the truth, and it is me who holds the truth because I saw it and because having seen it, I say it. This identification of truth-telling and having-seen-the-truth, this identification between the person speaking and the source, origin, and root of the truth, is undoubtedly a multiple and complex process that was crucial for the history of the truth in our societies.[72]

This is one of the most explicit formulations of an aspect of Foucault's history of truth that was already present in the 1970s, but that becomes full-fledged only in 1980, because of his new focus on the dimension of subjectivity: the genealogy of what I call the confessional regime of truth. Indeed, the problem that Foucault wants to examine is the emergence and historical transformations of a series of alethurgic procedures centered on the "I," the "myself," the *autos* as a crucial aspect of the Western history of truth. It is the problem of "self-alethurgy" and its multiple, protean relations with the art of governing human beings, or in other words, the problem of the "government of human beings through the manifestation of truth in the form of subjectivity."[73] How is it, Foucault asks, that in a society like ours "power cannot be exercised without truth having to manifest itself, and manifest itself in the form of subjectivity"?[74] And why do we expect from this manifestation of the truth in the form of subjectivity effects "that go beyond the realm of knowledge-*connaissance*" and belong instead "to the realm of the salvation and deliverance of each and all"?[75]

The received view is that *On the Government of the Living* marks the beginning of the last "phase"—the "ethical" phase—of Foucault's intellectual career insofar as it operates a series of methodological and conceptual shifts that place at the center of his work the dimension of subjectivity. This view is both correct and slightly inexact. It is correct because Foucault, in that lecture course, does focus his attention on the element of the first person in an unprecedented manner, thus paving the way for his analyses of the techniques of the self, aesthetics of existence, and *parrhesia*. It is slightly inexact, however, because the subject, as I mentioned above, *already* constituted a fundamental dimension of Foucault's work in the 1970s.[76] To be more precise, what emerges in *On the Government of the Living* is therefore not the dimension of subjectivity, but a *specific form* of subjectivity. The subject is no longer presented merely as an effect of the interplay between power mechanisms and knowledge procedures, as was the case in Foucault's lectures and writings from the 1970s, but as the indispensable element that makes possible the "government by the truth" in all of its aspects—both the government of others and the government of oneself.[77] This is the reason why, in *On the Government of the Living*, the subject acquires a conceptual autonomy it never had before in Foucault's work. At the same time, the notion of the "subject" that emerges in that lecture course does not correspond to a general or universal concept, but indicates a very specific entity—one that is capable of governing itself and being governed by others through a series of alethurgic procedures:

> What is the relationship between the fact of being subject in a relation of power and a subject through which, for which, and regarding which the truth is manifested? What is this double sense of the word "subject," subject in a relation of power, subject in a manifestation of truth?[78]

This subject is what I call an alethurgic subject. It is clearly the correlate to the question of the government—of self and others—by the truth that Foucault first (explicitly) formulates in *On the Government of the Living*, as

well as of the aspect of his history of truth that takes the form of a genealogy of the confessional regime of truth that still characterizes our society.

Confessional Sciences

As I briefly mentioned above, however, the questions that Foucault raises
in 1980—How is it that, in our society, power cannot be exercised without
a manifestation of truth in the form of subjectivity? Why do we expect
from this alethurgy effects that belong to the realm of the salvation and
deliverance of each and all?—are not *entirely* new. Similar formulations
can be found throughout his lectures and writings from the 1970s, and
notably in the first volume of his *History of Sexuality*, where, speaking of
confession (*aveu*) as "one of the West's most highly valued techniques for
producing truth,"[79] Foucault writes:

> The obligation to confess is now relayed through so many different points,
> it is so deeply ingrained in us, that we no longer perceive it as the effect of a
> power that constrains us; on the contrary, it seems to us that truth, lodged
> in our most secret nature, "demands" only to surface; that if it fails to do
> so, this is because a constraint holds it in place, the violence of a power
> weighs it down, and it can finally be articulated only at the price of a kind
> of liberation.[80]

Thus, in 1976, Foucault already establishes a clear connection between
the production of truth and the constitution of individuals as "subjects,"
"in both senses of the word," even though, to refer to the latter, he still
exclusively utilizes the term "subjection" (*assujettissement*).[81] What is
more, in a handful of pages from the chapter "*Scientia Sexualis*," Foucault
examines the transformations that confession underwent from the eighteenth century onward, which allowed it to spread far beyond the domain
of religion and to colonize the fields of pedagogy, medicine, psychiatry,
sexology, criminology, and so on.[82] In other words, he addresses the formation of the current confessional regime of truth.

The confession, Foucault argues, "was, and still remains, the general
matrix governing the production of the true discourse on sex"; this, of
course, does not entail denying that its (originally religious) technology
changed profoundly as soon as it lost "its ritual and exclusive location"
and began to be utilized in relationships such as those between "children
and parents, students and educators, patients and psychiatrists, delin-
quents and experts."[83] Foucault points to a series of specific transforma-

tions in the motivations, effects, and forms of confession: nineteenth-century psychiatry, for instance, requires individuals to voice "a discourse of truth" about their most singular pleasures, one that has "to model itself after that which speaks, not of sin and salvation, not of death and eternity, but of body and life—that is, the discourse of science."[84] Thus, owing to the dissemination of confessional procedures well beyond the domain of religion, and to the huge extension of their realm of application in the fields of medicine, psychiatry, pedagogy, sexology, and criminology, an "interference" was produced between the scientific technology of truth (which Foucault already addressed in *Psychiatric Power*) and the rituals of confession. Foucault characterizes this process in terms of the "improbable" emergence of a set of "confessional sciences."[85]

Confessional sciences rely on the coupling of confession and scientific discourse, thus combining knowledge-*connaissance* with the idea that the confession of the truth is able to *liberate* or *cure* the subject. In other words, "scientific" confession, just as religious confession, produces "rebound effects" on the subject, who thereby not only discovers the truth about herself, but in uttering such a truth can transform herself and regain the freedom, health, or "normality" she had lost. Consequently, confessional sciences clearly have the structure of "spirituality": they aim to produce effects on the subject that go well beyond the simple knowledge-*connaissance* of the subject herself.[86] The claim of these disciplines to be able to attain truth as knowledge-*connaissance*, that is, as neatly detached from the structure of truth-event and solidly installed in the "pure" realm of scientific truth unsullied by power, must therefore be problematized. Confessional sciences crucially aim to liberate, cure, or "save" the subject; they would not even exist if they did not promise to produce these effects. Hence, they clearly belong to the technology of truth-event.

In light of these remarks from 1976, it becomes easier to emphasize the ethico-political relevance of the project that Foucault fully elaborates in *On the Government of the Living*. By analyzing three forms of alethurgy, or better, of self-alethurgy in early Christianity—the preparation for baptism, the ecclesial or canonical penance, and spiritual direction (*direction de conscience*)—Foucault's aim is to write a genealogy of "the obligation to speak, the obligation to tell, the obligation to tell the truth, to produce a true discourse on oneself," in order to problematize the contemporary regime of truth centered on "scientific" confession.[87] As he argues, "this obligation to tell the truth about oneself has never ceased in Christian culture, and probably in Western societies": we are still "obliged to speak of ourselves in order to tell the truth of ourselves."[88] In other words, as part of his (political) history of truth, Foucault writes a genealogy of the confessional sciences in order to question their enduring hegemony and counteract the force that they derive, paradoxically, both from the technology of truth-event and from the technology of truth-demonstration—that is, both from the prestige of modern scientific discourse and from the long history of the relations between subjectivity and truth in the Christian West. Indeed, the truths that these disciplines discover (or better, produce) about the subject are presented as having features typical of scientific truths, such as universality and objectivity, but they are also supposed to induce effects that pertain to a completely different domain, thus giving the subject access to nothing less than a secular form of salvation.

Thus, if it is through a problematization of the status commonly attributed to the scientific standpoint of truth that Foucault justifies his project of a history of truth in the first place, the main aspect that such a project takes is that of a genealogy of the confessional sciences that emerged in the past two centuries as the result of the improbable combination of scientific procedures and confessional techniques. These disciplines, according to Foucault, play a crucial role in the current government of human beings by the truth—that is, in the contemporary regime of truth "indexed to subjectivity" that (still) requires individuals to say not only, "Here I am, me who obeys," but also "This is *what I am*, me who obeys."[89] "Why and how," Foucault asks,

> does the exercise of power in our society, the exercise of power as government of human beings, demand not only acts of obedience and submission, but truth acts in which individuals who are subjects in the power relationship are also subjects as actors, spectator witnesses, or objects in manifestation of truth procedures?[90]

The expression "truth act" (*actus veritatis*) is taken directly from the theological writings of the Middle Ages. Foucault utilizes it to designate "the part that falls to a subject in the procedures of alethurgy"—that of operator, of spectator, or of object itself of the manifestation of the truth.[91] Unsurprisingly, Foucault immediately points out that he will focus his attention on "reflexive" truth acts, that is, truth acts in which the subject is *at once* the operator, the spectator, and the object of the alethurgy.[92] Both from a methodological and from a conceptual point of view, however, the crucial expression that Foucault introduces once again in *On the Government of the Living* is that of a regime of truth, while also redefining it in order to make it play a new and fundamental role in his history of truth. It is to this concept, that of a regime of truth, that I will now turn my attention.

✳ 2 ✳

Regimes of Truth

In *On the Government of the Living,* Foucault evokes the concept of regime of truth without any further explanation at the end of the lecture
on January 30, 1980. He uses it to refer both to our society, characterized
by "a regime of truth . . . indexed to subjectivity," and to Christianity,
whose "regime of truth" is "very singular" and altogether different from
the regimes of truth that could be found in ancient Greece and Rome.[1] At
the beginning of the following lecture, however, Foucault discusses this
concept at length in what could be regarded as a thorough methodological
introduction to the topics addressed in the rest of the course—namely,
the three alethurgic techniques that characterize early Christianity's (confessional) regime of truth: baptism, ecclesial or canonical penance, and
spiritual direction.

In 1980, Foucault (re)defines a "regime of truth" as "that which determines the obligations of individuals with regard to the procedures of
manifestation of truth."[2] This definition is clearly different from the one
that I addressed in the previous chapter: in 1976, as we saw, the concept
of regime of truth referred to the reciprocal relation between power and
knowledge. But since in *On the Government of the Living* Foucault explicitly claims that he wants to get rid of the "now worn and hackneyed
theme" of power/knowledge by introducing the notion of the government
of human beings by the truth, it is no surprise that the concept of regime
of truth also needs to be newly defined.[3] Compared to 1976, Foucault's
definition of this concept in 1980 is premised on a new element, which was
not (explicitly) there before: subjectivity. Moreover, I shall argue that, by
clarifying the distinction between games and regimes of truth, in *On the
Government of the Living* Foucault also provides us with invaluable tools
to respond to one of the most common objections raised against his work:
that it risks amounting to nothing else than a reductionism captured in
"the view that reason is just another form of social power," or "that reason

is a fundamentally 'disciplinary' authority in the service of a 'regime of truth.'"[4]

Truth Obligations?

The new definition of the concept of regime of truth relies on an insight that, Foucault warns us, we will likely find problematic, for it contradicts a deeply rooted way of thinking about truth and power. The manifestation of truth, he argues, does not take place in a vacuum and (at least in practice) can never be *perfectly* separated from power relations. This does not mean, however, that truth *just is* power. To prove his point, Foucault introduces the notion of "truth obligations": the manifestation of truth, he claims, is always accompanied by specific obligations for the subject who is involved in it.

But why should we add this notion of obligation to the notion of manifestation of truth, and in what sense does the truth oblige?[5] If there is an obligation that binds individuals to something presented to them as true, and that compels them to recognize and posit it as such, it seems that we are not actually dealing with "the truth"—or so the objection goes—since the truth is "sufficient unto itself for making its own law": that is, it obliges by virtue of its *intrinsic* force and not an external "regime" of power.[6] Better still, the truth strictly speaking never *obliges*. Obligation and coercion do exist, of course, but only when and insofar as "the truth as such is not involved."[7] This objection challenges the legitimacy of the concept of regime of truth by expressing the commonplace idea that the notions of "regime" and "truth," or of "obligation" and "truth," cannot and should not be linked. While it seems perfectly legitimate to speak of a political regime or a legal regime, it would seem that we cannot speak of a regime of truth; while it might be entirely justified to speak of political constraints or legal obligations, we should not speak of truth obligations.

In formulating this objection, Foucault clearly gives voice to what, in *Psychiatric Power*, he referred to as the scientific standpoint of truth—the standpoint of truth-demonstration or truth as knowledge-*connaissance*—which denies the existence of any relation between power and truth, and radically rejects the idea that science can itself be regarded as "only one of the possible regimes of truth" among "many other possible and existing regimes of truth."[8] According to this standpoint, the truth needs nothing more than itself, its own manifestation, to be *freely* recognized, posited, and accepted by individuals: the truth is intrinsically valuable and belongs to the realm of freedom—it can only emancipate, it never subjugates. Therefore, for there to be a truth obligation, or again for something like an obligation to be added to the intrinsic rules of manifestation of the truth, it must either involve precisely something that cannot be manifested or demonstrated by itself as true and that needs as it were this supplement of force, this *enforcement*, this supplement of vigor and obligation, of constraint, which means that one really will be obliged to posit it as true, although one knows that it may be false, or one is not sure that it is true, or it is not possible to demonstrate that it is true or false.[9]

In short, if there is "obligation," if there is "regime," it just means that we are not actually dealing with the truth, but rather with the "coercion of the non-true or the coercion and constraint of the unverifiable."[10] It is worth noting that Jacques Bouveresse formulates this exact objection against Foucault without mentioning (or perhaps even realizing) that the latter already addressed it thirty-five years before:

What bothers me about this kind of argument [such as Foucault's] . . . is that truth itself is equated with power. . . . The more one has to use the notion of power to explain the fact that a theory or proposition is accepted as true, the less likely it is that such a theory or proposition is actually true. It is, in fact, error and illusion, rather than truth, that in some cases, and probably in many cases, require explanation in terms of power and strategies of subjugation and domination.[11]

Bouveresse's position, as I argued above, perfectly exemplifies the reduction of truth to the standpoint of knowledge-*connaissance*: the "force of truth" can only be found *in* the truth itself. In 1980, Foucault explicitly addresses (and problematizes) this position, thus responding to the above-mentioned objection. Following Nietzsche's plea to call the value of truth into question, Foucault elaborates a clearer distinction between games and regimes of truth, and a more refined account of the latter, in order to show that the truth is not *intrinsically* binding or valuable.

On the one hand, Foucault explains that he does not want—and that, in fact, he *never* wanted—to deny that the truth is *index sui*:[12] in any *game of truth*, that is, in any regulated system for the production of truth claims (when it is considered in terms of its formal structure, and not of the individuals who concretely engage with it), "only the truth can legitimately show the true" and establish the distinction between true and false statements.[13] On the other hand, however, Foucault argues that the truth is not *rex sui*, nor *lex sui*, nor *judex sui*: if we consider the *regime of truth*, thus taking into account the individuals who are concretely engaged in this or that game of truth, we must conclude, according to Foucault, that "the truth is not the creator and holder of the rights it exercises over human beings, of the obligations the latter have toward it, and of the effects they expect from these obligations when and insofar as they are fulfilled."[14] In other words, "it is not true that the truth constrains only by truth," because all reasoning and demonstration entail an assertion that does not itself belong to "the realm of the true or false" (that is, it does not pertain to the formal structure of the game of truth), but is rather "a sort of commitment, a sort of profession": "If it is true, then I will submit; it is true, *therefore* I submit."[15]

Even though it is sometimes made *imperceptible* by a given regime of truth—it "goes without saying," as in the case of "the logic of the sciences"—it is this "therefore" that gives binding force to the truth, including truth as knowledge-*connaissance*.[16] Indeed, in this "you have to" of the truth, Foucault argues, "there is something that does not arise from the truth itself in its structure and content."[17] In other words, this "you have to" of the truth cannot be justified or accounted for in terms of the game of truth: it is a "historical-cultural" and ethico-political problem that can only be addressed in terms of the regime of truth.[18] Thus, the "force" that the scientific standpoint of truth considers to be *intrinsic* to truth itself actually derives from the "therefore" that, at the level of the regime of truth, links the "it is true" to the "I submit." Within the scientific regime of truth, this "therefore" is *masked* by the structure of *évidence*, or obviousness, which ensures "the exact coincidence of the manifestation of truth and my obligation to recognize and posit it as true."[19] It is still there though: If it is true, and obviously true, then I will submit; it is obviously true, "therefore" I submit. The task that Foucault attributes to his genealogy of the regimes of truth that characterize contemporary society is precisely that of revealing, of *making us see* the (often imperceptible) "therefore" on which they rely.[20]

Games and Regimes of Truth

I will now further unpack Foucault's dense and complex argument. First of all, I should mark a—small but significant—point of disagreement with Philippe Chevallier's reading of these passages. In his book on Foucault and Christianity, Chevallier rightly argues that, in defining regimes of truth in 1976, Foucault does not (yet) distinguish "the interplay [*jeu*] of statements among themselves—which defines a proposition as being true according to rules independent of subjects—from the relation of subjects to these statements."[21] As we saw, it is only in 1980 that Foucault explicitly introduces the dimension of subjectivity in his definition of the concept of regime of truth. However, the conclusion that Chevallier draws from this—namely, that in 1976 Foucault denies "scientific propositions their own logic of truth, distinct from the organization of power relations in a given society"—is illegitimate.[22] Indeed, already in his inaugural lecture at the Collège de France, in 1970, Foucault clearly draws a distinction of scope, or rather of standpoints:

> Of course, if we restrict ourselves to considering a proposition within a discourse, the distinction between true and false is neither arbitrary nor modifiable, neither institutional nor violent. But if we adopt a wider scope, if we ask the question of what has been, and what continues to be, throughout our discourses, this will to truth [*volonté de vérité*] that has spanned so many centuries of our history, and what kind of distinction [*partage*] it is that, in its most general form, governs our will to know [*volonté de savoir*], then it is perhaps something like a system of exclusion (a historical system, one that is modifiable and institutionally constraining) that will begin to appear.[23]

It is undeniable that Foucault, in his lectures and writings from the 1970s and 1980s, almost exclusively adopts the latter standpoint.[24] Yet he never denies that every game of truth possesses a logic and structure that "autonomously" establish the distinction between truth and falsity— provided, of course, that we consider it from a standpoint *internal* to the game of truth itself, thus bracketing the sociopolitical, cultural, and historical context, as well as the flesh-and-blood individuals who concretely engage with the game of truth and bring it to life. Provided, in short, that we do not address it as a regime of truth.

The "autonomy" of the formal rules that establish the distinction between true and false statements within a given game of truth is nevertheless only partial: it depends, as I just mentioned, on the perspective we adopt. In 1980, Foucault argues that the truth is *index sui* because every game of truth (explicitly or implicitly) defines a set of rules that, within that game, make it possible to establish the distinction between truth and falsity without the need to refer to anything else—to any additional rule external to the game. Yet, as soon as we adopt the (broader) perspective of the regime of truth of which the game of truth is a part, we inevitably realize that these rules are not suprahistorical or universal, and that they do not derive their raison d'être, justification, and force from the truth(s) they establish. This is what Foucault means when he claims that the truth is not *rex sui, lex sui,* or *judex sui,* and that the "therefore" that links the "it is true" (of the game of truth) to the "I submit" (of the individuals who are concretely engaged in it) is a historical, cultural, and ultimately ethico-political problem that can only be addressed at the level of the regime of truth. Thus, the distinction between games and regimes of truth can be construed as a distinction between the epistemic acceptance of a given truth claim and the practical submission to that claim. While *acceptance* of the truth can be explained at the level of the game of truth, that is, by relying on its formal structure and rules, *submission* to the truth (giving the truth the right and power to govern one's, and others', conduct) must be addressed at a different level, that of the regime of truth.

Game of truth	Regime of truth
rules for the production of true and false statements	obligations of individuals with regard to true and false statements
pertains to the *epistemic acceptance* of the truth	pertains to the *practical submission* to the truth
the truth is *index sui*	the truth is **not** *rex sui, lex sui, judex sui*

Frantz Fanon's discussion of medico-legal practices in Algeria during the 1950s is helpful to clarify the upshots of construing the distinction between game and regime of truth in terms of the difference between acceptance of and submission to the truth. Fanon explains that, in normal circumstances, the colonized subject who committed a crime initially has no problem acknowledging it. However, when he is brought in front of a judge, the accused often denies everything and claims he is innocent.[25] His denial of the act is construed by the colonizer as the ultimate confirmation of the supposed untrustworthiness of the colonized subject, who is seen as a deceiver and a liar incapable of truth.[26] Yet Fanon convincingly argues against this conclusion, and drawing from the distinction between game and regime of truth we can indeed make perfect sense of the accused's conduct: while at the level of the game of truth the colonized subject is willing to *accept* the fact that he is the author of the criminal act, he voluntarily refuses to *submit* to the consequences of that truth by subjectively consenting to the sanction established by the juridical regime of truth.[27] In other words, the colonized subject rejects the "therefore" that links the "it is true" (that I committed the act) to the "I submit" (to the punishment dictated by an unjust colonial system). The colonized subject, who is always presumed guilty by the colonizer, thus refuses to submit to the colonial regime of truth; he thereby shows that admission of guilt cannot constitute a successful resolution of social and political problems where, as in colonized Algeria, there is no "pre-existing reciprocal recognition of the group by the individual and vice versa."[28]

The distinction Foucault draws between the notions of "game" and "regime" of truth has virtually gone unnoticed, but it is crucial for many reasons, not least that it constitutes the clearest possible rebuttal to the commonplace criticism according to which Foucault's history of truth, and more generally his genealogical method, rely on an illegitimate reduction of truth to power.[29] By contrast, as we saw, Foucault explicitly acknowledges that every game of truth possesses an internal logic and formal structure that autonomously establish the distinction between true and false statements: truth and power are therefore clearly distinct from one another on that level of analysis.[30] Yet this is only part of the story, for Foucault aims to problematize this "autonomy," albeit from a new perspective: the perspective of the regime of truth, which reveals the complex *interaction* between truth and power within the procedures that are used to govern human beings in contemporary society.

Consequently, while Foucault draws a clear distinction between games and regimes of truth (one that allows him to avoid any reductionism), it is crucial to emphasize that, on the other hand, his history of truth—or genealogy of regimes of truth—aims to show that there is no actual game of truth without or external to a regime of truth.[31] Concretely, no game of truth has the privilege of being "pure" and entirely autonomous. On the contrary, every game of truth is part of a broader regime of truth that determines the obligations of the individuals who are engaged in it and who—explicitly or implicitly, voluntarily or involuntarily, consciously or unconsciously, willingly or unwillingly—utter the "therefore" that links the "it is true" (defined by the game of truth) to the "I submit." This "therefore" is the crucial element on which the government of human beings by the truth ultimately relies: it is the (allegedly free) "commitment" though which the subject gives the governmental mechanisms of power the authority to conduct her conduct.

For instance, the contemporary medical and psychiatric game of truth defines the condition of "gender dysphoria" as the distress resulting from "the incongruence between one's experienced or expressed gender and one's assigned gender."[32] Imagine a conversation with my doctor focusing on relevant symptoms at the end of which, according to the criteria laid out in the DSM-5, it turns out that I do suffer from the condition. The rules of the game of truth allow us to reach the conclusion that "I am gender dysphoric." This truth that, within the contemporary medical and psychiatric game of truth, is *index sui*, nevertheless entails a series of major consequences in terms of the conduct of my conduct: if it is true that

I am gender dysphoric, then I must be medically treated.[33] Foucault's point is that my submission to this further claim ("I suffer from condition X, *therefore* I must be medically treated") cannot be explained at the level of the game of truth, but has to be addressed—and problematized—at the level of the regime of truth, which focuses on the obligations that derive from the truth claims established within a given game of truth.

As this example, along with the example drawn from Fanon, clearly show, the ethico-political relevance of the "therefore" that links the "it is true" to the "I submit" can hardly be overstated. By focusing precisely on that "therefore," that is, on the element that connects the game of truth with the regime of truth, Foucault does not reduce truth to power: he problematizes their concrete *interaction* and *effects* in terms of government of human beings. These effects, according to Foucault, invariably take the form of subjection and subjectivation—for every regime of truth ultimately requires individuals to constitute themselves as subjects in relation to it, through the (allegedly free) "commitment" they express by accepting the "therefore" that links the "it is true" to the "I submit."[34] Foucault here takes the example of the Cartesian subject, who can say "I think, therefore I am" if and only if she is "qualified in a certain way," that is, if and only if she is not mad.[35] Hence, the individual who opts to play the game of truth based on Cartesian obviousness (*évidence*) will constitute herself and be regarded by society as a "rational" subject, whereas the individual who cannot (or opts not to) say "when it is true, and obviously true, I will submit" will be deemed irrational or crazy and will be governed accordingly—submitted to medical treatment, confined in a psychiatric hospital, excluded from society. Thus, when the Cartesian subject says, "I think, therefore I am," between the "I think" and the "I am" there is an *explicit* "therefore" that seems unassailable, "but behind [which] is hidden another 'therefore,' which is this: it is true, therefore I submit."[36] In other words, beneath the explicit "therefore" of the Cartesian game of truth defined by obviousness (*évidence*) lies an *implicit* "therefore," which is that of "a regime of truth that is not reduced to the intrinsic character of truth."[37]

This example is important, because it shows that Foucault's conclusions also apply to games of truth that we would be tempted to consider "pure" and isolated from any "regime." Take one of the most extreme cases:

> Imagine two logicians who are arguing and whose reasoning together leads to a proposition that both acknowledge as a true proposition, although it was denied by one of them at the start of the discussion. At the end of this argument, the one who had denied the proposition at the start and who,

at the end, recognizes it, will say explicitly or implicitly: it is true, therefore I submit. What happens when she says "it is true, therefore I submit"? If she says "it is true," it is not insofar as she is a logician, well, I mean it is not because she is a logician that the proposition is true. If the proposition is true, it is because of the logic or that, anyway, the logic chosen was such and such, with its symbols, rules of construction, axioms, and grammar. Therefore, for the proposition to be true, it is necessary and sufficient that there was logic, that there were rules of this logic, rules of construction, rules of syntax, and that this logic works.[38]

Within the game of truth of logic, it is logic itself, "defined in its specific structure, that assures the fact that [a given] proposition is true"; however, when an individual who is playing this game says, "It is true, therefore I submit," this "therefore," according to Foucault, does not rely on (and cannot be explained by) logic itself.[39] The individual is bound by this "therefore" because and insofar as "she *is doing* logic," that is to say, "because she has constituted herself, or has been invited to constitute herself, as operator in a certain number of practices or as a partner in a certain type of game"—a "game" in which the truth is *itself* given binding force.[40] Consequently, the distinction between game and regime of truth seems to disappear in the case of logic, for logic *as a regime of truth* is characterized by the fact that "the demonstration as self-indexation of truth is accepted as having an absolute power of constraint," whereas in other cases (think of the example drawn from Fanon) the distinction between game and regime of truth is more evident, since it is clearer that a certain force must be "added" to the truth in order for it to take effect.[41] Foucault's point, however, is that such a distinction is *always* relevant: the game of truth of logic, too, is part of a "regime" insofar as the individuals who play it constitute themselves and are constituted in a specific way through the acceptance of the "therefore" that links the "it is true" (of logic) to the "I submit," that is, to their willingness to be conducted or governed on the basis of that truth.

In short, according to Foucault, there is no game of truth without or external to a regime of truth because every *actual* game of truth, when played by flesh-and-blood individuals, entails a process of subject-constitution that relies on the acceptance or refusal, by the individual, of the "you have to" of the truth defined by the game of truth. Consequently, in 1980, the complex dynamics of subjection and subjectivation are situated at the core of Foucault's political history of truth—thus adding an *ethico-political* dimension to it.[42]

A Critical (An)archaeology

In the lecture on January 30, 1980, of *On the Government of the Living*, Foucault claims that he wants to turn the traditional way of posing the "philosophical-political question" upside down.[43] Instead of posing the question of truth first by asking what the subject of knowledge-*connaissance*, on the basis of the voluntary bond that ties her to the truth, can say about "the involuntary bond that ties us and subjects us to power," Foucault wants to start with the question of power: "What does the systematic, voluntary, theoretical and practical questioning of power have to say about the subject of knowledge-*connaissance* and about the bond to the truth in which this subject is involuntarily held?"[44] Thus, for Foucault,

> it is no longer a matter of saying: given the bond tying me voluntarily to the truth, what can I say about power? But instead, given my desire, decision, and effort to break the bond that binds me to power, what then is the situation with regard to the subject of knowledge-*connaissance* and the truth? It is not the critique of representations in terms of truth or error, truth or falsity, ideology or science, rationality or irrationality that should serve as indicator for defining the legitimacy or denouncing the illegitimacy of power. It is the movement of freeing oneself from power that should serve as revealer in the transformations of the subject and the relation the subject maintains to the truth.[45]

Unsurprisingly, Foucault refuses to develop his philosophico-political analysis in terms of ideology.[46] Hence, in addressing early Christian technologies of confession, his aim is not to show that "inasmuch as human beings worry more about salvation in the other world than about what happens down here, inasmuch as they want to be saved, they remain quiet and peaceful and it is easier to govern them."[47] Instead, by developing an analysis in terms of regimes of truth and thus rejecting any clear-cut distinction between scientific knowledge and ideology, Foucault focuses on the relations "that link together manifestations of truth with their procedures and the subjects who are their operators, witnesses, or possibly objects."[48]

Is Foucault suggesting that science and religion are ultimately the same thing, and that it does not matter whether we base our belief system on one or the other? This is not his point. What Foucault is arguing here is that an analysis in terms of regimes of truth allows us to realize that *both* early Christianity and modern science are characterized by specific ways of linking the manifestation of truth to the subject who performs it, and that in *both* cases, while taking different forms, this link functions as a crucial element in the techniques employed to govern human beings. In short, adopting the standpoint of the regime of truth, instead of elaborating a critique of representations in terms of the well-known oppositions of truth and error, ideology and science, or rationality and irrationality, allows Foucault to seriously consider the early Christian texts he discusses and not to dismiss them as mere "ideologies" in which "the false, or the non-true, would have to arm itself or be armed by a supplementary and external power in order to improperly take on the force, value, and effect of truth."[49] Thus, when Foucault poses the "philosophico-political question," he aims to address the multiple ways in which people have been and still are governed by the truth, the different modalities in which they have accepted—or they have fought against—the "therefore," the "you have to" of the truth on which governmental mechanisms rely in order to conduct their conduct. This is clearly, for him, just another way of characterizing his project of a history of truth:

> This type of history will not therefore be devoted to the way in which truth succeeds in tearing itself away from the false and breaking all the ties which hold it, but will be devoted . . . to the force of truth and to the ties by which human beings have gradually bound themselves in and through the manifestation of truth. Basically, what I would like to do . . . is write a history of the force of truth, a history of the power of the truth, a history, therefore, to take the same idea from a different angle, of the will to know.[50]

Scholars have generally failed to notice that the philosophico-political perspective underpinning Foucault's history of (the force of) truth crucially builds on the ideas he develops in his 1978 lecture, "What Is Critique?"[51] Indeed, Foucault's project is predicated upon an "attitude" that relies on the postulate that "no power goes without saying, that no power, of whatever kind, is obvious or inevitable," and thus that no power has any "intrinsic legitimacy"—a *critical attitude* defined by "the movement of freeing oneself from power" and wanting to be governed otherwise.[52] In other words, in *On the Government of the Living*, Foucault suggests putting "the non-necessity of all power" (for "all power only ever rests on the contingency and fragility of a history"), and thus its "non-acceptability," at the outset of the philosophico-political task of questioning "all the ways in which power is in actual fact accepted."[53] This attitude clearly corresponds to the moral and political attitude Foucault discusses in 1978—"the art of not being governed like that and at that cost," the "art of not being governed quite so much" that he calls "critique."[54]

In 1980, however, Foucault no longer speaks of critique, but instead evokes "anarchy" and "anarchism"; however, he makes clear that he does not share the anarchist postulate according to which power is intrinsically bad, and that he still considers a society without power relations to be a mere dream. Foucault's philosophico-political project, that he here names "anarchaeology," only shares with anarchy—or, more precisely, with Paul Feyerabend's anarchist epistemology—a "theoretical-practical attitude" concerning the non-necessity of all power as a "principle of intelligibility of knowledge-*savoir* itself."[55]

The combination of this theoretico-practical attitude with a historical analysis in terms of regimes of truth defines what Foucault calls an "(an)archaeology of knowledge."[56] Its goal is to shift the emphasis from the "it is true" to the "*therefore* I submit," and thus to write the history of (the force of) truth in the form of a genealogy of the ways in which individuals have been bound or have bound themselves "to very specific manifestations of truth in which . . . it is *they themselves* who must be manifested in truth."[57] I say "genealogy" because, although Foucault never uses the term in *On the Government of the Living*, it is clear—contra Jeremy Carrette— that this kind of investigation is a genealogical one, which addresses the problem of the government of human beings through the manifestation of truth in the form of subjectivity by relying, more clearly than ever before, on the critical postulate of the non-necessity of all power.[58] If it is true, as I will argue in chapter 5, that Foucault's genealogies—of power/knowledge mechanisms or of regimes of truth—are always also genealogies of the critical attitude, then it is crucial to emphasize that, in *On the Government of the Living*, the critical attitude is not treated as an object of study, but as a theoretical-practical principle that Foucault places at the heart of his methodology.

What does this entail? By reiterating one of the main insights of his analytic of power—namely, that power is not intrinsically bad (although it is always potentially dangerous)—Foucault clearly indicates that the point of his anarchaeology is not to argue that *every* process of subject-constitution within a regime of truth or *every* "therefore" that links the "it is true" to the "I submit" is to be criticized and rejected. They may very well be innocuous, and oftentimes they likely are—think of the example of the two logicians. Foucault's point is rather that, in order to be able to realize that a specific "therefore" is problematic or dangerous, we first need to *see* it as such, to become aware of its existence and function; and to do so, we need to reject the idea that the truth, in addition to being *index sui*, is also *rex sui*, *lex sui*, and *judex sui*.

Take the gender dysphoria example: Foucault would argue that the main (potential) danger does not lie in the medical and psychiatric game of truth that defines the symptoms that allow my doctor to diagnose my condition, but in the "therefore" that links the "it is true" (that I am gender dysphoric) to the "I submit" (to the prescribed treatment). This "therefore" seems to go without saying within the contemporary medical and psychiatric regime of truth, and my doctor would probably present it to me as such. Yet Foucault aims to problematize precisely this "you have to" of the truth, to indicate that no "therefore" goes without saying or is automatically decided for us by the truth itself, and thus to make us *see* that it is possible to refuse to be governed "like that and at that cost." Indeed, my *acceptance* of the conclusion that I am gender dysphoric—according to the contemporary medical and psychiatric game of truth—does not entail that I must *submit* to its expected consequences at the level of the regime of truth: I do not have to recognize myself as a participant in this medical-psychiatric discourse, or change my behavior (or my body) accordingly. In other words, I do not have to submit to the "you have to" of this truth. But note that this also opens up the possibility of using the very rules of the regime of truth *strategically*: because diagnosis makes available intervention, if the latter is what I ultimately want, I may choose to submit to the "you have to" of such a truth merely as a way of accessing care. In this case, submission to a given regime of truth can be seen as a tactical move within a broader critical strategy.[59]

I already quoted Foucault's claim that he does not want to elaborate a "critique of representations in terms of truth or error, truth or falsity, ideology or science, rationality or irrationality," and use it as the foundation for a critique of power.[60] Thus, he does not want to say: This game of truth is wrong, you do not really suffer from gender dysphoria, and that's why you should resist. Indeed, the risk would be to suggest that one should resist because (and *only insofar as*) the exercise of medical power relies on errors and false conclusions—and conversely that, when it relies on the truth, one must *never* resist. By contrast, Foucault argues that the "movement of freeing oneself from power" should not depend on whether the truth that accompanies a given exercise of power is "really" true or not, but should instead target the "therefore," which gives *force* to that truth, allowing a given governmental apparatus to say: "It is true, therefore you must submit."[61] Indeed, this "therefore" is not necessary and can be rejected: whether we accept it or not should be an open question and not a foregone conclusion. Ultimately, the aim of Foucault's critical anarchaeology is to make us perceive all the "therefores" that silently govern our conduct, and to restore them to their actual status, that is, as historical, cultural, and ethico-political *problems*. As Foucault explains in 1978,

My problem is to see how human beings govern (themselves and others) by the production of truth. . . . How can one analyze the connection between ways of distinguishing the true from the false and ways of governing oneself and others?[62]

This is the problem that underpins Foucault's genealogy of the principal regimes of truth that characterize contemporary society.

Language Games and Games of Truth

The concepts of game and regime of truth—which Foucault uses, for example, to define science as a "family of games of truth all of which obey the same regime, although they do not obey the same grammar"—have a clear Wittgensteinian allure.[63] In his *Philosophical Investigations*, while assigning philosophy the task of "bring[ing] words back from their metaphysical to their everyday use," Wittgenstein clarifies one of the most striking claims of the *Tractatus*—namely, that language constitutes an insurmountable limit for us: "*The limits of my language* mean the limits of my world."[64] Thus, for Wittgenstein, "we cannot leave language to compare the logical form of language with the structure of reality," because "the world coincides for us with language."[65] The goal of the *Philosophical Investigations* is precisely to examine the complexity and richness of the world comprised within these limits—of our ordinary use of words and of the "inherited background against which I distinguish between true and false."[66] "Our mistake," Wittgenstein writes, "is to look for an explanation where we ought to regard the facts as 'proto-phenomena,'" and say: "This is the language game that is being played."[67] There is no "outside" to language games, no "meaning" that belongs to a reality external to the language games that are being played:

> The absolute inexpressible of the *Tractatus* thus becomes relative to this or that particular language game. We come up against such an inexpressible when we want to transport the grammar of a language game to another language game. One must respect the grammar of each language game, speak of feelings as feelings, of objects as objects, and acknowledge the insurmountable limits that are imposed on us within each given language game.[68]

When Foucault argues that the formal rules of each given game of truth autonomously establish, within it, the distinction between true and false statements, he seems to be making an analogous point: there is no truth external to the games of truth that are being played, just as there is no meaning external to the language games that are being played.[69] Thus, at first glance, Foucault's concept of game of truth looks very close to Wittgenstein's concept of language game. Indeed, Wittgenstein explains that he decided to use the term "language *game*" in order to "emphasize the fact that the *speaking* of language is part of an activity, or of a form of life."[70] Each given language game, as Pierre Hadot points out, "operates according to its own specific modes and rules";[71] and while at every moment in time the totality of the language games corresponds to all existing linguistic activities, "this diversity is not something fixed, given once for all," because "new language games" constantly "come into existence," while "others become obsolete and get forgotten"—just as Foucault's games of truth.[72]

Yet, notwithstanding the undeniable proximity between Foucault's concept of game of truth and Wittgenstein's concept of language game, I think it would be misleading to push the analogy too far, for at least two reasons. The most intuitive one is that, for Wittgenstein, the totality of language games existing at every moment in time corresponds to the *entire* field of linguistic activity, whereas for Foucault the totality of games of truth clearly does not exhaust the discursive field, insofar as some discursive practices—some language games—are not indexed to the truth.[73] The reason Foucault does not focus on them is to be found in the methodological principle that he formulates in *On the Government of the Living*, which I discussed above: no government (of self and others) without alethurgy.[74]

However, there is a second, more important reason for exercising caution when it comes to the analogy between games of truth and language games: the conceptual and practical connection that Foucault establishes between games and regimes of truth gives the former an ethico-political scope that it is difficult to find in Wittgenstein's notion of language games. Indeed, while it was in large part due to ordinary language philosophers such as Wittgenstein and Austin that Foucault came to conceive of discourse as a "strategic field"—as a "battle," a "weapon," a "force"—their analyses conducted "over a cup of tea, in an Oxford drawing room," remain too abstract in his eyes.[75] Foucault wants to "study the strategy of discourse in a more real historical context"—namely, the concrete networks of power relations that run through and shape discursive practices, and that the latter incite or trigger in turn.[76]

In 1978, Foucault famously refers to this project in terms of an "analytic philosophy of politics," or an "analytico-political philosophy," that, far from posing the issue of power in terms of good or bad, contents itself with posing it in terms of *existence*: "What do power relations fundamentally consist in?"[77] Just as ordinary language philosophy, which relies on the insight that "language is played" in order to describe what occurs in our everyday language games, Foucault relies on the hypothesis that "relations of power too are played" in order to describe "what ordinarily happens in power relations," and defines the latter as "games of power that we should study in terms of tactics and strategy, rule and accident, stakes and objective."[78] Thus, while drawing from ordinary language philosophy, Foucault explicitly *politicizes* its insights. This is even clearer when Foucault talks about the critical value of his analytico-political philosophy:

> We have known for a long time that the role of philosophy is not to discover what is hidden, but rather to make visible what precisely is visible, which is to say, to make appear what is so close, so immediate, so intimately connected with ourselves that, as a consequence, we do not perceive it.[79]

Here, Foucault is quoting almost verbatim the *Philosophical Investigations*, where Wittgenstein famously argues that

> philosophy just puts everything before us, and neither explains nor deduces anything. . . . The aspects of things that are most important for us are hidden because of their simplicity and familiarity. (One is unable to notice something—because it is always before one's eyes.)[80]

Yet Foucault imbues this task with a critical, ethico-political value that we do not (explicitly) find in Wittgenstein, who writes that "philosophy must not interfere in any way with the actual use of language," but must instead limit itself to describing it, and therefore "leaves everything as it is."[81] By contrast, in the first volume of his *History of Sexuality*, Foucault argues that "power is tolerable only on condition that it mask a substantial part of itself": its success "is proportional to its ability to hide its own mechanisms," and secrecy "is indispensable to its operation."[82] Thus, by making us see something that we could not see before—for instance, the "therefore" that links the "it is true" (of the game of truth) to the "I submit" (of the regime of truth)—philosophy is immediately critical for Foucault. His elaboration of the concepts of game and regime of truth, and his insistence on their conceptual and practical connection, do not serve a merely descriptive objective. Or better: description here has a crucial unmasking function that, while always avoiding formulating evaluative judgments, aims to "intensify the struggles that develop around power, the strategies of the antagonists within relations of power, the tactics employed, the *foyers* of resistance."[83] This is the critical, ethico-political dimension that characterizes Foucault's (mature) conception of games and regimes of truth, and that we would have a hard time finding in Wittgenstein's notion of language games: there is no game of truth without or external to a regime of truth that defines a specific modality of governing human beings and constituting their subjectivity.

By relying on the concepts of game and regime of truth, Foucault's history of truth calls into question the idea that the truth leaves us no choice, such that government is always good and legitimate if it is based on the truth. This idea is an ethico-political "trap" that Foucault's genealogy of the principal regimes of truth in contemporary society aims to unmask by showing the historicity of the "therefore" that links games and regimes of truth, thereby allowing us to problematize it.

The Value of Truth

The problematization of the "therefore" of truth is the form that Foucault's history of truth gives to the critical task that Nietzsche, in the *Genealogy*, characterizes as the calling into question of the value of truth. However, it could be asked why Foucault, after unmasking the above-mentioned ethico-political trap, did not decide to complement his genealogical project with the elaboration of a new critical theory that would avoid any reference to truth and rely on other, different values.[84] While a final answer to this delicate question will only be provided in chapter 5, a first (provisional) answer consists in emphasizing that Foucault always avoided elaborating ambitious and all-encompassing theories that would (allegedly) "solve" the problems of our time, just as he avoided calling for a global "revolution," preferring to focus instead on the analysis of more limited, ordinary, and humble counter-conducts in order to contribute to their intensification.[85] Thus, Foucault never places himself *outside* of the processes he addresses — including when he addresses the problem of the government of human beings by the truth. This is why, in his lectures and writings from the 1980s, his aim is not to develop an alternate theory of government, but to (genealogically) examine different ways in which the relation between the three "poles" of truth, government, and subjectivity has been shaped throughout the history of Western societies.

Therefore, in 1980, Foucault explicitly poses the question of the value of truth in ethico-political terms. While he no doubt agrees with Canguilhem that the value of philosophy is something other than the value of truth, what gives value to philosophy as a critical activity, according to Foucault, is the problematization of the value that has been and still is attributed to the truth, and consequently of the force that the latter exerts on people when it comes to governing their conduct.[86] This is the fundamental task that Foucault repeatedly attributes to his own analyses throughout the last five lecture courses given at the Collège de France. For instance, at the beginning of his 1981 course, *Subjectivity and Truth*, he schematically addresses three possible ways of conceiving of the relation between subjectivity and truth. First, the "philosophical" way, which has been prevalent from Plato to (at least) Kant, and which consists in asking how knowledge-*connaissance* as an experience specific to the knowing subject is possible: given that there can be no truth without a subject for whom this truth is true, how can the subject "actually have access to the truth?" (this is the question of "the possibility of a truth for a subject in general").[87] Second, the "positivist" way, which asks the same question, but the other way around: "Is it possible to have a true knowledge-*connaissance* of the subject, and on what conditions?"[88] In other words, the positivist question focuses on the possibility of an *objective* knowledge of the subject: "How can there be truth *of* the subject, even though there can be truth only *for* a subject?" (this is the question of "the possibility of telling the truth about subjectivity").[89]

Unsurprisingly, Foucault explains that he is not interested in either of these questions, but rather in a third way of conceiving of the relation between subjectivity and truth, which he terms "historico-philosophical": given that true discourses about the subject exist, circulate, and function in every human society, "what is the subject's experience of herself and what is the subject's relationship to herself in view of the fact of this existence of a true discourse about her?"[90] In other words,

> what experience may the subject have of herself when faced with the possibility or obligation of acknowledging something that passes for true regarding herself? What relationship does the subject have to herself when this relationship can or must pass through the promised or imposed discovery of the truth about herself?[91]

Given the existence in every human society, and certainly in ours (think of what Foucault calls confessional sciences), of discourses that aim to tell the truth about the subject, and given the set of truth obligations that bind the subject to them, Foucault wants to examine the problem of the subject's "experience" of herself and of how the latter is (trans)formed by these discourses. This is the question of the effects on subjectivity "of a discourse that claims to tell the truth about subjectivity"; hence the centrality of the dimension of subjectivity, or better, the focus on the alethurgic subject, which I discussed above in relation to Foucault's analyses in *On the Government of the Living*.[92] Indeed, in the historico-philosophical perspective, subjectivity is not conceived "on the basis of a prior and universal theory of the subject," but construed "as that which is *constituted* and *transformed* in its relationship to its own truth"—one that is not defined "by a certain content of knowledge-*connaissance* that is thought to be universally valid," nor "by a certain formal and universal criterion," but as a "system of obligations."[93] As Foucault already claimed in *On the Government of the Living*,

What is important in this question of truth is that a certain number of things actually pass for true, and that the subject must produce them herself, or accept them, or submit to them. So, what has been and will be at issue is the truth as bond, as obligation, and also as politics, and not the truth as content of knowledge-*connaissance* or as formal structure of knowledge-*connaissance*.[94]

What is important, in other words, is the "therefore" that links the "it is true" to the "I submit": not the formal rules of the *game* of truth, but the truth obligations of the *regime* of truth—or, as Foucault argues in *Subjectivity and Truth*, "the way in which subjectivities as experiences of self and others are constituted through obligations of truth," within "the political history of veridictions."[95] This approach, as mentioned above, characterizes the entirety of Foucault's lecture courses at the Collège de France from the 1980s, for it clearly underpins not only the distinction between philosophy and spirituality that he draws in the first lecture of *The Hermeneutics of the Subject*, but also the methodological introductions that he offers to *The Government of Self and Others* and *The Courage of Truth*.[96]

On the one hand, at the beginning of *The Government of Self and Others*, Foucault describes the theoretical shifts undergone in the previous ten years by the three main axes of his analyses: from the formation of knowledges-*savoirs* to the modes of veridiction; from the normative frameworks of behavior to the procedures of governmentality; from the subject (of knowledge-*connaissance*) to the forms of subjectivation examined in light of what Foucault now calls the techniques of the self, or the "pragmatics of the self."[97] Referring to these new axes, in the lecture on January 12, 1983, Foucault argues that his aim is to establish the correlation between them, and thus to pose "the question of the government of self and others" in order to see "how truth-telling [*dire-vrai*], the obligation and possibility of telling the truth in procedures of government can show how the individual constitutes herself as a subject in the relationship to self and the relationship to others."[98] This is the reason Foucault gives for putting *parrhesia* at the center of his analyses—for *parrhesia* is exactly situated "at the meeting point of the obligation to speak the truth, procedures and techniques of governmentality, and the constitution of the relationship to self."[99] It is thus not surprising that the topic of *parrhesia* ends up monopolizing Foucault's attention from 1982 to 1984, so much so that it no doubt deserves to be regarded as more relevant than his analysis of the ancient ethics of the care of the self—even though virtually all commentators still take the latter, along with the writing of the second, third, and fourth volumes of the *History of Sexuality*, as the defining project of the "final Foucault."

On the other hand, at the beginning of *The Courage of Truth*, Foucault explains that, while it is certainly interesting and important to analyze the "structures of those discourses which claim to be and are accepted as true discourses," that is, to undertake an "epistemological analysis" or a "study of epistemological structures," he chose to develop a different kind of investigation, which consists in the analysis of "the conditions and forms of the type of act by which the subject *manifests* herself when speaking the truth," that is, "constitutes herself and is constituted by others as a subject of a discourse of truth."[100] In other words, instead of analyzing the internal rules that define games of truth, Foucault decided to adopt the standpoint of the regime of truth and to undertake "the study of 'alethurgic' forms."[101] It is clear, therefore, that during the last four years of his life, the methodological and conceptual framework of Foucault's history of truth, as defined in *On the Government of the Living*, remains exactly the same.

Regimes of Truth and Spirituality

In 1980, Foucault insists on the *multiplicity* of regimes of truth that have emerged throughout the history of human societies, and argues that many of them, albeit "very distant from scientific regimes of self-indexation of truth," are "quite coherent and complex."[102] The last few years of Foucault's life will be devoted, precisely, to the analysis of several "non-scientific" regimes of truth, both in early Christianity and in Greco-Roman antiquity.[103] These ancient regimes of truth are all explicitly characterized, according to Foucault, by a structure of "spirituality": in order to have access to the truth, the subject must modify and transform herself through a series of exercises.[104] In other words, *askesis*—the work of the self on itself, the elaboration of the self by itself—plays a crucial role in these non-scientific "alethurgic forms."[105]

By examining the main features of these regimes of truth, so different from the modern ones centered on truth as knowledge-*connaissance* (even though, as we saw, truth-demonstration itself is actually only an aspect of truth-event), Foucault undertakes a complex operation. On the one hand, it is clear that some of his analyses, especially those addressing the Christian practices of *exomologesis* and *exagoreusis*, are part of his genealogy of the confessional regime of truth that characterizes our contemporary society.[106] On the other hand, as I will argue in more detail in chapter 5, Foucault's study of ancient *parrhesia* is also clearly part of another genealogy: the genealogy of the critical attitude, or the critical regime of truth in our society. The critical scope of Foucault's history of truth, as he develops it in the 1980s, is thus twofold: it aims both to question our unreflected acceptance of the "therefore" that links the "it is true" to the "I submit" in contemporary confessional sciences, and to examine historically situated forms of resistance and counter-conduct that rely on specific practices of truth-telling, or truth-*living* (as in the case of the Cynic philosophers).

Hence, on the one hand, Foucault's analysis of the technology of confession in early Christianity, and his study of the ancient (pagan) practices of the care of self and of *parrhesia*, aim to trace genealogical processes of "descent" and "emergence" that connect relevant features of these premodern regimes of truth with important aspects of the modern and contemporary (confessional) ones—and of their ways of organizing the relation between manifestation of truth, government of human beings, and constitution of subjectivity.[107] Yet, on the other hand, Foucault also emphasizes a series of genealogical *discontinuities*, or better, the fact that some of these ancient regimes of truth explicitly thematized in terms of "spirituality" (particularly those organized around the ethico-political practice of *parrhesia*) are at the same time part of a genealogy of critique that, in his eyes, plays a crucial role in the fight against contemporary governmental mechanisms.

Drawing from this Foucauldian insight, according to which *parrhesia*— a verbal activity rather than a mental experience—can be construed as a critical practice of truth that relies on a conception of truth as event and force rather than as knowledge-*connaissance*, in the next chapter I define parrhesiastic utterance as a (transhistorical) family of *critical* speech acts whose main effects are perlocutionary.[108] As I will show, the analysis of *parrhesia* as speech act builds on two of the main ideas that characterize Foucault's project of a history of truth: truth-demonstration is actually a form of truth-event, and no game of truth can exist outside of a regime of truth.

Truth as Force

To construe parrhesiastic utterance as a transhistorical family of critical speech acts that I suggest studying in terms of perlocutionary effect,
I will draw not only from Foucault's analyses of ancient *parrhesia*, but also
from Stanley Cavell's study of what he calls passionate utterance: a kind
or family of utterances in which "the feelings and actions I wish to provoke . . . or bring off . . . are ones I can acknowledge, or specifically refuse
to acknowledge, as appropriate responses to my expressions of feeling."[1]
I will clearly distinguish it from performative utterance as it is traditionally
understood—namely, in terms of the illocutionary act. My main goal,
however, is not to elaborate a full-fledged "theory" of parrhesiastic utterance, but rather to explore a possible redefinition of truth (and not just
of speech or words) as a critical, ethico-political *force*. To do so, I will
combine Foucault's analyses of ancient *parrhesia* and Cavell's "extension"
of J. L. Austin's theory of performative utterance in order to develop an
investigation of *parrhesia*'s perlocutionary effects—that is, what one does,
not *in* saying something, but *by* saying something. It is worth noting here
that Cavell himself conceived of his work on passionate utterance not—or,
at any rate, not primarily—as a contribution to the philosophy of language, but rather as a series of observations in service of something he
wanted "from moral theory, namely, a systematic recognition of speech as
confrontation, as demanding, as owed . . . , each instance of which directs,
and risks, if not costs, blood."[2]

Cavell, Austin, and the Perlocutionary

Since the "pragmatic revolution" in the philosophy of language of the
1950s, much ink has been spilled on the theory of speech acts, particularly on the notions of performative utterance and illocutionary force.

Yet some aspects of the performativity of language, that is, of its capacity to *do* things, remain significantly underexamined, most notably the domain of the perlocutionary. It could be said that, in this respect, Austin's project has been followed too literally, even by his critics. Indeed, in *How to Do Things with Words*, Austin explains that his main interest lies in the illocutionary act and, consequently, that his analysis of the locutionary and the perlocutionary acts merely aims to (try to) demarcate and emphasize the importance of the illocutionary dimension of speech.[3] Thus, it is no surprise that, in the first four decades following the publication of Austin's lectures, scholars have focused almost exclusively on the illocutionary act, while dismissing the perlocutionary act as unessential to the theory of speech acts.[4] It is mostly owing to Cavell's texts on passionate utterance, and to their emphasis on the need to overcome Austin's restriction of speech act analysis (and, more generally, of the performativity of language) to illocutions, that the perlocutionary domain has gained some traction in the past few years.[5]

Cavell famously presents his study of passionate utterance as an elaboration of Austin's idea of the perlocutionary effect—one that Austin himself, however, "for some reason did not make."[6] Indeed, according to Cavell, passionate utterance is "just one form in which perlocutionary effect structures itself: moralistic abusiveness is another; hate speech another; political oratory another."[7] Recall that, in *How to Do Things with Words*, Austin draws a distinction between the illocutionary and perlocutionary effects of a given speech act by arguing that the illocutionary effect consists in the performative function of the speech act at a conventional level (that is, in the "conventional consequences" of the utterance), while the perlocutionary effect corresponds to "the real production of real effects" on the (intended or unintended) audience or on the speaker—effects that are not entirely predictable because they are not conventionally defined.[8] Thus, according to Austin, any given speech act is composed of three deeply interconnected but theoretically distinct acts: the locutionary act (saying something meaningful), the illocutionary act (what one does *in* saying something), and the perlocutionary act (what one does *by* saying something).[9]

More precisely, Austin's idea is that to perform a locutionary act means also, in general, to perform an illocutionary act, such as asking or answering a question, giving information or assurance, announcing an intention or a verdict, and so on;[10] and that there is a further sense "in which to perform a locutionary act, and therein an illocutionary act, may also be to perform an act of another kind"—namely, a perlocution:

Saying something will often, or even normally, produce certain consequential effects upon the feelings, thoughts, or actions of the audience, or of the speaker, or of other persons: and it may be done with the design, intention, or purpose of producing them.[11]

However, while saying "I warn you" (a locutionary act) *is*, in the appropriate circumstances, to warn you (an illocutionary act), and it *may* also exasperate or intimidate you (a perlocutionary act), saying "I exasperate you" or "I intimidate you" will not *as such* exasperate or intimidate you.[12] Yet, as Cavell rightly argues, perlocutions constitute a dimension of our form of life as "creatures of language" that matters deeply to us, and that plays a fundamental role in our ordinary exchanges of words.[13] Building on this crucial insight, I will broaden Cavell's examination of the domain of the perlocutionary beyond what he calls passionate utterance and elaborate an analysis of *parrhesia* as another form in which the perlocutionary effect structures itself. This will allow me to clarify and extend Foucault's historical analyses of this peculiar practice of truth-telling, while situating them within a more explicit philosophical framework.[14]

In the first chapter of *Philosophy the Day after Tomorrow*, Cavell introduces his interest in "Austin's sense of the powers of speech" by linking it with his interest in "the voice in opera"—the latter being, in his view, "the Western institution in which . . . the human voice is given its fullest acknowledgement."[15] It is precisely this link that allows Cavell to ask whether Austin's theory of speech acts, that is, of speech as *action*, "may be extended, in a sense re-begun, in order to articulate a theory of speech as *passion*."[16] In addition to some well-known examples drawn from opera, literature, and cinema, Cavell claims that a theory of passionate speech should also be able to illuminate the status of utterances that lie more traditionally within the framework of moral philosophy, such as those discussed by A. J. Ayer in *Language, Truth, and Logic*: "You acted wrongly in stealing that money," "Tolerance is a virtue," "You ought to tell the truth."[17] These "moral judgments," according to Ayer, "do not say anything": they are compromised in their meaningfulness because, far from coming "under the category of truth and falsehood," they are "pure expressions of feeling" calculated to provoke "different responses."[18] Now, as Cavell rightly points out, Austin's theory of speech acts demonstrates the absurdity of this conclusion: in *How to Do Things with Words*, he "provides massive classes of counterexamples" to the idea that any sentence that does not come under the category of truth and falsehood is ipso facto meaningless;[19] and he discusses many cases in which to utter a sentence, in the appropriate circumstances, "is not to *describe* my doing of what I should be said in so uttering to be doing or to state that I am doing it: it is to do it."[20] Call this Austin's move.

Yet there are two aspects of this move that prove unsatisfactory. On the one hand, Austin does not explicitly discuss Ayer's above-mentioned examples of moral judgments, nor their descendants, and more generally he "seems unable to do much with the field of the perlocutionary comparable to his mapping of that of the illocutionary."[21] Thus, Cavell suggests that Austin's theory of speech acts should be *re-begun*, and that we should pay more attention "to the fact of the expressiveness and responsiveness of speech as such."[22] Call this Cavell's move. On the other hand, as we saw, Ayer claims that utterances such as "You acted wrongly in stealing that money," "Tolerance is a virtue," or "You ought to tell the truth" do not come under the category of truth and falsehood and *consequently* are not in the literal sense significant—they do not say anything. In criticizing Ayer's conclusion, however, neither Austin nor Cavell seems to be willing to also problematize his premise—namely, that these utterances do not come under the category of truth and falsehood. Indeed, Cavell's move consists in broadening Austin's theory of speech acts in order to shed new light upon the crucial philosophical "question of the relation of passion to speech."[23] According to Cavell, by focusing on performative utterance, Austin aimed "to lift the non-descriptive or non-assertional or non-constative gestures of speech to renewed philosophical interest and respectability, and to bring, or prepare the ground on which to bring, the philosophical concern with truth down to size."[24] Cavell is no doubt sympathetic to this project, but he is not ready to pay the price that seemingly goes with it, that of the "continued neglect of the passions, or say the expressive, in speech": according to him, Austin's theory of speech acts "pictures speech as at heart a matter of action and only incidentally as a matter of articulating and hence expressing desire."[25] Therefore, Cavell is not interested in the question of the truthfulness or falsity of our moral judgments.[26]

By contrast, I will take seriously Ayer's claim that these moral judgments do not come under the category of truth and falsehood in order to emphasize the novelty of an analysis of *parrhesia* as speech act—and to define what I call Foucault's move. Indeed, Foucault's lectures and writings (implicitly) suggest that *parrhesia* can be considered a specific family of speech acts characterized by the fact that the question of their truthfulness—which, as we shall see, does not correspond to the question of their (constative, logical, or epistemological) truth value—plays an essential role with regard to the act of uttering them, to the status of

the subject who utters them, and to the (intended and unintended) consequences they provoke. Thus, the analysis of *parrhesia* as speech act allows
us to examine a specific region of the perlocutionary domain, one that
overlaps with, but is philosophically distinct from, the region that Cavell
examines in his texts on passionate utterance: while the main function
of passionate utterance is to manifest human beings' (ethical) relation to
passion, the main function of parrhesiastic utterance is to manifest their
(ethico-political) relation to the truth. Clearly, Foucault's move—just as
Austin's and Cavell's—also aims to bring the philosophical concern with
(constative, logical, or epistemological) truth down to size, but it does
so in a different way, one that has not been adequately appreciated so far.

In short, if Austin's response to Ayer is to show that there is a vast
class of ordinary utterances (what he calls *performative* utterances) whose
meaning is not compromised by not being truth-evaluable; and if Cavell's
response to Austin is to broaden his theory of speech acts by offering a
detailed analysis of the perlocutionary in terms of what he calls *passionate*
utterances; then the response I will advance by drawing from Foucault's
historico-philosophical analysis of *parrhesia* consists in raising once more,
albeit from a different point of view, the question of the truthfulness or
falsity of certain utterances—namely, *parrhesiastic* utterances. By doing
so, my aim is to situate Ayer's warhorse examples of moral judgments
within a larger framework: that of an analysis of truth as a critical, ethico-
political force.

Parrhesia *as Speech Act*

There is of course a major difference between Foucault's analyses of *parrhesia* and Ayer's, Austin's, and Cavell's respective accounts of "moral,"
performative, and passionate utterances. Indeed, as mentioned above,
Foucault's study of *parrhesia* is part of a (twofold) genealogical project
and is therefore clearly not meant to be a contribution to the philosophy
of language. Foucault is not even interested in offering a systematic definition or characterization of *parrhesia* that would be valid in all times and
places.[27] *Parrhesia*, for him, is not (or, at any rate, not primarily) a class
of utterances to be analyzed in its ahistorical features, but a historical notion and practice whose meaning has significantly changed throughout
the centuries, and which he addresses as a crucial piece of his genealogy
of the confessional and critical regimes of truth in our society. Thus, in
the lectures and writings that he devotes to this topic between 1982 and
1984, Foucault offers several definitions of *parrhesia*, which are often quite
different from each other—since, clearly, *parrhesia* does not have the exact

same meaning in the context of fifth-century BCE Athenian democracy as in the texts written by fourth-century BCE Athenian elites, in Plato's dialogues, in Cynic philosophical practice, in Hellenistic and Roman spiritual direction, or in early Christianity.

Therefore, from a Foucauldian perspective, trying to systematize these historical analyses in order to elaborate a "theory" of what could be called parrhesiastic utterance would make little to no sense. However, it is possible to find, in the multiple historical forms taken by *parrhesia* as critical attitude (leaving aside, for the time being, Cynic *parrhesia* as *vraie vie* and *vie autre*), a certain number of common features that will allow me to talk about *parrhesia* in terms of a well-defined "family" of speech acts. Foucault himself seems to suggest this possibility when, in his lecture course *Discourse and Truth*, he offers "a brief survey of the meaning of the word [*parrhesia*] and the evolution of this meaning" throughout Greco-Roman culture from the fifth century BCE to the fifth century CE, concluding by defining the "general meaning" of *parrhesia* in the "positive sense of the word" as

> a certain verbal activity in which the speaker has a specific relation to truth through frankness, a certain relation to himself through danger, a certain relation to law through freedom and duty, and a certain relation to other people through critique (self-critique or critique of other people). More precisely, it is a verbal activity in which the subject expresses his personal relation to truth and risks his life because he recognizes that telling the truth is his own duty, so as to improve or to help other people. In *parrhesia*, the speaker uses his freedom and chooses truth instead of lies, death instead of life and security, criticism instead of flattery, and duty instead of interest and selfishness.[28]

Drawing from this definition, I will focus on two paradigmatic examples (apparently very different from one another) of the practice of *parrhesia* in antiquity, in order to enumerate and analyze the common features that characterize parrhesiastic utterance as a transhistorical family of critical speech acts.

The first example is addressed by Foucault in his 1983 lecture course at the Collège de France, *The Government of Self and Others*. It is actually the first concrete case of *parrhesia* he analyzes there, after speaking of Kant in the lecture on January 5, 1983, and offering some general remarks at the beginning of the following lecture. In order to transition from these introductory remarks, which no doubt risk appearing too abstract, to a "more precise" characterization of *parrhesia*, Foucault does not trace the history of this notion chronologically (as he would do a few months later at Berkeley), but chooses to focus on "an average text, . . . an average case, an average example of *parrhesia* from almost exactly mid-way between the classical age and the great Christian spirituality of the fourth to fifth century CE, in which we see this notion of *parrhesia* at work in a traditional but not very well-defined field of philosophy."[29] This example is drawn from Plutarch's *Parallel Lives* (959d), and in particular from the life of Dion, the brother-in-law of Dionysius, the tyrant of Syracuse, as well as Plato's disciple, sponsor, and host when the latter traveled to Sicily:

Their conversation having got underway, the basic theme of the discussion was virtue, but more especially courage. Plato showed that tyrants were anything but courageous; then, moving away from this subject, he elaborated on justice and showed that the life of the just man was happy and that the unjust man was unhappy. The tyrant could not bear these remarks, which he thought were directed at him, and he did not conceal his displeasure at seeing the other admiring auditors being charmed by the discourse of the great man. Finally, filled with anger and exasperation, Dionysius asked Plato: "What have you come to Sicily for?" And Plato replied: "I am looking for a good man." The tyrant replied: "By the gods, it is clear that you have not yet found one!" Dion thought that Dionysius' anger would end there, and he put Plato, who was in a hurry to leave, on a trireme taking Pollis, the Spartan, back to Greece. But Dionysius secretly asked Pollis to kill Plato on the journey, if it was possible, and if not, to at least sell him into slavery.[30]

Plutarch goes on to explain that Dion was about the only one whose frankness (*parrhesia*) the tyrant tolerated, and who was therefore allowed to speak his mind in front of him.[31] Yet I will focus on Plato's frankness: even though the word *parrhesia* is absent from the above-cited text, the idea is in fact clearly there. As Foucault argues, this is "an exemplary scene of *parrhesia*: a man stands up to a tyrant and tells him the truth."[32]

The second example is analyzed by Foucault in a lecture on *parrhesia* at the University of Grenoble in May 1982, given shortly after finishing his 1982 lecture course at the Collège de France, *The Hermeneutics of the Subject*. The "scene" described here is entirely different from the previous one: it is an instance of *parrhesia* within the framework of the care of the self, and more precisely of the philosophical practice of spiritual direction in ancient Rome—the context in which Foucault "discovers" the notion of *parrhesia* for the first time.[33] Both at Grenoble and at the Collège de France,[34] he focuses on a specific passage from Seneca's letters to Lucilius—the incipit of *Letter 75*, in which Seneca characterizes his own discourse as a parrhesiastic discourse (although, once more, neither *libertas* nor *libera oratio* appears in the text):

> My letters are not to your taste, not polished as they should be, and you complain about it. In truth, who thinks about polishing his style, apart from lovers of pretentious style? If we were idly sitting or strolling together, my conversation would be unaffected and easygoing. I wish my letters to be like this: there is nothing mannered or artificial about them. If it were possible, I would like to let you see my thoughts rather than translate them into language. Even in a regular lecture, I would not stamp my foot, wave my arms about, or raise my voice, leaving that to orators and judging my end achieved if I have conveyed my thought without ornament or platitudes. Above all, I would dearly love you to understand that I think everything I say, and not content with thinking it, I love it. . . . This is the most important point of my remarks: to say what one thinks, to think what one says, to see to it that language is in harmony with conduct. He who is the same when seen and heard has fulfilled his commitments.[35]

It is remarkable that the word "truth," just as the words *parrhesia* and *libertas*, does not appear in either of these texts: it is Foucault who introduces it, because he is convinced that these are two excellent examples of the practice of *parrhesia* and that, "in the first place, *parrhesia* is the fact of telling the truth."[36] However, as he immediately points out, it is clear that *parrhesia* "is not just any way of telling the truth": for instance, when Plato writes in his dialogues that "the life of the just is happy and that of the unjust unhappy," he is clearly not using *parrhesia*; instead, it is "only in this precise situation and context," when he utters those words in front of Dionysius, that he makes use of *parrhesia*.[37] Thus, according to Foucault, "*parrhesia* is a way of telling the truth, but what defines it is not the content of the truth as such": it is the specific form taken by the *act* of truth-telling.[38]

Defining *parrhesia* is therefore not an easy task: there is, and can be, no simple answer to the question "What is *parrhesia*?" when asked in the abstract. In 1983, Foucault argues that *parrhesia* "does not fall within the province of eristic and an art of debate, or of pedagogy and an art of teaching, or of rhetoric and an art of persuasion, or of an art of demonstration," because there is *parrhesia* every time that "telling the truth takes place in conditions such that the fact of telling the truth, and the fact of having told it, will, may, or must entail costly consequences for those who have told it."[39] Consequently, to define *parrhesia*, we should not focus on "the internal structure of the discourse, or [on] the aim which the true discourse seeks to achieve vis-à-vis the interlocutor," but rather on the speaker and "the risk that truth-telling opens up for the speaker."[40] By telling the truth to the tyrant, Plato opens up a certain "space of risk," of danger, of peril, in which his own life will be at stake—and, according to Foucault, "it is this that constitutes *parrhesia*."[41] *Parrhesia* should therefore be considered a specific verbal activity that "binds the speaker to the fact that what he says is the truth, and to the consequences which follow from the fact that he has told the truth": those who use *parrhesia*, Foucault concludes, "undertake to tell the truth at an unspecified price, which may be as high as their own death."[42]

These claims, however, far from dispelling all ambiguity, raise further questions: In what sense does the parrhesiast "tell the truth"? And how can Foucault's remarks about Plato *literally* risking his life in order to "tell the truth" to the tyrant Dionysius be applied to Seneca's perfectly civilized correspondence with his friend and disciple Lucilius?

To answer these delicate questions, in what follows I will develop a perlocutionary analysis of *parrhesia* as speech act. Here, it is worth noting that, even though Foucault never mentions the illocutionary-perlocutionary distinction, in the lecture on January 12, 1983, of *The Government of Self and Others*, he does refer to Austin's theory of speech acts. More precisely, Foucault draws a distinction between *parrhesia* and performative utterance (as defined by Austin at the beginning of *How to Do Things with Words*), arguing that the latter is "a form of enunciation which is exactly the opposite of *parrhesia*."[43] This sudden irruption of a discussion that pertains to the philosophy of language into Foucault's historico-philosophical analysis of ancient *parrhesia* should not appear too surprising. Indeed, as Arnold Davidson has convincingly argued, Anglo-American philosophy of language was for Foucault an important source of inspiration throughout his entire intellectual career.[44] As early as 1967, in a letter to Daniel Defert, Foucault claims that the Anglo-American "analytic" philosophers allowed him to understand how to study statements in their concrete functioning.[45] That same year, in a lecture given in Tunis, Foucault builds on the works of Luis Jorge Prieto and J. L. Austin to argue that the analysis of discourse cannot be reduced to the analysis of the linguistic rules that govern the combination of its elements, because "discourse is something that necessarily overflows language [*la langue*]."[46] Thus, he suggests that, in studying discourse, we should focus on what he calls "extralinguistic" elements, that is, the "contextual elements constituted by the very situation of the individual speaking" and "the speech act that is actually performed by the speaker at the moment when she speaks."[47] A few years later, as we saw, these same ideas led Foucault to conceive of discourse as a "strategic field" and a set of "strategic games"—as a struggle, a weapon, a force.[48] It would certainly be impossible to understand all the stakes involved in his analysis of *parrhesia* without taking into account this long-lasting philosophical interest in the *extralinguistic* analysis of discourse.[49]

If, in light of the above, Foucault's reference to Austin and speech acts in 1983 appears far less surprising, what is noteworthy is the parallel that can be established between Foucault's remarks on *parrhesia* and performative utterance and Cavell's claim that passionate speech *overturns*, "specifically and in detail," the six necessary conditions for the felicity of performative utterance.[50] Drawing from this parallel and building on the two above-mentioned examples, my perlocutionary analysis of *parrhesia* as speech act will take the form of a (provisional and open-ended) list of necessary conditions of parrhesiastic utterance. I will thus temporarily bracket the historical dimension of Foucault's study of *parrhesia* and, as a consequence, short-circuit the androcentric perspective that character-izes virtually all ancient philosophical texts referring to *parrhesia*.[51] The following analysis should therefore *not* be taken as applying exclusively to male parrhesiasts, for parrhesiastic speech acts can be performed (in the appropriate circumstances) by *anyone*, no matter their sex or gender.

Unpredictability, Freedom, and Criticism

In *Philosophy the Day after Tomorrow*, Cavell argues that there is "no con-ventional procedure for appealing to you to act in response to my expres-sion of passion (of outrage at your treachery or callousness, of jealousy over your attentions, of hurt over your slights of recognition)."[52] And he aptly points out that this "freedom" enjoyed by the interlocutor in her response (or absence of response) to the utterance addressed to her is a characteristic feature of all speech acts whose principal effects are perlo-cutionary.[53] Thus, Cavell claims that the "absence of convention" is "the first condition of passionate utterance," while in the case of performative utterance (at least as defined by Austin at the beginning of *How to Do Things with Words*) "there must exist an accepted conventional procedure for uttering certain words in certain contexts."[54]

In contrasting *parrhesia* with performative utterance, Foucault empha-sizes the exact same point:

> In a performative utterance, the given elements of the situation are such that when the utterance is made, the effect which follows is known and

ordered in advance, it is codified, and this is precisely what constitutes the performative character of the utterance. In *parrhesia*, on the other hand, whatever the usual, familiar, and quasi-institutionalized character of the situation in which it is effectuated, what makes it *parrhesia* is that the introduction, the irruption of the true discourse [that is, the parrhesiastic utterance] determines an open situation, or rather opens the situation and makes possible effects which are, precisely, not known.[55]

The first condition of parrhesiastic utterance is thus *the unpredictability of its effects*. Consequently, these effects belong to the domain of the perlocutionary—they are "real effects," as opposed to the "conventional consequences" that belong to the illocutionary domain. Does this mean that these (perlocutionary) effects are nothing more than "a chance by-product of our utterances"?[56] I think we should resist this conclusion because it risks suggesting that a coherent philosophical analysis of the perlocutionary domain is either uninteresting or impossible, and that at any rate it does not *really* belong to the theory of speech acts. Yet it is unquestionable that perlocutionary effects often constitute the most important aspect of what we do with words—the aspect that matters most to us. Asserting, for instance, would be a rather uninteresting activity if it was always and exclusively aimed at giving others reliable "testimony" on matters of fact. Luckily for us, this is not the case: the point of asserting something is often to convince or dissuade, amuse or anger, reassure or alarm, incite or scare, seduce or inspire, comfort or hurt. Therefore, the theory of speech acts would prove deeply deficient if it were to eschew perlocutionary effects, considering them merely as a chance by-product of our utterances, thereby dismissing the philosophical interest of (among others) passionate and parrhesiastic utterances.

Moreover, in emphasizing the unpredictability of the effects of passionate and parrhesiastic utterances, Cavell and Foucault (implicitly) provide us with a compelling argument for basing the distinction between illocutionary and perlocutionary acts on the degree of predictability and stability of their respective effects. Indeed, when felicitously performed, an illocutionary act entails a perfectly predictable sequence of illocutionary consequences: for example, when I promise something to someone, I commit myself in a well-defined way to keeping my word. In addition, these consequences possess a great degree of stability, because they cannot be modified or renegotiated *at will*, just by saying, "I'm sorry, I didn't mean my promise, forget it." (Of course, I *can* say that, but I would still have broken my word.) By contrast, perlocutionary effects are never entirely predictable and are structurally open to renegotiation: for instance, if I want to console you and end up angering you instead, I can always say, "I didn't mean to make you mad, forgive me, I was trying to comfort you"—thus (at least potentially) transforming the first perlocutionary effect into an open-ended process of renegotiation.

Of course, perlocutionary effects are not totally unpredictable, either. There are many social and cultural conventions that regulate our ordinary exchange of words as well as the production of perlocutionary effects: just as illocutionary consequences, perlocutionary effects are "constituents of social practices, . . . sustained by the practices of which they are themselves a part."[57] Consequently, we are *normally* right in expecting that a certain sentence, uttered in a certain context, will produce certain perlocutionary effects. As Cavell argues, "If I could not rationally expect, by variously expressing myself to you, to have the effect of alarming you or reassuring you, of offending or amusing you, boring or interesting you, exasperating or fascinating you, . . . I would lack the capacity to make myself intelligible to you."[58] However, I can never be entirely sure in advance that I will *actually* be able to make myself intelligible to my interlocutor in any given situation. Thus, acting perlocutionarily with words—including in the case of passionate and parrhesiastic speech—means exposing oneself to the freedom that other people have to respond in various ways (or not at all) to one's words.

From this stems another difference that Foucault emphasizes between *parrhesia* and performative utterance. In order for a performative utterance to be felicitous, and thus for its illocutionary consequence(s) to be realized, the institutional status or social position of the speaker is crucial, because "the person speaking [must have] the status which permits her to carry out what is stated by undertaking her utterance."[59] For instance, "the person who opens the meeting simply by saying 'the meeting is open' must have the authority to do so and be the chairman of the meeting";[60] or—to take a different, more ordinary, example—in order to be able to forgive someone by saying "I forgive you," one "must have suffered an offense" from that specific person.[61] By contrast, parrhesiastic utterance is characterized by the fact that "the parrhesiast is someone who emphasizes her own freedom as an individual speaking."[62] As Foucault clearly argues,

Whereas the performative utterance defines a definite game in which the status of the person speaking and the situation in which she finds herself determine precisely what she can and must say, *parrhesia* only exists when there is freedom in the enunciation of the truth, in the act by which the subject says the truth, as well as in the pact by which the subject speaking binds herself to the statement and enunciation of the truth.[63]

I will address the question of truth later. For the time being, I suggest that the second condition of parrhesiastic utterance is *the freedom of the speaker*. This condition clearly applies to passionate utterance as well: as Cavell argues, while a performative utterance "is an offer of participation in the order of law," a passionate utterance "is an invitation to improvisation in the disorders of desire."[64]

In *Language and Symbolic Power*, Pierre Bourdieu rightly remarks that the illocutionary force of our utterances cannot be found in words themselves, but should rather be sought in the institutional and social conditions of their use. The conclusion that he draws from this remark, however, is quite problematic: "Against all the forms of autonomization of a distinctly linguistic order," he writes, "*all speech* is produced for and through the market to which it owes its existence and its most specific properties."[65] Thus, according to Bourdieu, "the power of words is nothing other than the *delegated power* of the spokesperson, and her speech . . . is no more than a testimony, and only one among others, of the *guarantee of delegation* which is vested in her."[66] Now, my perlocutionary analysis of parrhesiastic utterance makes it possible to criticize not only the linguistic reductionism Bourdieu correctly denounces, but *his own* sociological reductionism as well. Indeed, the multiple examples of *parrhesia* Foucault discusses clearly show that the force of words, or of truth, extends well beyond the illocutionary dimension of speech, such that it is actually able to *break* the rules of the social market to which, according to Bourdieu, words must always conform or submit.

Let me take just two among many possible examples. In Euripides's tragedy *Ion*, Creusa, after having been seduced (today we would say raped) by Apollo, decides to confront the god's refusal to tell the truth: she thus overcomes her shame and finds the courage to publicly accuse him of wrongdoing. Hence, against the suddenly voiceless god of Delphi, Creusa raises her own voice, whose legitimacy is not guaranteed by any institutional or social rule of the time, and which clearly takes the form of a *claim*.[67] It is a "speech act" by which "someone weak, abandoned, and powerless proclaims an injustice to the powerful person who committed it."[68] As Dianna Taylor aptly argues, at the beginning of the #MeToo movement, the victims of sexual violence were analogously disempowered, as social structures for reporting were either absent or ineffectual; their public speech was thus neither institutionally nor socially legitimated—on the contrary, it *challenged* "influential institutional figures," thus threatening "the institutions themselves."[69] As these examples clearly show, the force of parrhesiastic utterances cannot be reduced to the institutional and social conditions that define the context of their enunciation, since what characterizes *parrhesia* is precisely the fact that it challenges and attempts to overturn (at least some of) these conditions. The #MeToo movement in particular is a clear example of profound social, political, and moral change brought about by parrhesiastic speech acts that contributed to breaking and reinventing existing social norms, even though they came from a position of powerlessness. Limiting the analysis of the force of words to the illocutionary domain therefore makes Bourdieu ultimately unable to see all the things that can be (perlocutionarily) done with words in order to transform the social norms that govern—but do not *determine*—the production of our utterances.

It is also noteworthy that many parrhesiastic utterances take the form of statements analogous to Ayer's above-cited examples of "moral judgements." For instance, Plato claims before Dionysius and his entire court that tyrants are not courageous and that the life of the just man is happy, whereas the life of the unjust man is miserable. As I mentioned above, Plato's statements, uttered in a different context (to himself, in front of a class, in a book), would not be considered parrhesiastic.[70] They *are* parrhesiastic, in this case, because Plato utters them in front of someone who has a reason to feel questioned by them—and questioned *from an ethical point of view*, that is, in his *ethos*, his way of behaving and living. Indeed, Plutarch explains that the tyrant could not bear these remarks because he (rightly) interprets them as directed at him: *he* is the cowardly tyrant, the unjust, unhappy man Plato was talking about.

Thus, the third condition of parrhesiastic utterance consists in the fact that the statement must be *intentionally* uttered in front of (or addressed to) someone who has a reason to feel questioned by it in his conduct, his *ethos*, his way of living and being. This condition also applies to Seneca's case: of course, not every proposition of Seneca's letters to Lucilius constitutes a parrhesiastic utterance, yet every statement explicitly addressed to Lucilius in order to question him in his *ethos* must be considered an instance of *parrhesia*. And note that Cavell too, in his analysis of passionate utterance, emphasizes an element that he calls "singling out": whether "I have the standing to appeal to or to question you—to single you out as the object of my passion."[71] I will therefore call this third condition of parrhesiastic utterance *criticism*, because the parrhesiast questions and singles out her interlocutor, not as object of her passion, but as target—precisely—of her criticism.[72]

Risk and Courage

As I mentioned above, Foucault is adamant that *parrhesia* always takes place in circumstances such that it will, may, or must entail *costly consequences* for the speaker. He characterizes this condition of parrhesiastic utterance in terms of the opening of a space of "unspecified risk" for the speaker, who undertakes to tell the truth "at an unspecified price," which may be as high as her own death.[73] It is easy to see how this condition applies to the example of Plato risking his own life by making use of *parrhesia* in front of the tyrant of Syracuse:

> When one finds oneself in a situation like this, the risk is in a way extremely open, since Dionysius' character, his unlimited tyrannical power, and his excessive temperament, the passions which drive him, may lead to the worst effects, and, as actually happens, to him wanting to kill the person who has told the truth.[74]

It is also clear why speaking out put, and continues to put, victims of sexual violence at indeterminate risk—from further humiliation to retaliation and physical violence.[75] By contrast, it is at first quite difficult to understand how this condition may apply to Seneca's case, because Seneca clearly does not risk his life by using *parrhesia* in his correspondence with Lucilius. From this standpoint, there is an obvious and fundamental difference between the two examples I chose in order to analyze parrhesiastic utterance as speech act. In Plato's case, the distribution of power among the interlocutors, or better, the strategic configuration of power relations that characterizes the context in which the exchange takes place, is radically asymmetrical: Dionysius has the "monopoly" of power and physical force, and consequently Plato finds himself entirely exposed to his anger—which, of course, Plato himself provoked by making use of *parrhesia*. In Seneca's case, by contrast, the strategic distribution of power is not *radically* asymmetrical, and it is the parrhesiast who seems to have the upper hand. Indeed, Lucilius freely decided to ask Seneca for help, thus declaring his willingness to listen and follow the advice of his spiritual director, who therefore clearly has ascendancy over him.

However, even though Lucilius freely decided to ask Seneca for help and clearly considers him to be the wiser of the two, it would be hard to deny that, in making use of *parrhesia* in his letters, Seneca too is risking something. To understand why, we have to take seriously Pierre Hadot's idea of dialogue as an "amicable but real" combat, and thus the risk of breakdown, of rupture, that always lies at its heart.[76] Seneca makes use of *parrhesia* because the critical remarks he addresses to Lucilius open up—even in the context of a relationship of spiritual direction or, for that matter, of a friendly conversation—a space of (unspecified) risk, which in this case is not the risk of death, but may still be as high as the irreparable rupture of the relationship between the two interlocutors.[77] In other words, what Seneca was constantly risking, and what each of us also risks when we use *parrhesia* in an ordinary conversation with a friend, is nothing less than the friendship itself—that is, our *shared* life with others:

> The parrhesiast is somebody who takes a risk. Of course, this risk is not always the risk of his life. When, for example, you see a friend doing something wrong, and when you take the risk of making him angry by telling him he is wrong, you are a parrhesiast. You don't risk your life, but you may hurt him, and your friendship may be hurt as a result.[78]

Consequently, parrhesiastic utterance always presupposes a certain dose of courage on the part of the speaker, since she makes use of *parrhesia* willingly and fully aware of the risks it may entail. At the heart of *parrhesia*, Foucault argues, we do not find the speaker's institutional or social status, but her courage:[79]

> [*Parrhesia*] involves some form of courage, the minimal form of which consists in the parrhesiast taking the risk of breaking and ending the relationship to the other person which was precisely what made her discourse possible. . . . This is very clear in *parrhesia* as spiritual guidance, for example, which can only exist if there is friendship, and where the employment of truth . . . is precisely in danger of bringing into question and breaking the relationship of friendship which made this discourse of truth possible.[80]

Risk and *courage* thus constitute the fourth and fifth conditions of parrhesiastic utterance.[81] Here, it is worth noting that Foucault insists on them in order to emphasize *parrhesia*'s difference from the "demonstrative procedure," that is, from what in *Psychiatric Power* he had called the technology of truth-demonstration, or truth as knowledge-*connaissance*.[82] In 1983, Foucault argues that "there is no *parrhesia* in the progressive steps of a demonstration taking place in neutral conditions, because the person who states the truth in this way does not take any risk."[83] This remark is crucial to understanding why not all forms of truth-telling are instances of *parrhesia*, and why *parrhesia* only constitutes *one* specific kind or family of veridictions—a point I return to below.

Yet the distinction between *parrhesia* and the technology of truth-demonstration should not be conceived in terms of a simple, clear-cut opposition. Indeed, as Foucault points out by referring to the case of Galileo, if the statement of the truth is an element of a demonstrative procedure, but also and at the same time "an irruptive event opening up an undefined or poorly defined risk for the subject who speaks," then of course it does merit being considered parrhesiastic—provided that all the other conditions are satisfied.[84] However, there can be no *parrhesia* if the statement of truth is *exclusively* envisaged "as an element in a demonstrative procedure."[85] In other words, it is the (extralinguistic) context in which the alethurgy occurs, and not the internal structure of the true discourse as such, that has to be taken into account to determine whether a given utterance is parrhesiastic or not. As we saw in examining the example of Plato and Dionysius, a statement such as "The life of the unjust man is unhappy," written in a book or uttered in front of a class as the conclusion of a syllogistic argument, would only exceptionally count as *parrhesia*, whereas it is clearly an instance of parrhesiastic utterance when addressed to a tyrant who will likely get angry and, potentially, kill the person who dared to tell him the truth. Thus, the analysis of *parrhesia* as speech act clearly relies on two of the main insights that characterize Foucault's project of a history of truth: truth-demonstration is but a form of truth-event, and there can be no game of truth external to a regime of truth.[86]

The conclusion that risk and courage are necessary conditions of parrhesiastic utterance may be rejected by referring to a notion that Foucault discusses several times in his lectures and writings on *parrhesia*: the notion of "parrhesiastic pact," or "pact of frankness."[87] By this, Foucault usually means a specific kind of engagement, on the part of the stronger, more powerful party, not to hurt or punish the weaker party for the truth they are about to speak. Now, the idea that a pact can be stipulated between the parrhesiast and her interlocutor(s) seems to contradict the two above-mentioned conditions concerning the space of indeterminate risk that *parrhesia* necessarily opens up and, as a consequence, the need for the parrhesiast to be courageous. However, even though the stipulation of a pact between the parrhesiast and her interlocutor(s) does "secure" (at least in part) their relationship, thus reducing the risk of rupture due to the parrhesiastic speech act, it is clear that the speaker still takes a risk and shows courage in choosing to make use of *parrhesia*. In fact, the parrhesiastic pact may always be broken. For instance, in Euripides's tragedy *The Bacchae*, a parrhesiastic pact is stipulated between Pentheus and the messenger who is to announce the disorders and excesses of the Bacchae.[88] Yet,

> since [Pentheus] is the master, since he is the king, since the other is a servant, he has the right to kill him or to punish him. [The parrhesiastic pact] is only a moral agreement, without any legal or institutional regulation. So, regardless, there is always a risk, but I don't mean that the risk is always the same all throughout the game. The risk is great in the beginning, but at the end, it is not.[89]

Similarly, Seneca and Lucilius also stipulate (albeit implicitly) a parrhesiastic pact: Lucilius asks Seneca for help and advice, thus placing himself under his guidance and making clear that he is willing to listen to his spiritual director's criticisms without getting angry at him. However, nothing ensures that Lucilius will actually be able to remain faithful to this commitment, just as nothing ensures that, after asking a friend to tell me what she really thinks of me, or of one of my actions, and after promising her that her truth-telling will not affect our relationship, I will not end up feeling deeply hurt by her remarks, such that our relationship may change or even end as a result. In short, by criticizing Lucilius's *ethos*, especially at the beginning of their relationship of spiritual direction, Seneca *is* risking something and giving proof of a certain dose of courage.

The existence of a parrhesiastic pact also suggests that the parrhesiast's interlocutor often plays a relevant, *active* role in what Foucault calls the parrhesiastic game (*jeu parrèsiastique*). As he argues in the first lecture of *The Courage of Truth*,

> *Parrhesia* may be organized, developed, and stabilized in what could be called a parrhesiastic game. For if the parrhesiast is someone who, by telling the truth, the whole truth, regardless of any other consideration, risks bringing her relationship to the other into question, and even risks her life, on the other hand, the person to whom this truth is told—whether the assembled people deliberating on the best decisions to take, or the prince, tyrant, or king to whom advice must be given, or the friend one is guiding—these agents, if they want to play the role proposed to them by the parrhesiast in telling the truth, must accept the truth, however much it may hurt generally accepted opinions in the Assembly, the prince's passions or interests, or the individual's ignorance or blindness. . . . Thus the true game of *parrhesia* will be established on the basis of this kind of pact, which means that if the parrhesiast demonstrates her courage by telling the truth in spite of everything, the person to whom this *parrhesia*

is addressed will have to demonstrate his greatness of soul by accepting being told the truth.[90]

Thus, in 1984, Foucault defines *parrhesia* as "the courage of truth in the person who speaks and who, regardless of everything, takes the risk of telling the whole truth that she thinks," but also as "the interlocutor's courage in agreeing to accept as true the hurtful truth that he hears."[91] However, as Foucault aptly points out by referring to Aristotle's *Nicomachean Ethics*, in the case of the interlocutor, we should actually speak of *megalopsukhia* (greatness of soul) rather than courage per se.[92] Alternatively, a clear distinction should be drawn between two types of courage: on the one hand, the courage of the parrhesiast, which is bound up with the space of indefinite risk opened up by the critical force of her *parrhesia* against her interlocutor(s); on the other hand, the courage of the interlocutor, which (at least initially) is limited to his commitment to taking the words of the parrhesiast seriously. Only later can this initial commitment (potentially) give rise to the interlocutor's active attempt to question and change his own way of behaving and living, thus translating the received criticism into *self*-criticism.

Does the latter type of courage merit consideration as a necessary condition for parrhesiastic utterance? The answer is no. Indeed, it is clear that for an utterance to be considered parrhesiastic it is not necessary that a pact or a game be (explicitly or implicitly) established between the speaker and her interlocutor(s): the parrhesiastic speech act does not *depend* on the interlocutor's willingness to actually listen to it. For instance, even though he did not stipulate any explicit pact with Diogenes, Alexander resists the impulse to kill him and continues listening. We could no doubt speak retroactively of a parrhesiastic pact or game established between them;[93] yet Dio Chrysostom's text constantly emphasizes how fragile the latter really is—always at risk of being broken.[94] *That* is what makes Diogenes's words parrhesiastic. In short, the establishing of a parrhesiastic pact or game—whether explicit or implicit—must be considered an issue extraneous to the necessary *conditions* of parrhesiastic utterance.[95]

Finally, it is worth emphasizing that the fourth and fifth conditions of parrhesiastic utterance (especially in Seneca's case) also apply, albeit in a slightly different way, to passionate utterance. Indeed, as Cavell argues, "failure to have singled you out appropriately in passionate utterance characteristically puts the future of our relationship, as part of my sense of my existence, on the line."[96] This analogy is even clearer in Cavell's discussion of remarriage comedies. As is well known, each of these movies focuses on the path that the members of an older pair must undertake in order to "get *back* together, together *again*," that is, in order to fix their marriage threatened by the risk of divorce and reestablish their relationship in the form of "a meet and happy conversation"—which, according to John Milton, is the "chiefest and noblest end of marriage."[97] This is why Cavell claims that, in these films, the central pair's relationship has "the quality of friendship": for them, "talking together is fully and plainly being together, a mode of association, a form of life" characterized by "articulate responsiveness [and] expressiveness," through which they learn "to speak the same language."[98] In other words, their conversation does not chiefly aim to attain mutual agreement, nor pure and simple understanding, but more importantly mutual acknowledgment—and yet the latter is also what the interlocutors must constantly risk, because it can only be obtained if one courageously takes the chance of exposing oneself (over and over again) to the unpredictable responses and reactions of the other person.[99]

Transparency, *or* Parrhesia *and Rhetoric*

It is now necessary to address the fundamental but problematic distance that separates *parrhesia* (at least as Foucault construes it) from rhetoric and all other arts of discourse. Indeed, *parrhesia* is, by definition, a non-artificial way of speaking: it is direct, clear, and transparent—in short, it is rhetoric "degree zero" (*degré zéro*).[100] In his *Letter 75* to Lucilius, Seneca clearly emphasizes this crucial feature of *parrhesia*: just as an "unaffected and easygoing" conversation, he writes, there is "nothing mannered or artificial" about my letters because, "if it were possible, I would like to let you see my thoughts rather than translate them into language." Thus, *parrhesia* can be characterized as a way of letting the interlocutor(s) *see* one's thoughts, without embellishing them through an elegant rhetorical style or altering them using oratorical tricks: it aims to convey "the thought purely and simply, with the minimum embellishment compatible with this transparency."[101] Thus, I call the sixth condition of parrhesiastic utterance *transparency*.

Paul Allen Miller has recently argued that, in his final lectures at the Collège de France, Foucault draws a clear distinction between *parrhesia* and rhetoric, or "philosophy's traditional adversary."[102] While "rhetoric is concerned with the manner of speaking," and with persuasion, Miller contends that *parrhesia* is "fundamentally concerned with speaking the truth."[103] Yet he is well aware that things are more complicated than they appear, since "clearly these are not mutually exclusive concerns."[104] In his critique of Foucault's account of the relations between *parrhesia* and rhetoric, Arthur Walzer picks up on this issue and claims that Foucault selectively favors unartful and bold forms of *parrhesia*, thus reducing rhetoric to mere flattery in order to exclude the rhetorical aspects of *parrhesia* from his analysis. Yet, according to Walzer, this is historically and philologically illegitimate: rhetoric and *parrhesia* cannot and should not be entirely pulled apart, because, throughout history, the latter has more often than not taken on a rhetorical character.[105]

Both Miller and Walzer, however, overlook the fact that Foucault's views on the relations between *parrhesia* and rhetoric undergo some significant changes between 1982 and 1984, while becoming progressively more convincing. It is only in 1984, when he takes up the perlocutionary dimension, that Foucault is finally able to clearly distinguish the two.[106]

In 1982, Foucault addresses the issue of *parrhesia*'s alleged "transparency" within the context of the traditional polemic in antiquity opposing philosophy to rhetoric. He argues that, while rhetoric is "the inventory and analysis of the means by which one can act on others by means of discourse," philosophy can be defined as "the set of principles and practices available to one, or which one makes available to others, for taking proper care of oneself or of others."[107] Even though there appears to be an overlap here, since it seems necessary that, in order to realize its objective (that is, taking care of self or others), philosophy as a discourse make use of rhetoric, Foucault immediately points out that philosophical discourse invariably strives to tell the truth, whereas rhetoric is indifferent to the truth: its essential goal is persuasion.[108] However, Foucault is aware that the relations between philosophy and rhetoric are much more nuanced than the relations between philosophy and flattery or sophistry.[109] Indeed, philosophical discourse clearly has its own "materiality," its own "plasticity," and thus also its own "rhetoric" on which its effects depend, at least in part.[110] To deny this would contradict Foucault's own conception of games and regimes of truth, treating philosophy as a "pure" game of truth existing outside of all regimes.

Thus, in *The Hermeneutics of the Subject*, Foucault defines *parrhesia*— within the context of the philosophical practice of spiritual direction in the first two centuries of the Roman Empire—as "that kind of appropriate rhetoric, or nonrhetorical rhetoric, which philosophical discourse must employ":

> *Parrhesia* is the necessary form of philosophical discourse, since . . . when we employ the *logos*, there is necessarily a *lexis* (a way of saying things) and the choice of particular words rather than others. Therefore, there can be no philosophical *logos* without this kind of body of language with its own qualities, its own figures, and its own necessary effects at the level of

pathos. But if you are a philosopher, it is not the art or *technē* of rhetoric that is needed to control these elements (verbal elements, elements whose function is to act directly on the soul). It must be this other thing, which is both a technique and an ethics, an art and a morality, and which is called *parrhesia.*[111]

In other words, Foucault suggests that, at least in the context of the practice of spiritual direction in Roman philosophy, *parrhesia* is different from rhetoric because it is not merely a technique or an art of discourse (aiming at persuasion), but also an *ethics*: the spiritual director makes use of it in order to take proper care of his directee(s), that is, to help them acquire autonomy and self-mastery. Thus, "the master's discourse must not be an artificial, sham discourse subservient to the rules of rhetoric, seeking only to produce effects of pathos in the disciple's soul," but should be such that the disciple(s) can autonomously "subjectify" it.[112] *Parrhesia*, as a *technē* employed by philosophical discourse in the ancient practice of spiritual direction, aims to define a set of rules—rules of prudence, rules of skill, *kairos*—which do not pertain to "the truth of the [master's] discourse" but to "the way in which this discourse of truth is formulated."[113] Yet it cannot be equated to rhetoric because it is not indifferent to the truth and does not aim to persuade, but rather to give form to a discourse of truth that is supposed to help the disciple to autonomously take care of himself.[114]

Consequently, rather than *parrhesia*'s "mortal enemy" (which, according to Foucault, is flattery), rhetoric is presented as both its "technical adversary" and its "technical partner": *parrhesia* must dissociate itself from rhetoric not in order to do away with it once and for all, but to be able to *make use* of it "within strict, always tactically defined limits, where it is really necessary."[115] Indeed, as opposed to rhetoric, *parrhesia* is what allows the transmission of true discourse, "in all its naked force," from master to disciple—it is, in other words, one of the main instruments through which, in antiquity, (philosophical) truth was given force.[116] In *The Hermeneutics of the Subject*, the relation between *parrhesia* and rhetoric is thus portrayed as a complex, nuanced, ambiguous, and ultimately *strategic* one.

In the following two years, Foucault's analysis of *parrhesia* significantly broadens, no longer focusing exclusively on the practice of spiritual direction in Roman philosophy. As a consequence, his account of the relations between *parrhesia* and rhetoric also undergoes some relevant changes. While maintaining that *parrhesia* "as a technique, a process, and a way of saying things can and frequently must make an effective use of the resources of rhetoric," Foucault now seems increasingly interested in emphasizing what *undoubtedly* differentiates *parrhesia* from rhetoric—and in making clear that *parrhesia* has no specific rhetorical form and "cannot just be defined as an element falling within the province of rhetoric."[117] The crucial difference between the two still seems to lie in the fact that, while rhetoric aims to persuade and is indifferent to the truth, "it is not so much or not necessarily a matter of persuasion in *parrhesia*."[118] Yet this is not an unproblematic claim, because Foucault immediately adds that, "when Plato gives Dionysius a lecture, he *is* trying to persuade him," and that it is precisely in this kind of situation, that is, when *parrhesia*'s goal is *also* persuasion, that it can and must "call upon methods of rhetoric."[119] This goal and these methods, however, do not define the "nature" of *parrhesia*: they are not necessary conditions of parrhesiastic utterance, but additional elements that may or may not characterize specific instances of it. Similarly, it is clear that sometimes *parrhesia* takes the form of defiance, of insult, of psychagogy, but that none of these forms is *necessarily* entailed by it. By contrast, what *does* constitute a necessary condition of parrhesiastic utterance is what I called transparency: *parrhesia* always conveys the speaker's thoughts as clearly and openly as possible, and exactly as they are.

Consequently, in order to depict Socrates as a paradigmatic parrhesiastic figure, Foucault ends up downplaying the importance of what likely constitutes the most famous form that his discourse takes: irony. In his 1982 Grenoble lecture, for instance, Foucault still does not present Socrates as a parrhesiast because he thinks that "there is a structural opposition between *parrhesia* and irony."[120] But it does not take him long to change his mind. In his 1983 lecture course, *The Government of Self and Others*, Foucault portrays Socrates as a parrhesiast, while still emphasizing that "nothing is more distant than *parrhesia* from the well-known Socratic, or Platonic-Socratic irony": in his eyes, *parrhesia* remains "a veritable antiirony."[121] Socrates's discourse is not always parrhesiastic: it is parrhesiastic only when it is "without embellishment," thus directly conveying his thoughts, and only insofar as it "employs the words, expressions, and phrases which come to mind"—a discourse that "the person who utters it believes to be true."[122] In short, when he uses irony, Socrates does not speak as a parrhesiast.

Foucault further elaborates on these ideas in addressing the Greek notion of *logos etumos*, that is, discourse "in the naked state," devoid of any "embellishment, apparatus, construction, or reconstruction," and therefore "closest to the truth."[123] According to the ancient Greeks, Foucault argues, "language, words, and phrases in their very reality have an original relationship with truth," since they "bring with them what is essential (*ousia*), the truth of the reality to which they refer."[124] Consequently, any "addition, transformation, trick, or shift in relation to the distinctive, original form of language" inevitably distances it from the truth: parrhesiastic discourse, as opposed to rhetoric, is *etumos* because it is not "chosen, fashioned, and constructed in such a way as to produce its effect on the other person," but is "so bare and simple, so in keeping with the very movement of thought that, just as it is without embellishment, in its truth, it will be appropriate to what it refers to."[125] In short, its transparency ensures that it is able both to tell the truth about reality and to express "the soul of the person who utters it."[126]

It will be important to keep these remarks in mind to shed light on Foucault's enigmatic claim that

> the parrhesiast says what is true because he thinks that it is true, and he thinks that it is true because it is really true. Not only is the parrhesiast sincere, not only does he state his opinion frankly, but his opinion is also the truth. He says what he knows to be true. In *parrhesia*, there is a coincidence, an exact coincidence, between belief and truth.[127]

Does the parrhesiast say what she *knows* to be true, or just what she *thinks* or *believes* to be true? Is she truthful because her *parrhesia* expresses knowledge, or just in the sense that she is sincere? I will address these delicate questions in the next chapter, but it should be clear by now that we can hope to understand Foucault's remarks on *parrhesia* as a form of truth-telling only if we are willing to take seriously the main insights of his history of truth, thus refraining from interpreting these questions in light of the (currently dominant) conception of truth as knowledge-*connaissance*.

To go back to the issue of the complex relations between *parrhesia* and rhetoric, it is worth noting that, in the first lecture of *The Courage of Truth*, Foucault draws an even more radical distinction between the two. While in 1983 Foucault still seemingly presents *parrhesia* as a specific (philosophical) kind or "limit case" of rhetoric, in 1984 he claims that *parrhesia* "is opposed to the art of rhetoric in every respect."[128] His way of characterizing this opposition also importantly changes: rhetoric is no longer said to be indifferent to the truth, but is instead portrayed as indifferent to the relation between the speaker and what she says, for it "does not involve any bond of belief between the person speaking and what he [states]"; its aim is to produce effects in the form of beliefs, convictions, and conducts in the audience, so as to establish "a constraining bond between what is said and the person or persons to whom it is said."[129] By assuming this perspective, which explicitly focuses on the perlocutionary effect, it becomes easier for Foucault to explain why *parrhesia* is the opposite of rhetoric: on the one hand, *parrhesia* entails a strong, manifest, and constitutive bond between the speaker and what she says; on the other, by openly expressing her thoughts, the parrhesiast also exposes herself and her bond with her interlocutor(s) to an indefinite risk.[130] In short,

> rhetoric does not entail any bond between the person speaking and what is said, but aims to establish a constraining bond, a bond of power between what is said and the person to whom it is said. *Parrhesia*, on the other hand, involves a strong, constitutive bond between the person speaking and what she says, and, through the effect of the truth, the injuries of truth, it opens up the possibility of the bond being broken between the person speaking and the person to whom she has spoken. Let's say, very schematically, that the rhetorician is, or at any rate may well be an effective liar who constrains others. The parrhesiast, on the contrary, is the courageous teller of a truth by which she puts herself and her relationship with the other at risk.[131]

The standpoint of the perlocutionary, that is, of what is done not *in* but *by* saying something, thus allows Foucault to find a clearer way of distinguishing *parrhesia* from rhetoric: while the latter does not rely on any bond of belief between the speaker and what she says, and aims to establish a bond of power between what is said and the person(s) to whom it is said, the former relies on a constitutive bond between the speaker and what she says, and exposes the speaker, as well as the bond between her and her interlocutor(s), to an unspecified risk in order to try to open the latter's eyes (albeit not in the mode of persuasion) to aspects of their beliefs or conduct that need to be changed. In other words, most of the time, the parrhesiast does hope to change the beliefs and conduct of her interlocutor(s), but refuses to do so by establishing a bond of power between her speech and the person(s) to whom it is addressed. Instead, she leaves her interlocutor(s) entirely free to respond as they want to her words, including by breaking their bond with her. This is a far subtler and more convincing argument than those routinely attributed to Foucault when it comes to characterizing (and criticizing) his account of the relations between *parrhesia* and rhetoric.[132]

This conclusion is remarkable: the evolution of Foucault's views on this topic and the pain he takes to distinguish *parrhesia* from rhetoric should give pause to all scholars who have criticized him for his alleged reduction of truth claims to the power effects they have on their audience, or who have characterized his own (critical) approach as a rhetorical or fictional one.[133] It also clearly shows that we should resist all simplistic reduction of the perlocutionary to rhetoric, acknowledging instead, as Cavell does, the rich and multifaceted nature of the perlocutionary domain.

Equipped with these insights, it is now time to address the most delicate of all the conditions of parrhesiastic utterance, and attempt to clarify in what sense, according to Foucault, the parrhesiast speaks "the truth."[134]

Dramatics of Truth

As mentioned above, at the beginning of his 1984 lecture course at the Collège de France, *The Courage of Truth*, Foucault claims that the analysis of *parrhesia* as a specific modality of truth-telling constitutes an aspect or a piece of a more general project that he calls "the study of 'alethurgic' forms"—where "alethurgy" designates "the production of truth, the act by which truth is manifested."[1] We saw that, starting in 1980, the notion of alethurgy plays a crucial role in Foucault's history of truth, allowing him to emphasize that the procedures through which truth is obtained and manifested are numerous, multifaceted, complex, and that they cannot be reduced to those pertaining to what, in *Psychiatric Power*, he had called the technology of truth-demonstration, or truth as knowledge-*connaissance*—which is "only one of the possible forms of alethurgy."[2] Now, alethurgy, or the manifestation of what is true as opposed not only to what is false, but also to what is "hidden, inexpressible, unforeseeable, or forgotten," clearly plays an essential role in Foucault's analysis of *parrhesia* as well.[3] Indeed, as he repeatedly makes it clear, Foucault considers *parrhesia* as a way of speaking or manifesting the truth. Consequently, I call *alethurgy* the seventh condition of parrhesiastic utterance, the last I will address here—even though the list of conditions of *parrhesia* as a speech act considered from the perspective of the perlocutionary effect can only be provisional and open-ended.

Alethurgy

If we follow what A. J. Ayer, J. L. Austin, and Stanley Cavell claim about moral judgments, we would need to admit that, in most cases, parrhesiastic utterances also have no truth value: statements such as "The life of the unjust man is unhappy," just as moral judgments such as "Tolerance is a virtue," do not come under this tradition's definition of the (constative, logical, or epistemological) category of truth and falsehood. Yet it is clear that, in the case of *parrhesia*, we cannot do away with the question of truth so quickly: that would be to concede that the (philosophico-scientific) technology of truth-demonstration is the *only* legitimate standpoint of truth, the touchstone of *all* alethurgy. But this is precisely the conclusion that Foucault's history of truth aims to challenge, thus proving essential for understanding why *parrhesia*, albeit often devoid of truth value, still merits consideration as a way of speaking or manifesting the truth.

Foucault repeatedly argues that, for an utterance to be considered parrhesiastic, it is crucial that the speaker actually believe what she says. However, this is not enough: the parrhesiast does not only *believe* what she says, but through the verbal act of *parrhesia*—one that, as we saw, requires courage, for it opens up a space of indefinite risk for the speaker—she also *binds* herself to her utterance and to the truth she believes it manifests. This is why *parrhesia* cannot be reduced to mere sincerity: in addition to believing what she says, the parrhesiast chooses to engage in a courageous form of alethurgy that may entail costly consequences for herself.[4] Yet this is still insufficient: the parrhesiast, by engaging in this risky and courageous alethurgy, shows her interlocutor(s) that what she thinks and says is also reflected in her own *ethos*, that is, in her way of behaving and living.

In his *Letter 75* to Lucilius, Seneca writes: "I think everything I say, and not content with thinking it, I love it."[5] He immediately makes clear that this is "the most important point" of his remarks: "to say what one thinks, to think what one says, to see to it that language is in harmony with conduct," so that one "is the same when seen and heard."[6] In commenting on this passage in his 1982 Grenoble lecture, Foucault argues that *parrhesia* is "the presence, in the person who speaks, of his own form of life rendered manifest, present, perceptible, and active as model in the discourse he delivers."[7] In other words, the parrhesiast "says what she thinks not in the sense that she expresses her opinions or says what she thinks is true, but by saying what she loves, that is to say, by showing what her own choice is, her *proairesis*."[8] Speaking in the first person, and thus assuming for a moment the parrhesiast's perspective, Foucault concludes:

> I must be myself, the exact way I am, in what I say; I must myself be implicated in what I say, and what I affirm must show me really true to what I affirm. . . . I do not content myself with telling you what I judge to be true. I tell this truth only inasmuch as it is in actual fact what I am myself; I am implicated in the truth of what I say.[9]

These remarks show what the alethurgic condition of parrhesiastic utterance consists in: the parrhesiast is *implicated* in what she says, not only
because she believes it is true, but because, on the one hand, she is willing
to accept an undefined risk in order to tell this truth, and, on the other
hand, her own *ethos* bears witness of the "harmony" that exists between
her *logos* and her *bios*—between what she thinks, what she says, and her
own way of behaving and living.

Foucault examines in more detail this (twofold) condition in his analysis of Socrates's *parrhesia*, whose distinctive feature consists precisely
in the perfect "homophony" that he establishes between what he thinks,
what he says, and the way in which he lives. Indeed, as the *Apology* and the
Laches make it clear, Socrates's life—his *bios*—constitutes the *basanos* or
"touchstone" of his *parrhesia*.[10] But what is more noteworthy is that Foucault addresses this point, albeit from a slightly different angle, even when
he compares performative and parrhesiastic utterance. As mentioned
above, in the case of performative utterance, the institutional or social
status of the speaker is "indispensable for [its] effectuation" because, for
instance, to be able to open a meeting by saying "the meeting is open" the
speaker must have the authority to open the meeting. However, Foucault
argues that "there does not have to be a . . . personal relationship between
the person undertaking the utterance and the utterance itself for the latter
to be performative."[11] In other words, "it does not matter whether the
chairman who says 'the meeting is open' is really bored by the meeting
or if he dozes off": provided that he utters that sentence, he will open
the meeting regardless.[12] By contrast, as we noticed when we addressed
the delicate distinction between *parrhesia* and rhetoric, this "indifference"
with regard to the relation between the speaker and her utterance is out
of the question in the case of *parrhesia*: the latter, Foucault argues, is "the
affirmation that in fact one genuinely thinks, judges, and considers the
truth one is saying to be genuinely true."[13]

Here, Foucault seems to overlook an entire class of performative utterances ("I congratulate you," "I condole with you," "I promise") that, to be
felicitous, *do* require that the speaker has "certain thoughts, feelings, or
intentions"—in other words, that she be sincere.[14] From this standpoint,
the distinction he draws between performative and parrhesiastic utterance does not appear to be so radical: the condition Γ.1 for performative
utterance—"where, as often, the procedure is designed for use by persons
having certain thoughts or feelings, . . . a person participating in and so
invoking the procedure must in fact have those thoughts or feelings"—
may be considered analogous to the "first step" of the alethurgic condition

for parrhesiastic utterance.[15] Indeed, as mentioned above, for an utterance to be parrhesiastic it is necessary that the speaker *believe* in it—just as a condition for the felicity of passionate utterance as defined by Cavell is that "the one uttering a passion must have the passion."[16] However, not only is there no predetermined "procedure" in the case of *parrhesia*, but in addition, the alethurgic condition is clearly not reducible to sincerity, as the speaker's "implication" in the truth of her utterance goes beyond the simple correspondence between what she thinks and what she says. Parrhesiastic utterance manifests the perfect harmony that exists between the speaker's words and her way of living, while at the same time expressing and reinforcing such harmony through the risky event of the utterance itself: in opening up a space of indeterminate risk for the speaker, parrhesiastic alethurgy renders her a "visible statue of the truth" that she utters.[17] In other words, the harmony between the speaker's *logos* and her *bios* is not only a *precondition* of parrhesiastic utterance, but, more importantly, a *consequence* of it: *parrhesia* has "rebound effects" on the speaker herself, because "in producing the event of the utterance the subject modifies, or affirms, or anyway determines and clarifies her mode of being insofar as she speaks."[18] Parrhesiastic utterance relies on, expresses, and contributes to the constitution of the speaker's *ethos* in a dynamic, transformative circularity.

Thus, in *The Government of Self and Others*, Foucault gives a new meaning to the notion of parrhesiastic pact, which is no longer stipulated by the speaker and her interlocutor(s), but by the speaker *with herself*, at two different but interconnected levels:

> That of the act of enunciation and then [that], explicit or implicit, by which the subject binds herself to the statement she has just made, but also to the act of making it. This is what makes the pact double. On the one hand, the subject in *parrhesia* says: This is the truth. She says that she really thinks this truth, and in this she binds herself to the statement and to its content. But she also makes a pact in saying: I am the person who has spoken this truth; I therefore bind myself to the act of stating it and take on the risk of all its consequences.[19]

This is why Foucault defines *parrhesia* as an ethics, "the ethics of truth-telling, in its risky and free act," and claims that the analysis of it belongs to the domain of the "dramatics"—as opposed to the "pragmatics"—of discourse.[20] Indeed, the pragmatics of discourse can be defined as "the analysis of what, in the real situation of the person speaking, affects and modifies the meaning and value of the utterance"; in other words, it is "the analysis of the elements and mechanisms by which the situation of the enunciator modifies the value or meaning of the discourse."[21] Here, Foucault is clearly referring to what, in the 1960s, he had called the extra-linguistic elements of discourse: both the context defined by the situation of the speaker and the speech act that she carries out.[22] By contrast, *parrhesia* corresponds to "a whole family of completely different facts of discourse which are almost the reverse, the mirror projection," of those analyzed by the pragmatics of discourse: in the case of *parrhesia*, what matters is the way in which "both the statement and the act of enunciation" affect "the subject's mode of being."[23] Foucault suggests calling the *dramatics of discourse* "the analysis of these facts of discourse, which shows how the very event of the enunciation may affect the enunciator's being," and hence conceiving of *parrhesia* as one of the main forms taken by the "dramatics of true discourse."[24] Foucault's focus, in this definition, on the rebound effects of the utterance on the speaker herself is nevertheless too narrow: indeed, as mentioned above, a perlocutionary analysis of *parrhesia* as speech act requires us to take into consideration its effects on the interlocutor(s) as well.

At any rate, assuming the standpoint of the dramatics of discourse allows us to clearly see that the main function of *parrhesia* is to express or manifest the speaker's relation to the truth—where "truth" should here be conceived as an ethico-political force. In *How to Do Things with Words*, Austin famously argues that the problem of truth merits being posed not only when it comes to constative utterances and locutionary acts, but also, albeit differently, when it comes to performative utterances and illocutionary acts. This establishes a complex relation between the dimension of truth and falsity, on the one hand, and the dimension of felicity and infelicity, on the other:

> It is essential to realize that "true" and "false," like "free" and "unfree," do not stand for anything simple at all; but only for a general dimension of being a right or proper thing to say as opposed to a wrong thing, in these circumstances, to this audience, for these purposes, and with these intentions. . . . The truth or falsity of a statement depends not merely on the meanings of words but on what act you were performing in what circumstances.[25]

According to Austin, assertions are illocutionary acts that must meet a series of pragmatic conditions—"conditions of use and practice, taking into account context features which are not semantic features"—in order to be felicitous, that is, to qualify as assertions in the first place, and thus for the question of their truth or falsity to even be pertinent.[26] Consequently, the truth or falsity of a statement depends not only on semantic, but also on pragmatic conditions.[27] Yet, if Austin is right in maintaining that, to avoid the "descriptive fallacy," the truth or falsity of a statement must always be assessed in light of the specific *act* the speaker is performing in a given context—or, as Foucault would say, in light of its extralinguistic elements—there seems to be no good reason to limit the analysis of such an act to its illocutionary dimensions.[28] Indeed, as the study of *parrhesia* in terms of the dramatics of discourse clearly shows, such performance also has perlocutionary dimensions. Therefore, "true" does not only stand for a general dimension of being "a right or proper thing to say," but can also stand for a general dimension of being a *courageous* or *risky* thing to say—in these circumstances, to this audience, and so on. In other words, in addition to semantic and pragmatic conditions, the truth of a statement can also depend on ethical and political conditions.[29]

As I argued above, the truth(s) manifested by the parrhesiast should not be assessed in light of the "truth value" of her statements, even though the latter can *also* be true from a constative, logical, or epistemological perspective. It was not the (constative or scientific) truth value of Galileo's claim according to which the earth revolves around the sun that made his utterance a parrhesiastic one: Galileo was a parrhesiast because of the risk he took by courageously making his views public, even while knowing the Catholic Church would deem them heretical. An analogous conclusion applies to the scientists who, in the context of the Covid-19 pandemic, had the courage to keep informing (and alerting) people about the dangerousness of the virus, the need for social distancing and face coverings, or the importance of vaccination, even though, by doing so, they were putting themselves and their careers at risk—as was the case, for instance, in Brazil.[30] In many other cases, however, the parrhesiast's statements cannot even be attributed a (constative, logical, or epistemological) truth value: think, for instance, of Pericles in front of the Athenian Assembly claiming that "we should not yield to the Peloponnesians," or of Plato in front of Dionysius of Syracuse claiming that "tyrants are not courageous."[31] These are what Foucault calls ethical and political truths:

> It's quite clear and obvious that the Greeks won't say, for instance, that a naturalist or that a historian or that an architect . . . use *parrhesia* when they . . . tell the truth about the living beings or about a historical event or about their *technē*, their art as architects. The truth which is put in question in *parrhesia*, this truth, first, always belongs to a specific field, or to two specific fields: the field of ethics and the field of politics. A scientific truth

does not need to be . . . transported by *parrhesia*. But, in several cases, several important cases, ethical and political truth needs *parrhesia*. And the second character of this truth is that this truth is dangerous or, more precisely, that it may be dangerous for the speaker to tell this truth and unpleasant or wounding . . . for the hearer to hear it. It is an ethical or political truth which has by itself a kind of danger, which implies a kind of danger. . . . *Parrhesia* refers to the dangerous game of telling the truth in the political and ethical field.[32]

However, it should be clear by now that politics and ethics are not the only fields in which *parrhesia* takes place: scientific, historical, and literary alethurgies, for example, can all be considered instances of *parrhesia*, in the appropriate circumstances.[33] Instead, the point is that, no matter the field (or better, the regime of truth), what is at stake in *parrhesia* are the ethical and political *dimensions* of the practice of truth-telling: parrhesiastic utterance is an alethurgy, a manifestation of truth, because it expresses and reinforces the perfect harmony between the speaker's thoughts, words, and deeds, while at the same time criticizing the *ethos* of her interlocutor(s) and thus courageously opening up a space of unspecified risk for the speaker—who accepts being held (perlocutionarily) responsible for her words.[34]

From this perspective, it could be said that a parrhesiastic speech act is "happy" when the speaker's interlocutor(s) are willing to listen to her without getting angry, without threatening her, without damaging their relationship, but instead do their best to transform their *ethos* according to the criticisms she voices.[35] By contrast, instances of *parrhesia* could be considered "unhappy" when the speaker is not actually heard or is punished for what she says, and at any rate when her words fail to produce any consequences at the level of the *ethos* of her interlocutor(s). However, it does not seem appropriate to talk about "felicitous" and "infelicitous" instances of *parrhesia* on the basis of its perlocutionary effects, because by definition there is no established conventional procedure for the production of certain perlocutionary effects instead of others. Moreover, as I mentioned above, although parrhesiastic utterance *may* contribute to changing the opinions and *ethos* of the parrhesiast's interlocutor(s), its main objective is not to persuade, but to courageously voice a critical truth regardless of the consequences: the point of *parrhesia* is not persuasion or moralization, but the violent "irruption" of the truth.[36]

Borrowing Foucault's words from *Psychiatric Power*, it is clear that this mode of truth should be conceived as an *event*: it is a "truth-thunderbolt" that establishes a relationship, not of knowledge-*connaissance*, but of "shock or clash" between the speaker and her interlocutor(s).[37] This is why parrhesiastic alethurgy can only take place in the encounter between two or more individuals, and never in the solitary, "intimate" experience of the discovery of an inner truth. The truth that *parrhesia* manifests is an ethical and political *force* that challenges the way the parrhesiast's interlocutor lives, while also expressing and reinforcing the speaker's own mode of being.

Now, especially if we consider Seneca's written conversation with Lucilius, characterized by the "reciprocal opening" of the two partners,[38] we can see that the alethurgic condition of parrhesiastic utterance finds a—no doubt imperfect—parallel in the seventh condition of passionate utterance that Cavell establishes: indeed, parrhesiastic exchanges as well can constitute (more or less confrontational) "instances of, or attempts at, moral education."[39] The idea that a specific mode of conversation is conducive to moral education runs throughout most of Cavell's analyses of remarriage comedies.[40] As he argues in the fifth chapter of *Philosophy the Day after Tomorrow*, "What makes marriage worth reaffirming is a diurnal devotedness that involves friendship, play, surprise, and mutual education," which are all manifested "in the pair's mode of conversing with each other (not just in words), which expresses an intimacy or understanding often incomprehensible to the rest of the depicted world, but in which consists the truth of the marriage."[41] Echoing Foucault and Hadot, Cavell concludes:

> The education of the pair by each other is not to provide an increase of learning but (as in Wittgensteinian instruction) a transformation of existence; those who cannot inspire one another to such an education are not married; they do not have the right interest for one another.[42]

However, even though they allow us to examine crucial aspects of the perlocutionary domain and do significantly overlap in certain instances, passionate and parrhesiastic utterances remain two different kinds or families of speech acts, pertaining to two distinct (albeit interconnected) "regions" of the perlocutionary: while the main function of passionate utterance is to express human beings' (ethical) relation to passion, the primary function of parrhesiastic utterance is to show their (ethico-political) relation to the truth. The perlocutionary analysis of *parrhesia* as speech act therefore makes it possible to shed light on a family of utterances so far overlooked, but which are crucial not only in our everyday lives and in literary, theatrical, and cinematographic works, but also in the history of philosophy itself from ancient Greece to the present. Indeed, if it is true that one of philosophy's most constant features has been what we may call its "critical function," and that "the philosopher has always more or less the profile of the anti-tyrant," then *parrhesia* clearly merits consideration as a fundamental form of *philosophical* utterance.[43] This is what Foucault has in mind when he argues that the analysis of ancient *parrhesia* is a component of the genealogy of the critical attitude in our society.[44]

Sincerity, Authenticity, Avowal

My perlocutionary analysis of *parrhesia* has resulted in a list of seven conditions that an utterance must meet in order to be considered parrhesiastic:

1. unpredictability of the effects of the utterance
2. freedom of the speaker
3. criticism of the *ethos* of the interlocutor(s)
4. indeterminate risk taken by the speaker
5. courage shown by the speaker
6. transparency of the utterance, which conveys the speaker's thoughts "purely and simply"
7. alethurgy—manifestation or "irruption" of the truth as an ethico-political force

This list is neither definitive nor exhaustive. On the contrary, just as Cavell's list of perfectionist themes derived from his reading of Plato's *Republic*, my list is also provisional and open-ended. Indeed, these conditions are *necessary* but likely not *sufficient* to define parrhesiastic utterance, and each of them can take many different forms.[45] Nonetheless, this list is crucial to distinguishing the specificity of *parrhesia* from a series of other forms of truth-telling with which it might be mistakenly identified.

As I mentioned above, Foucault himself emphasizes the distinction between *parrhesia* and sincerity on several occasions. In the lecture on March 2, 1983, of *The Government of Self and Others*, he offers a reading of Plato's *Apology* that shows the gulf separating philosophical truth-telling from rhetorical speech. Indeed, in the *Apology*, Socrates is presented as "the man of truth-telling without any *technē*"—as the one who always tells the truth and never makes use of any art of persuasion.[46] More precisely, Socrates gives three reasons why his own way of speaking is radically foreign to the institutional, political, and judicial fields: first, the language he uses in front of the assembly that has to judge him is in no way different from the one he uses "every day in the public square, the market, and elsewhere"; second, this language "is no more than the series of words and phrases which occur to him"; third, he always "says exactly what he thinks," and thus, at the heart of his speech, lies "a sort of pact between himself and what he says."[47] I already examined the features of *parrhesia* that differentiate it from rhetoric and, building on the Greek notion of *logos etumos*, I explained why Foucault considers the former to be not only a sincere, but a true mode of discourse.[48] However, the perlocutionary analysis of parrhesiastic utterance, and its constituent list of conditions, allow us to further clarify the difference between *parrhesia* and sincerity, as well as the even more delicate difference between *parrhesia* and authenticity.

In his book on the philosophy and history of sincerity, Andrea Tagliapietra elaborates several helpful distinctions, while offering a convincing summary of the philosophical *doxa* on sincerity.[49] To begin with, it is clear that saying something false is conceptually distinct from lying, because the person who lies *intends* to tell a falsehood, whereas a person can say something false without deliberately intending to do so — she can simply be mistaken about it. Consequently, sincerity is the contrary to lying, not to saying something false. Yet sincerity is often not just an act, nor simply an attribute of a given statement, but a *mode of being* of the subject. What does it mean, then, to be sincere?

A first sense of sincerity, the most ordinary but also the most general and in a sense ambiguous, corresponds to the notion of *truthfulness*: it consists in saying what one thinks or believes to be true, thus indicating a correspondence between one's thoughts and one's words.[50] Yet *parrhesia* should not be reduced to sincerity-truthfulness, and this is not because it is closer to frankness ("to tell *all* the truth" at all times) than to truthfulness ("to truthfully say *all that one says*"), but because the alethurgic condition of parrhesiastic utterance requires the establishment of a perfectly harmonic relation not only between what one thinks and what one says, but also between what one says and what one does.[51] Moreover, while *parrhesia* always opens up a space of unspecified risk for the speaker, most instances of sincerity-truthfulness do not, since they do not aim to criticize the speaker's interlocutor(s) and thus require no courage on her part. In short, even though sincerity-truthfulness *is* an aspect — or what I called the first step — of the alethurgic condition for parrhesiastic utterance, *parrhesia* cannot be reduced to it and must be situated on a different plane.

There is a second sense of sincerity, more engaging on a personal level, that corresponds to what could be called *veracity*, that is, the fact of behaving in accordance with what one says. Here, not only does the person say what she thinks or believes to be true, but she also behaves accordingly, because "from the standpoint of veracity, *words are facts*."[52] Sincerity-veracity is therefore more demanding, and no doubt less common, than sincerity-truthfulness; it comes closer to *parrhesia*, but still does not exactly correspond to it.[53] Indeed, if in the case of sincerity-veracity the speaker advances one step further toward *parrhesia* by saying what she thinks *and* doing what she says, *parrhesia* still requires something more: as mentioned above, the parrhesiast is "implicated" in the truth of what she says not only because she is true to her words, but also because she is willing—and courageous enough—to accept an indefinite risk in order to utter them, one that may be as high as her own death. Thus, *parrhesia* cannot and should not be reduced simply to sincerity-veracity.

Yet there is a third sense of sincerity, which "does not immediately concern the relationship with others, but rather the intimate agreement with oneself": indeed, if "through our words and deeds we can reveal our thoughts to others and communicate to them what we believe to be true, we remain the sole witnesses of this actual *sincerity*," because we are the only ones who, in the intimacy of our conscience, can know "the intention with which we say the things we say or do the things we do."[54] We can call this third sense of sincerity *authenticity*.[55] This typically modern sense of sincerity, according to which sincerity-authenticity corresponds to "the individual's mode of being, the sentimental and social life through which she affirms her singularity and truth," might seem to come even closer to *parrhesia*, but in fact should be carefully distinguished from it.[56] Indeed, *parrhesia* does not require the examination of one's interiority or the discovery of an intimate truth that allows one to "actualize oneself" or to "become what one is."[57] In short, *parrhesia* (as I defined it above) should not be confused with the Christian hermeneutics of the self and its injunction to discover the truth of ourselves in order to better renounce who we are, nor with the modern hermeneutics of the self and its invention of "the positive figure of man" as the essential correlate to the interpretive operations of the human sciences.[58] It is precisely this invention that has sustained the development of a "morality of authenticity"—the secular form taken by the Christian injunction to discover the secret truth about ourselves, but this time in order to "actualize" ourselves and express our inner, unique voice.[59]

Foucault opposes this idea that one must incessantly strive to "become what one is," which he terms the contemporary "cult of self," to the Greco-Roman culture of the self and, with it, the ancient practice of *parrhesia*.[60] Indeed, as we saw, the parrhesiast does not strive to "realize" herself or to express her "true nature": the truth that is at stake in her speech is not an intimate one that she manifests after having discovered it in the depths of her own soul, but a critical and risky one that plays the role of an ethico-political force vis-à-vis her interlocutor(s).

Foucault's study of *parrhesia*, and the perlocutionary analysis of par-rhesiastic utterance I advance in this book, should therefore not be considered components of an "archaeology of sincerity."[61] As Alain Lhomme rightly argues, the invention of interiority was necessary "to transform sincerity into a virtue," for it made it possible to ask "not only to what extent the other is reliable, credible, or sincere, but to what extent I can call *myself* sincere."[62] This "sincerity device" (*dispositif de sincérité*), tightly connected with the modern idea of an authentic self, with self-analysis, and with the emergence of scientific psychology and "confessional sciences" more generally, still constitutes the main framework within which we pose the question of truth-telling.[63] It should now be clear that the study of *parrhesia*, far from reinforcing this framework, is instrumental for criticizing it, along with the modern injunction to authenticity and the subjugating effects of the confessional sciences.[64]

Consequently, it is crucial not to confuse *parrhesia* with avowal, no matter if religious, medical, juridical, psychoanalytical, or other. In the inaugural lecture of his Louvain series, *Wrong-Doing, Truth-Telling*, Foucault offers an analysis of avowal—the "obligation to tell the truth about oneself"—which does not refer to any of its historically situated forms, but rather addresses it as a specific kind of speech act or language game.[65] After mentioning the famous episode of psychiatrist François Leuret forcing his patient to avow his madness through several ice-cold showers, Foucault declares that he would like to study the long history of avowal by pursuing an "ethnology of truth-telling," and in particular of truth-telling about oneself.[66] What, then, is an avowal? We could begin by saying that avowals are characterized by the fact that "the one who speaks affirms something about himself," but this is clearly insufficient, because an avowal is more than a simple claim about what one has said or done, or what one is.[67] Hence, building on Leuret's example, Foucault advances a list of four necessary conditions of avowal as speech act.

First, an avowal always entails a certain "cost of enunciation," for it consists in "passing from the untold to the told, given that the untold had a precise meaning, a particular motive, a great value."[68] Second, "in the strictest sense, an avowal is necessarily free" and entails a commitment: "It does not obligate one to do such and such a thing," but it "entails that he who speaks commits himself to being what he affirms himself to be, precisely because he is just that"—because "it is true."[69] Third, an avowal "can only exist within a power relation," and it is the avowal itself that

"enables the exercise of that power relation over the one who avows";
this is why "all avowals are 'costly.'"[70] Fourth, by binding the subject to
what he affirms, an avowal also "qualifies him differently with regard to
what he says": the fact of saying "I am mad" alters the patient's relation
to his own madness and opens up the possibility for him to be cured.[71]
Foucault thus concludes that an avowal is "a verbal act through which the
subject affirms who he is, binds himself to this truth, places himself in a
relationship of dependence with regard to another, and at the same time
modifies his relationship to himself."[72]

If we compare these conditions with the conditions for parrhesiastic
utterance established above, we can easily notice some similarities but
also several important differences between the two families of speech acts.
First, *parrhesia* entails a certain cost of enunciation as well, but the shift
from the untold to the told has a very different meaning: indeed, in the
case of *parrhesia*, it is not the fact of *not telling*, but rather the fact of *telling*
that has value, and the cost of enunciation—that is, the opening up of a
space of indefinite risk for the speaker—is a price that the parrhesiast
intentionally agrees to pay in order to tell the truth. Second, *parrhesia* also
relies on the freedom of the speaker and requires a commitment on her
part; yet, by saying what she thinks and by showing the harmony between
her thoughts, her words, and her deeds, the parrhesiast's main objective
is to question her interlocutor's *ethos*. Thus, while *parrhesia* can also only
emerge in a power relation between two or more interlocutors, it nevertheless plays a radically different role within it than avowal does: parrhesiastic utterance is a critical force directed at the speaker's interlocutor(s);
it does not enable power to be exercised over her. Finally, the parrhesiast
does not speak in order to be *differently* qualified in relation to what she
says: *parrhesia* does not entail any self-renunciation or self-sacrifice. On
the contrary, the rebound effects induced by the parrhesiastic utterance
on the speaker's mode of being have the function of *ethical intensifiers*:
the truth that the parrhesiast utters is "authenticated" by her *ethos*, but
her *ethos* is in turn "affirmed" or "reinforced" by her speech act—which
requires courage and opens up a space of undefined risk. In short, while
one avows his sins in order to stop being a sinner, or his madness in order
to stop being mad, when one makes use of *parrhesia*, one continues being
what she is—and in fact, her risky utterance affirms and reinforces her
own way of behaving and living.

Parrhesia should therefore be conceived as a specific, well-defined family of speech acts, clearly distinct from other forms of truth-telling such as
sincerity, authenticity, or avowal. The provisional and open-ended list of
conditions of parrhesiastic utterance elaborated above better grasps this

specificity and distinguishes *parrhesia* from other kinds of veridiction, thus opening up the possibility of elaborating an ethics and politics of truth-telling.

Putting the Truth to the Test of Life

I have characterized *parrhesia* as a courageous verbal activity that consists in introducing a risky discourse that functions as a critical force within a given context and a specific configuration of power relations. Yet this is not the only form of *parrhesia* that Foucault examines in his analyses of Greco-Roman antiquity. In particular, he famously defines Cynic *parrhesia* as a way of living rather than as a way of speaking: the Cynic *bios*—both a "true life" (*vraie vie*) and an "other life" (*vie autre*)—is an alethurgy in and of itself, one that may be accompanied by words, but one that does not *need* them in order to be performed. Cynicism "presents itself essentially as a certain form of *parrhesia*, of truth-telling, but which finds its instrument, its site, its point of emergence in the very life of the person who must thus manifest or speak the truth in the form of a manifestation of existence."[73] As Frédéric Gros rightly argues, "What interests Foucault in the Cynics is that they refuse the discursivity of truth: truth is not something to be discussed, but something to be lived; it is not something to be demonstrated, but something to be shown."[74] Can this non-verbal *parrhesia* also be addressed in light of the perlocutionary analysis of parrhesiastic utterance I developed above?[75]

In his texts on passionate utterance, Cavell argues that perlocutionary effects are "readily, sometimes more effectively, achievable without saying anything," because "the urgency of passion is expressed before and after words."[76] Hence, "passionate expression makes demands upon the singular body in a way illocutionary force (if all goes well) forgoes";[77] the body, in fact, is often the best image of the soul, inasmuch as "it gives expression to it."[78] Foucault himself argues that *parrhesia* "does not necessarily or exclusively go through *logos*, through the great ritual of language in which one addresses the group or even an individual," for after all *parrhesia* "may appear in the things themselves, it may appear in ways of doing things, it may appear in ways of being."[79] Building on these insights, and keeping in mind that Foucault defines alethurgy as the set of verbal *or non-verbal* procedures by which the truth is manifested, in what follows I will develop an analysis of the perlocutionary effects of Cynic (non-verbal) *parrhesia*.[80] Such an analysis will shed light on the specificity of Cynic *parrhesia* while emphasizing the "embodied" nature of the alethurgy that, at bottom, characterizes *all* forms of *parrhesia*. Of course, this entails broadening the scope of Austin's definition of the perlocutionary in order to take into account the consequential effects upon the feelings, thoughts, or actions of the audience or the speaker that can be produced, not only by an utterance, but also by a *gesture* or a *behavior*.

While the verbal dimension remains central even in Socratic *parrhesia* (as I mentioned above, in the *Apology* and the *Laches*, Socrates's *bios* is presented as the touchstone of his *logos*, and not directly as the site of emergence of the truth), Foucault argues that the Cynics operate a shift from *logos* to *bios*: their *parrhesia* becomes incarnated, embodied—it is itself a mode of conduct and a way of life. Thus, by radicalizing Socratic *parrhesia* through the practice of a "truth-telling" that, paradoxically, no longer needs words, the Cynic philosopher leads a life of active poverty, irreverence, and animality that is scandalously "other," fighting *in* and *against* this world to keep open the possibility of a different world, that is, to transform *this* world into an *other* world—"the same *transfigured*."[81]

A specific kind of truth-*telling* in Socrates, Plato, Seneca, and virtually all other philosophers in antiquity, *parrhesia* thus becomes a form of truth-*living* with the Cynics:

Cynicism is not satisfied with coupling, or establishing a correspondence, a harmony or homophony between a certain type of discourse and a life conforming to the principles stated in that discourse. Cynicism links mode of life and truth in a much tighter, more precise way. It makes the form of existence an essential condition of truth-telling. It makes the form of existence the reductive practice which will make space for truth-telling. Finally, it makes the form of existence a way of making truth itself visible in one's acts, one's body, the way one dresses, and in the way one conducts oneself and lives. In short, Cynicism makes life, existence, *bios*, what could be called an alethurgy, a manifestation of truth.[82]

Hence, unsurprisingly, the core of Foucault's study of Cynicism, in *The Courage of Truth*, is constituted by the analysis of the ethico-political effects of this *parrhesia*-as-life, this *parrhesia*-as-existence.[83] We should not forget, however, that in 1983, at Berkeley, while stressing that the Cynics "were interested in choosing and practicing a certain way of life more than anything else," and that their *parrhesia* made use of "very short words, always linked to a certain physical and social behavior, and also related to a scandalous attitude," two of the three Cynic parrhesiastic practices that Foucault analyzes are verbal.[84] Indeed, besides the Cynics' "scandalous behavior," Foucault focuses his attention on their "critical preaching" and their "provocative dialogue."[85] Now, to these (more traditional) forms of

Cynic *parrhesia*, it is clearly possible to apply the conclusions reached in the analysis of *parrhesia* as speech act that I developed above: in its verbal forms, Cynic *parrhesia* too can be conceived as a critical, ethico-political force in a battlefield, for the Cynic parrhesiast also courageously accepts facing a "permanent danger" in order to tell the truth.[86] By contrast, in 1984, at the Collège de France, the verbal aspects of Cynic *parrhesia* almost completely disappear from Foucault's analysis, which instead revolves entirely around an embodied *parrhesia* that manifests itself through the gestures, the behavior, and the (extra)ordinary way of living of the Cynic philosopher. Indeed, Foucault's aim is now to address "the emergence of the *true life* in the principle and form of truth-telling."[87] What does this "true life" consist in, then?[88]

According to Foucault, the Cynic *bios* is characterized by four main features, which mark the "transvaluation," or the scandalous reversal, of four traditional features of philosophical life in antiquity. First, the Cynics transform the unconcealed life—the rule of non-concealment as an ideal principle of conduct—into a life that is "really, materially, physically public."[89] For instance, Diogenes eats, sleeps, and satisfies all his needs in public, under the eyes of everyone; he leads "a life of blatant and entirely visible naturalness, asserting the principle that nature can never be an evil."[90] Second, the Cynics transform the unalloyed life—the ideal of a life without mixture and dependence on anything external to itself—into a life of real, active, and indefinite poverty, a life of physical ugliness, filth, begging, humiliation, and dishonor. The Cynic life is one of *restless* poverty, which "strives to get back to the ground of the absolutely indispensable."[91] Third, the Cynics transform the life led in accordance with nature, but also with the laws, rules, and customs of human society, into a scandalously animal life: "When need is a weakness, a dependence, a lack of liberty, human beings must have no other needs than those of the animal, those satisfied by nature itself."[92] Consequently, the Cynics criticize and reject the institution of marriage, family obligations, food taboos and conventions, even the prohibition of incest. Finally, they transform the unchangeable life—the principle of a sovereign life, of perfect self-mastery nevertheless in the service of others—into a *militant* life that takes the form of "an explicit, intentional, and constant aggression directed at humanity in general," aiming "to change its moral attitude (its *ethos*) but, at the same time and thereby, its customs, conventions, and ways of living."[93]

This is what Cynic *parrhesia* consists in, as it literally becomes embodied in a specific *bios*—in a conduct, a series of gestures and behaviors that *themselves* possess an alethurgic function. If, as suggested above, we broaden the scope of Austin's notion of the perlocutionary, then it can be

argued that the Cynic true life meets the seven conditions that I established for parrhesiastic utterance. First, the effects of the Cynic scandalous
behavior or shameless conduct cannot be known in advance: just as verbal
parrhesia, the "irruption" of the *bios kunikos* in a given situation is likely
to produce a number of unpredictable effects (*unpredictability*). Second,
the situation itself does not determine what the Cynic philosopher can
or should do; on the contrary, he remains entirely free to choose which
parrhesiastic gesture or action to perform, or to refrain from performing
any (*freedom*). Third, the Cynic behavior is parrhesiastic only insofar as it
takes place in public, and thus in front of someone who is likely not only
to be scandalized by it, but also to feel their own *ethos* questioned by the
Cynic philosopher's militant impudence and animality (*criticism*). Fourth
and fifth, the Cynic conduct always takes place in conditions such that it
may entail costly consequences for the parrhesiast: it opens up a space of
indeterminate *risk* (which can entail many consequences, from dishonor
to exile or even death), and therefore requires a great deal of *courage* on
the part of the Cynic philosopher, who willingly chooses to behave in
this way. Sixth, the *bios kunikos* is radically opposed to "artificial" ways of
life that focus on appearance and worldly goods: indeed, the Cynic life is
organized around the principle that everything that comes from nature
is good, whereas all that is normally sought after in human society (fame,
wealth, power) is bad and thus must be rejected. The Cynic philosopher
thereby embodies in physical form the wish expressed by Seneca in his letter to Lucilius ("If it were possible, I would like to let you see my thoughts
rather than translate them into language"): everything he does is before
the eyes of all, and nothing of his (extra)ordinary way of living is hidden
or embellished (*transparency*).[94] Finally, as I pointed out above, the Cynic
life is an *alethurgy*, a manifestation of a truth that, as in the case of verbal
parrhesia, is to be conceived as an ethico-political force.

Thus, on the one hand, it is clear that it is the Cynic philosopher's *bios*,
and not his *logos*, that fulfills a parrhesiastic function, as the (perlocutionary) effects of Cynic *parrhesia* are achieved normally without saying
anything—simply by making a gesture or performing an action in front
of other people. From this standpoint, there is no doubt a very close link
between *parrhesia* as speech act and the Cynic "true life."

Yet, on the other hand, we should not downplay the significant differences that separate these two forms of *parrhesia*. First, it should be noted
that criticism takes on a peculiar form with the Cynics. In the case of
verbal *parrhesia*, the speaker normally questions the *ethos* of her interloc-
utor(s) by focusing on a specific, often "tailored" point: you think you are
happy, but no unjust man can be happy; you think you are courageous, but

no tyrant can actually be courageous; and so on. By contrast, in the case of Cynic (non-verbal) *parrhesia*, criticism is hyperbolic and totalizing, and is rarely tailored to the parrhesiast's interlocutor(s). Indeed, when Diogenes masturbates in public, what is he really doing?[95] His gesture has no doubt a critical function (against social conventions and sexual taboos), yet it is not addressed to any *specific* person, just as it does not formulate any *targeted* criticism. Cynic scandalous behavior, as Foucault repeatedly points out, is usually addressed to "humanity in general," since it is the *ethos*—the moral attitude and way of living—of *all* human beings that the Cynic philosopher criticizes and aims to change through the perpetual scandal of his shameless life that he puts on display for all.[96] At the same time, this criticism necessarily remains, to a certain extent, *indeterminate*: what exactly is the meaning of Diogenes's gesture of masturbating in the marketplace? To criticize his fellow citizens for hiding such perfectly natural activity behind their home's walls? Certainly. But also, more generally, to criticize them for constantly behaving according to "artificial" conventions and rules rather than using nature as their guide; and to criticize the other philosophers as well, who all claim to lead their lives in accordance with nature, but are not actually willing to accept the most radical consequences of this resolution. In short, Cynic parrhesiastic practices possess a *polysemy* that is only very rarely found in verbal forms of *parrhesia*. Thus, while Cynic behavior systematically scandalizes, it is easy to ignore or fail to grasp its critical function: as it is not explicitly addressed *to me*, I may not feel questioned by it in my own *ethos*, and simply label the Cynic philosopher as a fool who does not even merit my attention.

Second, while verbal *parrhesia* (just as passionate utterance) normally takes place in a dialogical context, that is, a conversation, exchange, or confrontation between two interlocutors, Cynic (non-verbal) *parrhesia* is almost always addressed to a large audience.[97] The Cynic scandalous behavior is not addressed to the prince or the tyrant, nor to a disciple or a friend. Indeed, in confronting Alexander, Diogenes makes use of verbal *parrhesia* and does not perform any scandalous gesture; his *bios* is always there, of course, to authenticate his *logos*, but in this case his *parrhesia* is very close to Socrates's.[98] By contrast, Cynic behavior does not aim to initiate a dialogue, but rather to create a rupture and a reaction of rejection from others, who turn their backs on the Cynic philosopher, scandalized by his actions. Thus, the Cynic philosopher is alone: indeed, it is crucial for his "mission" that he remain alone, because in order to be able to care for humanity *as a whole*, he must criticize *everyone*.[99] As I pointed out above, Plato and Seneca try to produce a positive effect on their respective interlocutors by courageously telling them the truth: Plato wants to convert Dionysius to philosophy, Seneca struggles to help Lucilius advance on his path toward virtue. While putting their relationships on the line, their *parrhesia* does not aim to *break* them. By contrast, Cynic scandalous behavior has *as its objective* to break all bonds—indeed, the very possibility to establish a bond. This rupture is therefore not merely a risk taken by the Cynic philosopher, but constitutes a deliberately sought-after effect of his parrhesiastic practice. Perhaps the clearest example of this can be found in Dio Chrysostom's *Eighth Discourse*. During the Isthmian Games, Diogenes gives a long speech on virtue and the need to endure the difficulties of life and to fight against pleasure. The crowd listens attentively and seems to be persuaded by his arguments. However, realizing that he is winning the crowd over, Diogenes suddenly "ceases speaking and, squatting on the ground, performs an indecent act"; the crowd "scorns him and calls him crazy," turning their attention back to the Sophists.[100] This episode is emblematic because the rupture produced by Diogenes's "indecent act" is in no way required by the logic of his speech. While parrhesiastic utterance rarely *aims* to break the relationship between the speaker and her interlocutor(s), *the goal* of Diogenes's scandalous behavior is precisely to create such a fracture and make mutual agreement impossible.[101] Indeed, it is only from a position of marginality that the Cynic philosopher, "king of poverty," can lead his militant "life of battle and struggle against himself and for himself, against others and for others."[102]

Third, and consequently, the risk that the Cynic philosopher takes and the courage he evidences both have a specific meaning. Indeed, while it is undeniable that the Cynic philosopher's parrhesiastic behavior opens up a space of indeterminate risk (refusal, dishonor, exile, death), this risk is not only accepted by him as a *possible* consequence of his *parrhesia*, but is actively *sought* and willingly *produced*. Moreover, the Cynic philosopher considers everything not connected with virtue or freedom to be strictly indifferent to him—from this perspective, his life has many common features with the Epicurean and Stoic "stylistic of independence, self-sufficiency, and autarchy," but radicalized through a "material, physical, bodily dramatization of the principle of life without mixture or dependence."[103] In other words, for the Cynic philosopher, dishonor, humiliation, and exile are not actually evils, but morally indifferent events to be utilized as tests (*épreuves*) of self-mastery; nor is death an evil, as long as it does not undermine his fundamental freedom. Thus, while from *our* point of view, it is certainly legitimate to argue that the Cynic philosopher, by behaving as he does, takes great risks and gives proof of great courage, from the point of view of the *Cynic himself,* it would no doubt be more appropriate to conclude that he does not actually "risk" anything; rather than courage, what he gives proof of is his perfect self-sufficiency.

Finally, as mentioned above, an important difference between verbal *parrhesia* and the Cynic scandalous behavior is situated at the level of what I called the alethurgic condition. The Cynic philosopher's *bios,* in fact, is not (only) the *basanos,* the touchstone capable of authenticating the truth of his *logos,* even though it does sometimes play this role: every time the Cynic philosopher speaks, it is clear that what he says corresponds not only to what he thinks, but also to his *ethos,* his way of behaving and living. However, his gestures and behavior need not be accompanied by words, as they themselves usually take on the task of manifesting the truth. But what does this alethurgy consist in? It would be tempting to answer that the Cynic life, stripped of everything artificial and scandalously animal, manifests the "truth of nature." This conclusion, however, does not take into account that the Cynics, far from conceiving nature and the *cosmos* as entities organized according to a rational order or set of immutable laws, see the universe as devoid of meaning and rationality, and nature as dominated by fate.[104] The Cynic philosopher's constant reference to nature plays the role of a tactical weapon in his struggle against the conventions and norms of human society: nature gives him the opportunity to constantly put his life to the test, pushing him to asymptotically reduce the extent of his dependencies on others. As Foucault aptly argues, for the Cynic philosopher, nature, in particular animality, is not "a given," but "a duty": it is a task, a challenge, a "way of being in relation to oneself, a way of being which must take the form of a constant test" and "exercise."[105] Consequently, the *bios kunikos* does not manifest the "truth of nature," but puts itself to the test of nature in order to unmask and criticize every human norm that presents itself as universal and necessary, even though it is actually "singular, contingent, and the product of arbitrary constraints."[106] In short, the Cynic philosopher's constant reference to nature functions as a "broken mirror" in which all universals are turned upside down in order to reveal their historical and contingent character.[107] It is precisely this strategic, militant reversal that characterizes the Cynic *bios* as an alethurgy.

Scandal is therefore essential to Cynic alethurgy, which does not exactly show the harmony between the parrhesiast's *logos* and her *bios,* but rather consists in the manifestation of the *disharmonious* relation between the Cynic philosopher's life and the opinions, habits, and customs of human society. Cynic *parrhesia* always aims to create a rupture, a break; it takes the form of a provocation, an explicit and radical aggression against social norms and conventions. This is why Foucault repeatedly describes the Cynics' "mission" in terms of a "philosophical militancy."[108]

Here, a point of clarification is in order. In the lecture on February 29, 1984, of *The Courage of Truth*, Foucault offers an excursus on Cynicism as a "trans-historical category," that is, a "historical category which, in various forms and with diverse objectives, runs through the whole of Western history."[109] More specifically, he analyzes three main examples of the transfer and penetration of the theme of "life as a scandal of the truth," of "*bios* as alethurgy," throughout the history of the West.[110] The first is Christian asceticism, from Peregrinus to the spiritual movements of the Middle Ages, notably the Franciscans and the Dominicans.[111] The second is revolutionary militantism, that is to say, revolution conceived not only as a political project, but also as a form of life, particularly in nineteenth-century Europe.[112] Finally, the third example is modern art beginning in the mid-nineteenth century as a practice of "laying bare, exposure, stripping, excavation, and violent reduction of existence to its essentials."[113]

Now, revolutionary militantism poses a particularly delicate problem: that of the use of physical violence. Certainly, militantism construed as "bearing witness by one's life in the form of a style of existence" that must "break with the conventions, habits, and values of society" and manifest "the concrete possibility and the evident value of an other life, which is the true life," is very close to my characterization of Cynic parrhesiastic practices.[114] However, the only violence that the Cynic philosopher performs against others, by permanently living before their eyes, consists in forcing them to listen to his words and look at his body and gestures. In other words, it is the (moral) violence of the scandal produced by his shameless and animal life, since the Cynic philosopher, like all other parrhesiasts, only puts *his own life* in danger, and never exerts any physical violence on others. Nevertheless, the radicality of his militancy should not be downplayed. Essentially non-violent, the revolution advocated by the Cynic philosopher is nonetheless real: through his scandalous behavior, he incessantly creates a space of *moral danger* for his fellow citizens, shaking the habits and norms that give their everyday life its (apparent) stability and thereby opening up the possibility of sociopolitical transformations in the present.

In the lecture on March 2, 1983, of *The Government of Self and Others*, Foucault argues that we should not assess the discourses that claim to tell the truth by measuring them "against a history of knowledge-*connaissance* which would permit us to determine whether or not [they tell] the truth."[115] In other words, we should not write the history of truth by taking truth-demonstration as our paradigm, but instead outline "a history of the ontologies of veridiction" that poses three major questions: first, the question of "the mode of being peculiar to this or that discourse, as distinct from others, when it introduces a certain specific game of truth into reality"; second, the question of "the mode of being that this discourse of veridiction confers on the reality it talks about, through the game of truth it practices"; third, the question of "the mode of being that this discourse of veridiction imposes on the subject who employs it, such that this subject can play this specific game of truth properly."[116] The study of *parrhesia*, both as a verbal activity and as a scandalous behavior, is clearly part of such a history of the ontologies of veridiction, for it shifts the problem of truth toward *ethos*, that is, the way of living and being of the person who courageously takes risks in order to (try to) change the mode of being of her interlocutor(s) and, more generally, the world in which they live.

As I mentioned above, the main goal of this book is to shed light on a family of utterances—and attitudes—whose key function is to manifest the ethical and political relation of human beings to truth, thereby paving the road for (non-violent) critical practices and struggles aimed at the transformation of oneself, others, and society as a whole.

* 5 *
Critique and Possibilizing Genealogy

In the previous chapter, I argued that the perlocutionary analysis of *parrhesia* as speech act lends support to Foucault's insight that the performativity of language must not be reduced to its pragmatic force, but also encompasses dramatic dimensions, and thus contributes to shaping subjectivity itself—of both the speaker and her interlocutor(s). Yet the fact that, with words, we do not only do *things*, but also create and transform *ourselves as subjects*, has so far largely been overlooked by philosophers of language. Thus, by suggesting we pay renewed attention to the perlocutionary, I hope the analysis of *parrhesia* as speech act developed in chapters 3 and 4 also makes it possible to examine some of the most relevant ethical and political dimensions of our life as speakers—as "creatures of language," as Stanley Cavell would say.[1]

However, Foucault's study of *parrhesia* is not primarily intended as a contribution to the philosophy of language; it is instead an integral part of his project of writing a history of truth. In chapters 1 and 2, I argued that this project has a critical function insofar as it allows Foucault to unmask the historical and contingent nature of two of the most pervasive contemporary regimes of truth, the scientific and the confessional. It shows that every regime of truth, far from being necessary or universal, must be addressed as a historical, cultural, and ultimately ethico-political problem. Yet this is not the only critical function performed by Foucault's history of truth, or genealogy of regimes of truth. Indeed, as I argue in this chapter, Foucault's conception of critique is not only a subversive or problematizing endeavor; it is also a "possibilizing" one. This neglected dimension of Foucault's genealogical method is evident in his analysis of ancient *parrhesia*, which he presents as one component in a broader genealogy of a third regime of truth—the critical regime of truth, or the "critical attitude" in our society. It is by taking this claim seriously that I will be able to show that Foucault's genealogical inquiries, and his history of truth more specifically, are part and parcel of a compelling critical practice with normative force.

Beyond the Vindicatory-Subversive Dichotomy

In recent years, genealogy—conceived, in very general terms, as a narrative describing how a certain belief, concept, value, or practice came about, or might be imagined to have come about—has increasingly become central to debates in both analytic and continental philosophy.[2] In analytic philosophy, genealogy has been mostly employed as a "state of nature epistemology" to explain the emergence of concepts and values such as knowledge, truthfulness, and testimonial justice.[3] In continental philosophy, by contrast, following Nietzsche and Foucault, genealogy has been posited as a basis for social and political critique.[4] Thus, in either camp, the use of genealogy has so far been motivated by the need to reassure or foster "anxiety" as to the epistemic or sociopolitical validity of our beliefs, concepts, values, or practices.[5] In other words, genealogy has been employed either for *vindicatory* aims, to show that if certain features of a concept originated with the concept, they are essential to it and should not be questioned; or for *subversive* aims, to show that if a belief or practice emerged in a contingent way or, worse, as a consequence of ignoble historical events, it must be criticized, if not straightforwardly abandoned.[6]

In what follows, I will argue that this dichotomy has prevented scholars from grasping a further, crucial dimension of genealogical inquiry. And while scholars such as Colin Koopman and Amy Allen, building on Foucault, have already defended an alternate approach that they call *problematizing* genealogy, I will suggest that they too have missed an important aspect of (Foucauldian) genealogy, which I call *possibilizing*.[7] This aspect has virtually gone unnoticed, even though it constitutes an essential feature of Foucault's genealogical project at least from 1978 on, when he first coins the notions of "counter-conduct" and "critical attitude."[8] A few years later, it is through genealogy that Foucault explicitly relates the notion of counter-conduct to the analysis of ancient *parrhesia*: "In analyzing this notion of *parrhesia*, I would like also to outline the genealogy of what we could call the critical attitude in our society."[9] For Foucault, however, the genealogy of the critical attitude is neither vindicatory nor purely subversive or problematizing, but has a crucial possibilizing function: it allows us to "separate out, from the contingency that has made us what we are, the *possibility* of no longer being, doing, or thinking what we are, do, or think."[10] This "possibility," far from just being abstract, is to be conceived in terms of the elaboration and practice of concrete forms of counter-conduct in the present.[11] And even though genealogy does not legislate the specific *content* of these counter-conducts, it does define their *form*, since each aims to criticize and destabilize a given power/knowledge apparatus, or better, a given regime of truth with its "therefore" that still governs (certain aspects of) "our" conduct today.

But who is the subject here—who is this "we"? I will argue that Foucauldian genealogy provides us with an answer to this question, one that, however, is not and cannot be situated prior to the genealogical endeavor. By tracing the emergence of past counter-conducts against a given set of governmental mechanisms that are still operative (albeit transformed) in the present, Foucault's genealogy of the critical attitude contributes to making the future "formation of a 'we' *possible*."[12] This is what I call the we-making dimension of possibilizing genealogy.

By focusing attention on this neglected aspect of the genealogical method, I hope to provide a definitive rebuttal to one of the main criticisms that has been raised against genealogy in general, and Foucauldian genealogy in particular. It has been argued that Foucault's genealogies are at best capable of emphasizing the historically contingent origins of concepts and practices such as disciplinary control, punishment, sexuality, and truth and truth-telling—and of showing that, right from the start, these concepts and practices have been inextricably enmeshed in relations of power.[13] However, Foucauldian genealogy has so far not been considered capable of giving us any indication as to "what we should do": Should we reject these concepts and practices, or at least try to change them? And what alternate concepts and practices should we elaborate? Most importantly, why bother at all, since according to Foucault—or so it is posited—power is everywhere, and thus escaping from it is ultimately impossible?[14]

To date, the most influential articulation of this line of criticism is found in Nancy Fraser and Jürgen Habermas, who famously claim that Foucault's genealogical project lacks normative grounding and is therefore incapable of telling us why we should resist the mechanisms of power it nevertheless reveals in an empirically insightful way.[15] This conclusion, I argue, is mistaken because it conceives of Foucauldian genealogy exclusively as a subversive method, whereas Foucault's genealogical project also encompasses a possibilizing dimension. By this I mean that it aims not only to demonstrate the contingent nature of our concepts and practices by revealing the power dynamics that presided over their establishment (subversive genealogy), nor exclusively to make them problematic once more (problematizing genealogy); it also aims to show that each governmental apparatus or regime of truth was already contested in the past—and is no doubt still contested in the present—by multiple forms of counter-conduct, which are "normatively significant" because they concretely embody the possibility of no longer being, doing, and thinking what we are, do, and think.[16] Thus, by emphasizing that the genealogy of the critical attitude is intrinsically connected with the other genealogical inquiries that Foucault undertook in the course of his intellectual career, and that his "analysis of truth" and his "critique of power" are the two sides of the same coin, or better, two complementary aspects of his history of truth, I will also provide a stronger argument in favor of the thesis that his work equips us with effective critical tools while possessing normative force—albeit one that resists being translated into definite prescriptions.[17]

Foucault, Habermas, and the Question of Normativity

It has been observed that the so-called Foucault/Habermas debate has received disproportionate attention in the past thirty years, given that it never ultimately took place and is therefore essentially a product of the scholarly literature on these thinkers.[18] I will thus refrain from attempting to reconstruct the debate as it would or should have happened. Instead, I will argue that the form this debate has taken in the secondary literature demonstrates how critics and apologists of Foucault alike have so far failed to grasp the possibilizing dimension of his genealogical project, and with it its specific normative force.

In addressing Foucault's work in *The Philosophical Discourse of Modernity*, Habermas argues that "genealogy is overtaken by a fate similar to that which Foucault had seen in the human sciences": since genealogy claims for itself the "reflectionless objectivity of a nonparticipatory, ascetic description of kaleidoscopically changing practices of power," it cannot but end up taking the form of "the *presentistic, relativistic, cryptonormative* illusory science that it does not want to be."[19] Foucault's genealogies aim to be descriptive and value-neutral, and yet, according to Habermas, Foucault draws on them in order to formulate (subversive or critical) judgments that rest on masked, and therefore illegitimate, normative assumptions. More precisely, Habermas argues that, since Foucault's "theory of power" entails that "the meaning of validity claims consists in the power effects they have," Foucault's genealogical project is ultimately self-defeating. Indeed, if it succeeded, it would "destroy the foundations of the research inspired by it as well."[20] If the truth claims associated with Foucault's genealogies amounted to no more than their effects on readers, "the entire undertaking of a critical unmasking of the human sciences would lose its point," because no distinction whatsoever could then be drawn between discourses in power and counter-discourses: they would both consist in "nothing else than the effects of power they unleash."[21] Thus, according to Habermas, Foucault's genealogical inquiries cannot truly be critical, for their conclusions cannot claim to fall outside the reach of his all-encompassing theory of power. Consequently, genealogy should not be conceived as critique, but "as a tactic . . . for waging a battle against a normatively unassailable formation of power"—a tactic that is ultimately unable to tell us why we should fight against power, so pervasively conceived.[22]

In short, the core of Habermas's criticisms of Foucault consists in casting doubt on the normative validity of his genealogical method, suggesting that it cannot help but be self-defeating. In analogous fashion, a few years before, Fraser had already argued that Foucault's views fall prey to "normative confusions," since they claim to be at once value-neutral and politically engaged, and yet lack grounds to articulate why struggle is preferable to submission, and why domination should be resisted.[23]

Much ink has been spilled in the attempt to either strengthen Fraser's and Habermas's line of criticism against Foucault, or defend Foucault's genealogical inquiries against these objections.[24] In the latter case, two main strategies have been deployed. On the one hand, scholars have argued that Foucault's genealogies of power/knowledge, and his philosophical-political project more broadly, are consistently non-foundational: far from being normatively confused, they are perfectly coherent in their non-normative endeavor.[25] On the other hand, scholars have claimed that Foucault's philosophical-political project is in fact normative, but disagree on how it should be cashed out: either his conception of freedom or autonomy, variously characterized in terms of self-transformation or self-determination, *does* constitute the normative grounding that Fraser and Habermas demand;[26] or his normative commitments are of a different kind than what Fraser and Habermas would likely accept.[27] Bridging these two camps, some scholars have even tried to combine Foucault's and Habermas's views, arguing that they are closer than they seem, or even complementary.[28]

While entering into the details of these debates is outside the scope of this chapter, it is important to emphasize that virtually every scholar sympathetic to Foucault ends up conceding a strategically crucial point to Fraser and Habermas: (subversive) genealogy aims first and foremost to open up a space of freedom, but it is not its task to "fill" such a space, nor to commit us to doing so. It unmasks the fact that our beliefs, concepts, and practices, far from being natural and necessary, are historical and contingent; hence, by "denaturalizing" everything that presents itself as ahistorical and universal, it opens up new possibilities for action, as well as for personal and sociopolitical transformation.[29] However, its capacity to open up these new possibilities is construed as intrinsically non-normative. As David Couzens Hoy aptly puts it, genealogy recognizes

> that it does not change the world, but it does prepare the world for change. By disrupting the fatalism resulting from resignation to the inevitability of oppressive social institutions, genealogy frees us for social transformation, even if it does not tell us precisely what to do or where to go.[30]

The work undertaken by (Foucauldian) genealogy is thus considered to be at worst *parasitical* and at best merely *preparatory*.[31] By revealing "historically constituted objects" to be "historically contingent and therefore changeable," genealogy is able to "free us from captivity to a picture or perspective" that constrains "our capacity for self-government," but it does not thereby commit us to capitalizing on the "sense for the non-necessary" it creates.[32] Its emancipatory effects are conceived as mere potentialities that always stand in need of actualization.

Scholars such as Koopman and Allen have attempted to more precisely delineate the specificity of Foucault's genealogies, but an analogous conclusion nevertheless applies. What they call problematizing genealogies "critically investigate the conditions of the possibility of the practical exercise of [our] concepts," and are therefore different both from vindicatory and from subversive genealogies.[33] In Koopman's view, Foucauldian genealogy aims to show how and why certain concepts and practices became a problem at a given historical moment in order to make them *problematic* once more: revealing how those concepts and practices have been constituted and concretely exercised facilitates social and political transformations in the present.[34] This interpretation does capture a crucial aspect of Foucault's genealogies by explaining how they make transformation possible: they diagnose the "limits of the present," thereby preparing the ground for the work of "transgression" and "experimentation."[35] Yet, on this view, Foucauldian genealogy does not commit us to anything in particular, since it does not possess any normative force per se.[36]

Consequently, all the defenses so far elaborated in response to Fraser's and Habermas's criticisms ultimately fall short. Indeed, they all too readily concede that Foucault's genealogies are structurally unable to tell us why we should fight against the mechanisms of power whose subjugating effects they nevertheless insightfully reveal, and therefore do not possess any normative force. As a result, Foucauldian genealogy is reduced to a mere ladder, to be used only to be kicked away. However, this conclusion

holds only if we continue to focus exclusively on the subversive or problematizing dimensions of genealogy as Foucault practiced it. While I do
not want to deny that these two dimensions constitute essential aspects of
Foucault's genealogical inquiries—and of his philosophical project more
broadly—emphasizing a further dimension that I call possibilizing puts us
in the position to see that Foucauldian genealogy *does* possess normative
force. Although it does not tell us precisely what we should do, genealogy constitutes a concrete framework for action—an ethico-political
"we"—that *commits* us to resisting certain aspects of the governmental
mechanisms and regimes of truth it reveals, thus inciting us to elaborate
alternate ways of conducting ourselves.

The Genealogy of Critique

In order to bring out the possibilizing dimension of Foucault's genealogical inquiries, we need to shift our focus from the exclusive attention
scholars have paid to the issue of genealogy *as* (a form of) critique. This
narrowness of scholarly focus has obscured the crucial role that the genealogy *of* critique plays in Foucault's work starting from at least 1978—and,
as I will argue, even before this date, albeit implicitly. The turning point is
Foucault's 1978 lecture, "What Is Critique?," in which he "plays" one Kant
(that of *Was ist Aufklärung?*) against another Kant (that of the *Critiques*)
in order to radically redefine the critical project so as to take it up on his
own terms.

If Foucault concurs with a long tradition in thinking that the question
of critique, at least in its modern sense, was inaugurated by Kant, he dis-
sents from it in arguing that such a question in fact originated in Kant's
text on the *Aufklärung* rather than in the *Critiques*.[37] He thus shifts the
question of transcendental critique toward what he calls the "critical attitude," connecting the issue of the relations between knowledge and power
with an "individual and collective" *ethos* defined by the "will not to be
governed" quite so much.[38] As a result, the epistemologico-transcendental
question "What can I know?" becomes a "question of attitude," that is,
an ethico-political question, and critique is redefined by Foucault as "the
movement by which the subject gives herself the right to question truth
on its effects of power and question power on its discourses of truth"—
a movement that, as I mentioned above, aims at the "desubjugation of the
subject [*désassujettissement*] in the context of . . . the politics of truth."[39]
   Far from aiming to elaborate a critical *theory*, then, Foucault's project
focuses on the analysis of a series of concrete critical *attitudes*—and does
so genealogically. From this perspective, for Foucault, *parrhesia* clearly

constitutes a specific critical attitude. In *Discourse and Truth*, as we saw, he defines it as a verbal activity in which the speaker has "a certain relation to other people through critique (self-critique or critique of other people)."[40] Indeed, "*parrhesia* has always the function of criticism[:] criticism of oneself, the speaker himself, or criticism of the interlocutor."[41] In short, Foucault clearly conceives of *parrhesia* as a historical form, or better, a "family" of different but interrelated historical forms taken by the critical attitude. And not only does he argue that "Kant's text on the *Aufklärung* is a certain way for philosophy . . . to become aware of problems which were traditionally problems of *parrhesia* in antiquity," but, as elaborated above, he claims that, in analyzing the notion of *parrhesia*, his main goal is to "outline the genealogy of what we could call the critical attitude in our society."[42]

This genealogical project—the last one Foucault had the chance to undertake—has generally not been noticed.[43] Yet it is hard to downplay its relevance, since it extends far beyond the analysis of the notion of *parrhesia* in Greco-Roman antiquity. Indeed, virtually all of Foucault's genealogical inquiries comprise important moments in which the focus is not on subjugating and normalizing governmental mechanisms, but is squarely on critical attitudes or "counter-conducts," that is, struggles "against the processes implemented for conducting others."[44] To name just a few examples:

1. In the fourth volume of his *History of Sexuality*, while tracing the genealogy of the subject of desire, Foucault refers to the "angelic nature [*angélisme*] of virginity" as a form of counter-conduct that aimed to undermine the existing "sexual social contract."[45]
2. In his investigation of pastoral power as part of a genealogy of modern governmentality, Foucault focuses on five medieval counter-conducts: asceticism, communities, mysticism, the "problem of Scripture," and eschatological beliefs.[46]
3. In his genealogy of modern psychiatry, Foucault analyzes convulsion both as an embodied resistance to religious and medical practices of examination and as what would later become the "neurological model of mental illness."[47]
4. In tracing the birth of the repressive juridico-political apparatus in France, Foucault devotes the first half of his 1971–72 lecture course at the Collège de France to the 1639 rebellion of the Nu-pieds in Normandy.[48]
5. In his analysis of psychiatric power as part of the broader project of a genealogy of modern disciplinary power, Foucault repeatedly focuses on the

"insurrection of the hysterics" and their struggle against the medicalization of their own bodies.[49]

6. As mentioned above, in the larger context of his genealogy of the relations between subjectivity and truth Foucault refers to "militantism" and "revolutionary life" as well as the "artistic life" in nineteenth-century Europe as two of the main examples of the extension of the theme of the Cynic "true life" throughout the history of the West.[50]

7. Foucault's publication of the "dossier" *Herculine Barbin*, an aspect of his genealogy of the modern notion of sexual identity, investigates how emerging medical strategies of normalization to universally impose a "true sex" could nevertheless be contested by the experience of the "happy limbo of a non-identity."[51]

8. With regard to his genealogical analysis of biopolitics, and more precisely the modern and contemporary medicalization of life and death, Foucault famously discusses suicide as a form of counter-conduct.[52]

This list is obviously not meant to be exhaustive, and Foucault's analysis of *parrhesia* should of course be added to these examples as the main "critical moment" in his genealogy of the modern Western subject and, as I argued in chapters 3 and 4, in his broader project of a history of truth.[53] These forms of contestation and resistance are also each very different from one another: not all are deliberate, organized, or even effective. However, they constitute significant moments in which (individual and collective) critical attitudes appear in the context of Foucault's genealogical inquiries.[54] This should not come as a surprise, since, after all, one of Foucault's crucial methodological principles is that "where there is power, there is resistance, and yet, or rather consequently, this resistance is never in a position of exteriority in relation to power."[55] To be consistent with this principle, in revealing the contribution of historically constituted governmental formations and regimes of truth in the shaping of our current beliefs, concepts, and practices (and of our own selves), Foucauldian genealogy must also reveal the multiplicity of points of resistance that played "the role of adversary, target, support [*appui*], or stepping stone" for the emergence and concrete functioning of those formations and regimes.[56] As Foucault claims in 1983, the most fundamental objective of his philosophical and ethico-political project is to link together "the historical and theoretical analysis of power relations, institutions, and knowledge" and "the movements, critiques, and experiences that call them into question in reality."[57] Consequently, *every* genealogy that Foucault advances should also be conceived as (an element of) a genealogy of the critical attitude: far from limited to the historical analysis of *parrhesia* or the development of modern governmentality, Foucault's genealogical attention to critical attitudes runs throughout virtually all of his lectures and writings of the 1970s and the 1980s, and is an integral part of his project of a history of truth.[58]

The dimension of Foucauldian genealogy that focuses on critical attitudes corresponds to what I call possibilizing genealogy, insofar as it does not aim to "deduce from the form of what we are what is *impossible* for us to do and to know," but to concretely "separate out, from the contingency that has made us what we are, the *possibility* of no longer being, doing, or thinking what we are, do, or think."[59] Yet this dimension of genealogy is not reducible to the idea, emphasized by many scholars, that one of the main effects of subversive or problematizing genealogies is to open up new possibilities for action, since merely being able to do so suffices neither to say anything further about what these possibilities might be nor to commit us to undertaking them. By contrast, Foucault's genealogy of the critical attitude focuses on moments in which people actually *tried* to no longer be, do, or think what they (were told they) were or had to do or think.[60]

This mode of genealogy is therefore possibilizing insofar as it directly sustains Foucault's "hyper- and pessimistic activism": "My point," Foucault famously argues in 1983, "is not that everything is bad, but that everything is dangerous, which is not exactly the same as bad. If everything is dangerous, then *we always have something to do*."[61] Hence, this pessimistic activism is necessarily connected with a "postulate of absolute optimism," since Foucault's genealogical analyses of power mechanisms aim to allow "those who are inserted in these relations of power" to "escape them, to transform them, not to be subjugated any longer because of their actions, their resistance, and their rebellion."[62] As Foucault puts it, "I do not conduct my analyses in order to say: this is how things are, you are all trapped. I say these things only to the extent to which I see them as capable of permitting the transformation of reality."[63] Now, far from remaining an abstract ideal, this postulate of absolute optimism finds a concrete instantiation in the genealogy of the critical attitude: individuals in history have always been immersed in, and subjugated by, complex governmental formations, but they were never entirely trapped, since they were able to elaborate a multiplicity of specific, contingent, fragile, but nevertheless *real* forms of counter-conduct. If it was possible for them, Foucault's argument goes, it is possible for us as well.

However, the "possibilization" entailed by Foucault's genealogy of the critical attitude is concrete not only because it reveals the history of the constitution of governmental apparatuses and regimes of truth to include an at least equally relevant history of struggles and resistances, but also because it thereby constitutes an ethico-political "we" encompassing the individuals who endured and fought against those apparatuses and regimes in the past. As I will now show, this ethico-political "we" generates a normative commitment for us to giving a new and no doubt different life to these struggles in the present.

Genealogy and We-Making

In "On the Concept of History," Walter Benjamin defends a conception of (the writing of) history and the relation between the present and the past that is of direct relevance to the account of genealogy I am advancing here. In the XVII thesis, he argues that "thinking involves not only the movement of thoughts, but their arrest as well," and that when thinking "comes to a stop in a constellation saturated with tensions, it gives that constellation a shock" by which it is "crystallized as a monad"; for the materialist historian, every such monad constitutes "a revolutionary chance in the fight for the oppressed past."[64] Instead of writing history from the standpoint of the victors, the materialist historian thus commits herself to writing it from the standpoint of the vanquished, adopting the discontinuous perspective of their fights against oppression that interrupt the continuity of domination throughout history.[65] Thereby, in a "moment of danger"—namely, "the danger of becoming a tool of the ruling classes" and falling prey to their way of narrating history—the materialist historian aims to produce a shock that imbues the past struggles fought by the oppressed classes with new life. She thus interrupts the "homogeneous, empty time" of historicism, "blast[ing] open the continuum of history" and the concepts of progress and telos along with it.[66]

Foucault never explicitly referred to Benjamin's theses in "On the Concept of History." On the one occasion he was ever asked if he would like to write the history of the vanquished, he responded positively, but immediately raised two objections. First, he claims that this project entails a delicate methodological problem, because "the vanquished . . . are those who, by definition, have been prevented from speaking," or those on whom "a foreign language has been imposed."[67] Consequently, is it even possible to hear them or give them back their voice? Second, Foucault is (unsurprisingly) critical of the concept of class struggle, as well as of the more general idea that power can be neatly characterized in terms of a war between two well-defined social groups: "Aren't the processes of domination far more complex and complicated than war?"[68] Finally, Foucault would no doubt also have objected to Benjamin's seemingly clear-cut distinction between ruling and oppressed classes and his appeal to a (proletarian) revolution, as well as to his claim that every generation is endowed by the previous ones with a *"weak* messianic power."[69]

Even though Foucauldian genealogy is not to be confused with the peculiar kind of historiography that Benjamin advocates, in at least one sense Benjamin and Foucault are much closer than we might expect.[70] In the previous section, I argued that Foucault's genealogical inquiries focus both on specific governmental apparatuses and regimes of truth, and on the struggles engaged against those very apparatuses and regimes. They thus tell a story both of subjugation and of resistance. For Foucault, the writing of genealogy, just as the writing of history for Benjamin, is therefore never neutral nor merely descriptive: it generates specific ethico-political commitments. While for Benjamin "the present is brought into a state of crisis that demands action, by its transformed relation to the past," for Foucault the genealogical method calls on us to recognize our own forms of subjection/subjectivation and to realize that we are part of the same history as the "infamous" people of the past.[71] Like them, we are enmeshed in complex power relations and regimes of truth—relations and regimes that they have endured, but also fought against. Thus, just as Benjamin, Foucault does not write history, or genealogy, in order to anachronistically make the past present again, but in order to instill in his audience a sense of ethico-political commitment toward the vanquished, or better, the subjugated individuals of the past—a commitment to carrying on their struggles in the present, albeit in a different form.[72] Consequently, the possibilizing dimension of Foucauldian genealogy cannot be found in fictional genealogies, nor in any other fictional narrative, including novels, even though Foucault was also interested in the transformative powers of fiction.[73] As Hilary Putnam rightly argues, literature is crucial in allowing us to imagine other possible ways of life.[74] Yet Foucauldian genealogy is about *real* lives and *actual* struggles, such that its ethico-political force is of a very different kind than a fictional narrative's.[75]

Yet we could ask: Who exactly counts as "vanquished"? Marxism provides Benjamin with an easy answer: the oppressed classes, and in particular the proletariat. But what about Foucault? Is his genealogical project able to rule out the problematic idea that a possibilizing genealogy could also legitimately be written, for instance, by neo-Nazis claiming that they are fighting for the vanquished German Nazis of the past century? The answer to this crucial question can be found in the "we" that possibilizing genealogy helps to constitute. Indeed, genealogy's capacity to instill a sense of ethico-political commitment in its audience relies on the constitution of a specific "we" as a *trans*historical (and not *supra*historical or *a*historical) subject of resistance. As Judith Butler aptly argues, while Fraser and Habermas postulate the existence of a stable, known, and agential "we" in asking the question "What should *we* do?" or "Why should *we* resist?" Foucault refuses to appeal to any stable and predetermined "we."[76] This rejection, however, is not to be interpreted as a rejection of any possible form of collective subjectivity. On the contrary, as I mentioned above, Foucault claims that the problem is "to make the *future* formation of a 'we' possible" (a "we" that "would also be likely to form a community of action"), because "the 'we' must not be prior to the question; it can only be the result—and the necessarily temporary result—of the question."[77]

Foucauldian genealogy, and more precisely the genealogy of the critical attitude, plays a crucial role in this process of we-making. Indeed, far from being given in advance, the "we" is constituted in the course of genealogy itself, but such a process can never be fully accomplished. This "we" is therefore not to be understood in terms of a fixed and shared "identity": it is never stable, never defined once and for all, but fluid, heterogeneous, multiple, and *structurally open*. In other words, Foucauldian genealogy refuses to make use of history in substantiating a "we" that is already presupposed—a totalizing "we" that would exclude all other possible "we"s, or would set itself in opposition to a "they." Consequently, a history of the past century written with a view to carrying on the neo-Nazi project of German national socialism into the present (one that presupposes a fixed, totalizing, and exclusionary "we") could never be considered an instance of possibilizing genealogy.

Moreover, Foucault's genealogy of the critical attitude does not aim to "tell a single story that is true for everybody."[78] For instance, it explicitly refuses to interpret history in terms of class struggle and to consider the proletariat as the subject of such a history. Rather than postulating a single subject as the subject of a suprahistorical critical attitude, or a universal "we" as the normative foundation of critique, *each genealogy* constitutes a different, specific, and structurally open "we": a "we" made by all the individuals who endured and fought against the governmental mechanisms and regimes of truth delineated in the course of the genealogy, and by those who are carrying on or will carry on their fight in the present. To avoid any misunderstanding, we should therefore more appropriately talk of the constitution of a *multiplicity* of non-totalizing, structurally open, and potentially overlapping "we"s that genealogical inquiries and contemporary struggles progressively populate with *real* people of different historical times.[79]

Foucault's (genealogical) history of truth, in addition to problematizing our unreflected acceptance of the "you have to" of the truth, also aims

to show that the governmental mechanisms and regimes of truth that individuals endured and fought against in the past are still at play, albeit transformed, in the present: each of us is a constituent of one (or more) of these
transhistorical "we"s that genealogy creates. Although not prescriptive or
"normativistic," since it does not rely on "external normative standards,"
nor does it measure reality "against an 'abstract ought,'" Foucauldian genealogy is nonetheless "normatively significant" and allows us to coherently
articulate a "normativity without foundations."[80] By recounting a history
that is still *ours* (a history not only of subjection, but also of contestation and resistance), Foucauldian genealogy situates each of us within a
(multiplicity of) "we"(s), each carrying with it, in an immanent fashion,
an ethico-political commitment to questioning, criticizing, and fighting
against a given governmental mechanism and regime of truth.[81] This is the
specific normative force that characterizes possibilizing genealogy, and
thereby Foucault's project of a history of truth.

From this perspective, the genealogist can be seen as a sui generis parrhesiast, who is not only personally implicated in what she writes insofar
as she is herself part of the history of subjection and resistance she tells,
but who also "speaks the truth" at the perlocutionary level. Think, for
instance, of the crucial role that Foucault's activism in the Prisons Information Group (GIP) played in his decision to write a genealogy of the
prison, and of his claim that the truthfulness of his books is to be assessed
in terms of the effects they are able to produce both on their author and
on their readers.[82] As Foucault famously argues in 1978, his books aim to
function, for himself as well as for those who read them, as an *experience*:

> It is clear that, in order to have such an experience through a book like *The
> History of Madness*, it is necessary that what it asserts is "true," in terms
> of academic, historically verifiable truth. It cannot just be a novel. But
> what is essential is not found in a series of true or historically verifiable
> observations; it rather lies in the experience which the book allows us to
> have.[83]

In other words, Foucault conceives of his books as truthful first and
foremost in terms of their perlocutionary effects, and more specifically—
I would argue—of their capacity to incite their readers to engage in the
forms of critique and counter-conduct that have been and still are opposed
to the governmental mechanisms and regimes of truth they describe. "I
try to produce an interference between our reality and what we know
about our past history," Foucault explains in 1979, one that, if success-

ful, will in turn produce "real effects on our present history."[84] Foucault's "experience-book[s]" thus aim to produce "a transformation, a metamorphosis," one that "has a certain value, a certain character accessible to others": it "must be linkable, to a certain extent, to a collective practice and way of thinking," such as, for instance, the anti-psychiatric movement or the prisoners' movement in France.[85] This picture of the genealogist as a sui generis parrhesiast is entirely consistent with Foucault's conception of the role of the intellectual who, as Verena Erlenbusch-Anderson rightly argues, is not "a prophet or lawgiver who imposes normative prescriptions about what is to be done on the practices of those who fight on the ground," but instead someone who "excavates, or helps excavate, norms from the practices of those who are fighting" or have fought in the past.[86]

Foucault once claimed that "the ethico-political choice we have to make every day is to determine which is the main danger."[87] This choice constitutes the prerequisite of any genealogical inquiry: How do we decide *which* genealogy to write? The answer to this question necessarily lies external to (and *precedes*) the genealogical endeavor; it is linked to the ethico-political choice Foucault refers to.[88] The answer to the question "What should we do?"—if we expect it to take the form of a series of specific prescriptions—also lies external to (and *follows*) the genealogical endeavor; it is linked to yet another series of delicate ethico-political choices. What I hope to have demonstrated is that, although it is not the task of genealogy to answer these two questions, and although Foucault consistently refuses to adopt any Archimedean point as a normative grounding for critique, Foucauldian genealogy is nevertheless not merely descriptive or value-neutral—or worse, normatively confused. On the contrary, because of its possibilizing dimension, Foucauldian genealogy's normative force derives from its capacity to constitute a concrete framework for action (a transhistorical "we") allowing *genealogy itself* to answer the question "Why resist?" by generating a sense of ethico-political commitment in its audience.[89]

Thus, even though Foucault's genealogies do not provide us with ready-made solutions to our current problems, nor do they tell us precisely "what is to be done," they nevertheless aim to commit us to carrying on, in one form or another, the struggle against the subjugating effects of the governmental mechanisms and regimes of truth that still permeate our lives, and whose functioning they insightfully reveal.[90] Foucault's history of truth is no exception. Indeed, its aim is not only to unmask and problematize the "therefore" of truth, or the procedures that lead people to submit to certain truth claims and give them the power to govern their conduct. Foucault's history of truth also shows us how individuals in the past concretely fought against such "therefores," thus emphasizing that there have been (and still are) many critical or counter-hegemonic ways to make use of what I have called the force of truth—*parrhesia* being the clearest example.

CONCLUSION

Rethinking Critique

In this book, my aim has been to offer the first comprehensive interpretation of Foucault's project of a history of truth—which I consider to
be the common thread that connects his 1980s analyses of *parrhesia* and
techniques of the self to his 1970s interest in Nietzschean genealogy and
the politics of truth—and to assess its philosophical and ethico-political
relevance. By shedding light on this ambitious critical project, and by re-
lating it to the elaboration of an ethics and politics of truth-telling, I hope
this book will contribute to overcoming two of the main misconceptions
that still loom over Foucauldian scholarship. First, that Foucault's later
work on *parrhesia* and the techniques of the self constitutes a departure
from his prior interest in politics and power/knowledge mechanisms; by
contrast, as I showed above, his work from the 1980s remains thoroughly
political in focusing on the issue of the government of human beings by
the truth. Second, that Foucault's so-called turn to ethics signals the aban-
donment of the methods of archaeology and genealogy; by contrast, we
saw that Foucault keeps referring to archaeology and genealogy until the
end of his life, sometimes adding a more explicit critical dimension to both
in talking about anarchaeology and the genealogy of the critical attitude
in our society.

I also hope this book will help shift the recent focus of scholars away
from the unproductive and worn-out discussion about Foucault, postmodernism, and post-truth. Rethinking the current relation between critique, truth, and truth-telling is a very delicate and politically urgent task.
Indeed, the proliferation of lies, fake news, and "alternative facts" on social
media and other news outlets presents us with an uncomfortable dilemma:
either we concede that truth does not really matter, since everything just
depends on power, propaganda, and persuasion; or we strenuously defend
the—political, ethical, social—value of truth, especially scientific truth.[1]
While the choice is clear for most of us, the uncomfortable part of this task

comes with the temptation to think that, in order to defend the value of truth, one has to construe it as *intrinsic* or *unconditional*. Critical thinkers such as Nietzsche and Foucault therefore immediately become suspect: in our post-truth era, we are told, we should not be allowed to problematize the value of truth, or to elaborate a critique of the will to truth. In fact, any project of the sort must be considered a dangerous way of giving in to relativism, science denialism, and alternative facts. However, this conclusion does not take into account that truth and facts alone do not possess any *intrinsic* critical force on their own. For instance, as Martina Tazzioli and I have recently argued, the accumulation of evidence and facts to document the violence perpetrated against migrants at Europe's borders, while indisputably showing the deadly effects of the EU's policies of migration containment, has so far been largely unable to disrupt those policies, as well as the rise of racism, xenophobia, and far-right political parties.[2] I take this to show that truth and facts alone are often not enough to sustain effective critical practices, since they have no critical force *in and of themselves*, as the repeated failures to implement appropriate responses to climate change at a global level also clearly show.

Consequently, Foucault's analyses of truth and truth-telling, correctly understood, seem to be of utter importance today. As we saw, Foucault incessantly raises the question of truth, of its value, and of its ethico-political effects, thus inciting us to ask the crucial question of the conditions under which "telling the truth" can be an effective critical practice—and what it actually means to speak "the truth" at an ethical, social, and political level. What Foucault puts at the core of his critical project, more precisely, is the "therefore" of truth, that is, the often imperceptible procedures that lead us not only to *accept* certain truth claims, but to *submit* to them and give them the power to govern our conduct. This is what I have called the problem of the *force of truth*. Examining and problematizing our reasons to give in to the "therefore" that links the "it is true" to the "I submit" constitute the core of Foucault's genealogical project of a history of truth, while also opening up the space for the elaboration of an ethics and politics of truth-telling that, instead of concealing the existence of such a "therefore," puts it at the forefront by shifting the attention toward the question of the speaker's *ethos* and the ethico-political effects of her truth-telling. When combined with the we-making effects that characterize all Foucauldian genealogies, I have argued that this ethics and politics of truth-telling is imbued with a normative force that offers a compelling response to the charge of relativism and reductionism, on the one hand, and the pitfalls of foundationalism, on the other.[3]

It should therefore be clear by now that Foucault's rejection of "the Truth" as a timeless and suprahistorical concept does not amount to a rejection of truth altogether. On the contrary, Foucault considers the question of truth—of its manifestation, its value, and its effects—as *the* crucial philosophical and ethico-political question. Throughout his intellectual career, he never ceased to interrogate and problematize our desire to attain the truth and the "will to truth" that characterizes our societies, along with the attempt of philosophers and critical thinkers alike to lay out a truthful picture of the human being and society that would serve as a foundation for their theories. In arguing that one of his main principles is "never to accept anything as definitive, sacrosanct, self-evident, or fixed," Foucault is criticizing precisely the claim that a universal, suprahistorical truth is needed in order for our personal and political lives, as well as our critical theories and practices, not to dissolve into chaos.[4] His aim, however, is not to do away with truth altogether, but to reveal the multiple ways in which human beings engage in historically situated regimes of truth that govern their conduct through the "therefore" that links the "it is true" to the "I submit"—or, in other words, the multiple ways in which we give "truth" the right to tell us what to do and how to live. Yet, while Foucault follows Nietzsche in encouraging us to question the unconditional value attributed to truth, he is also aware that we cannot simply "jump" outside of all games and regimes of truth, just as we cannot jump outside of all power relations. Even though each game and regime of truth is historically situated and therefore (up to a certain point) contingent and transformable, Foucault implicitly acknowledges that human beings *need* to establish and engage in games and regimes of truth in order to survive and be able to live together.[5]

This is why, in Foucault's view, the genealogical analysis of the various regimes of truth that emerged throughout human history to connect a certain way of manifesting the truth to a certain modality of governing people and a certain form of subjectivity is paramount to address (and criticize) the workings of power in *any* given society. Far from being a solution that finally sets us free, the truth is for Foucault an inescapable *ethico-political problem.*[6] As I argued in chapter 2, the object of Foucault's history of truth, and the target of his genealogical critique (at least in its final, most mature version), are not constituted by the formal rules that define each game of truth, but by the "therefore" that links the "it is true" of the game of truth to the "I submit" of the individuals who are concretely engaged in it. Indeed, one of Foucault's main insights is that no game of truth exists outside of a regime of truth, that is, without being connected with a specific bundle of relations linking truth, power, and subjectivity to each other. Consequently, Foucault's history of truth is not an epistemological endeavor, but a thoroughly ethico-political one.

Emphasizing the distinction Foucault draws between games and regimes of truth allows us to extricate his analysis of truth and truth-telling from what Colin Koopman calls "the impasse between foundationalism and relativism."[7] Indeed, for Foucault, each game of truth has an internal logic and formal structure that, within that specific, historically situated game of truth, autonomously establish the distinction between true and false statements: within each game of truth (that is, at a first-order normative level), truth is *index sui* and is therefore not "relative" nor reducible to power. Now, while the concept of regime of truth clearly problematizes this first-order autonomy of the truth, it does so at a different level: by revealing the necessary interaction between truth and power within the procedures that are used to govern human beings, taking the perspective of the regime of truth allows us to see that (at a second-order or metanormative level) truth is not *rex sui*, *lex sui*, or *judex sui*—that is, it does not possess any normative force per se.[8] The distinction between games and regimes of truth, combined with the insight that every game of truth is concretely linked (but not reducible) to a specific regime of truth, thus allows Foucault to respond to the charge of both foundationalism and relativism, as well as naive reductionism. It constitutes a viable rebuttal to the worry that, by disqualifying all claims to objectivity and reducing truth to a historically situated epiphenomenon of power dynamics, Foucauldian genealogy—and even more so his history of truth—removes out from under us all stable ground for drawing a coherent distinction between what we have reason to think and what relations of power do to our thinking.[9]

In his recent, important book, *Critique and Praxis*, Bernard Harcourt argues that "it never makes sense to speak of Truth with a capital T" in the political realm.[10] Indeed, in that context, "the imposition of a foundation, the claim to truth, is itself a power play," one that indicates "the quest for a solid foundation on which to ground oneself or to convince others," and consequently one that "critical philosophy must avoid."[11] My reading of Foucault's history of truth as a genealogy of the most pervasive contemporary regimes of truth (namely, the scientific and confessional regimes of truth) aims precisely to elaborate a conception of social and political critique as a foundationless task consisting in the incessant questioning of the value of truth—one that, however, avoids first-order relativism and reductionism. Yet I am not convinced that this entails that political philosophers and critical thinkers alike should stop, not only referring to the Truth, but also using the word "truth" altogether, as Harcourt suggests.

On the contrary, following Foucault, I argued that critique itself can be fruitfully conceived as a regime of truth.

This move, on the one hand, has the advantage of emphasizing the historical, contingent, partial nature of all forms of critique (and of critical truth-telling), and thus the importance of questioning the will to truth that is at play even in our own critical discourses and practices. In other words, it is crucial to elaborate a critique of critique itself: (genealogical) *self*-criticism is the necessary correlate to one's engagement in critical thinking and practice. Critique, understood as the incessant attempt to challenge and reverse the governmental mechanisms that conduct our conduct, or as "the art of not being governed quite so much," is a battle *immanently* fought on the terrain of truth.[12] This is why I argued in favor of the elaboration of an ethics and politics of truth-telling that does not try to ground itself on a solid foundation, nor to impose on others— one that, therefore, is situated at the level not of the illocutionary, but of the perlocutionary. By combining Foucault's analysis of *parrhesia* with J. L. Austin's and Stanley Cavell's respective insights into performative and passionate utterance in chapters 3 and 4, I listed seven conditions of parrhesiastic utterance as a critical speech act whose effects pertain to the domain of the perlocutionary: unpredictability, freedom, criticism, risk, courage, transparency, and alethurgy. These conditions enable us to rethink the role that truth-telling plays within our critical discourses and practices, and to newly define critique as a historically situated and foun-dationless *activity* that incessantly attempts to transform oneself, others, and the world. They also allow us to see that the "force of truth," that is, its capacity to produce effects on reality, is necessarily contextual: at the level of the regime of truth, truth is not an epistemic force to be analyzed in terms of illocutionary effects;[13] it is an ethico-political force that operates in a perlocutionary battlefield. Hence the suggestion that truth should be redefined in terms of *ethos*—and, as Foucault argues in 1983, that the critical thinker's attitude should be "demanding, prudent, 'experimental,'" for "at every moment, step by step, one must compare what one is thinking and saying with what one is doing, with what one is."[14] Critique does not only consist in unmasking and problematizing the received "therefores" that characterize contemporary regimes of truth, but also in creating and experimenting with new "therefores" of truth—and instead of concealing them, making them (and their consequences) as explicit as possible in our words, in our actions, and in our lives.

On the other hand, conceiving and genealogizing critique itself as a re-gime of truth has the advantage of emphasizing critique's historical depth. As I argued in chapter 5, Foucault's genealogical project should be construed not only as a subversive or problematizing endeavor, but also as a possibilizing one, that is, as a way of showing that, at every given moment in history, governmental mechanisms and regimes of truth leave open a multiplicity of possibilities for resistance and counter-conduct that have been and still are *concretely used* by specific individuals. In other words, albeit always contextual and historically situated, critique is not an activity that begins each time from scratch: there is no "origin" of critique, and those who engage in critical practices are always already part of a long history of struggles, or what I defined in terms of a transhistorical, open, and mobile "we" that constitutes the unavoidable framework for "collective social experimentation and political transformation."[15] It is only within this framework that the Nietzschean task that Foucault sets for his (genealogical) history of truth, that is, *experimentally* calling the value of truth into question, can be accomplished.

This we-making dimension is also what gives genealogy its specific normative force: even though Foucault's genealogies do not tell us precisely "what is to be done," they nevertheless commit us to carrying on, in one form or another, the (collective) struggle against the subjugating effects of the governmental mechanisms and regimes of truth that still permeate our lives. Seen from this point of view, Wendy Brown's famous objection to Foucault appears misplaced: Foucault does not "*tacitly assume* the givenness and resilience of the desire for freedom," thus overlooking the ways in which power operates on that very desire by negating or redirecting it.[16] On the contrary, Foucault's genealogical inquiries, and most notably his genealogy of critique, empirically reveal the existence throughout history of multiple forms of "voluntary inservitude" and "reflective indocility."[17] That is, they show us *the fact* that counter-conducts, no matter how small or limited, have been (and still are) enacted against each and every governmental mechanism and regime of truth. Therefore, genealogy is ultimately necessary to concretely substantiate the "theoretical-practical attitude concerning the non-necessity of all power" that Foucault, in 1980, terms "anarchaeology."[18]

By offering a new reading of Foucault's history of truth in terms of a genealogy of the most relevant contemporary regimes of truth (scientific, confessional, and critical), and by elaborating an ethics and politics of truth-telling derived from the perlocutionary force of truth, I thus hope this book will contribute to a reevaluation of Foucault's critical project as a whole, demonstrating that the latter can still play a decisive role in our own way of conceiving and practicing critique today.

Acknowledgments

This book is the result of many years of patient, at times frustrating, but enormously enriching engagement with Michel Foucault's work on truth and *parrhesia*. The material that constitutes it has already, in a sense, lived three different lives. The first one corresponds to my earlier attempts, roughly between 2012 and 2015, to figure out what Foucault means when he talks about games and regimes of truth, while also trying to find a way to use J. L. Austin's analysis of speech acts to clarify Foucault's study of *parrhesia*. It was only after transforming my PhD dissertation into a monograph in 2015 (published by Vrin as *Éthique et politique de soi: Foucault, Hadot, Cavell et les techniques de l'ordinaire*) that I decided to give my work on Foucault's history of truth and *parrhesia* the form of a book. *La force du vrai: De Foucault à Austin* was eventually published in French by Le Bord de l'Eau in 2017, in a series edited by Fabienne Brugère and Guillaume le Blanc. Those two years correspond to the second life of this book. Soon thereafter, however, the conversations sparked by this first publication enabled me to realize that I had many more (and sometimes quite different) things to say on the topic, and more importantly that the link between Foucault's history of truth and his practice of genealogical critique warranted closer examination. The past few years have been devoted to working out this connection and rethinking the whole project, thus giving the book a third life as my first monograph in English, thanks to Kyle Wagner and the interest and generous support of the University of Chicago Press. The introduction and chapters 1–4 of this book are a significantly revised and expanded version of the French book, while chapter 5 and the conclusion are new additions. Chapter 5, forthcoming in *Inquiry* as "On Possibilising Genealogy" (2020, © Taylor & Francis, available online: https://www.tandfonline.com/doi/10.1080/0020174X.2020.1712227) appears here in a modified version. Portions of chapters 3 and 4 also found their way into initial publication in English as "Performative, Passionate, and Parrhesiastic Utterance: On Cavell, Foucault, and Truth as an Ethical Force" (*Critical Inquiry* 41, Winter 2015, © The University of Chicago, available online: https://www.journals.uchicago .edu/doi/10.1086/679074), but have since been extensively revised.

Yet, above all, this book is the result of the myriad encounters and conversations that allowed me to have something to say about Foucault, the history of truth, and genealogical critique at all. From this perspective, the list of people I am indebted to is endless. It unquestionably begins with Arnold Davidson: when I was an undergraduate at the University of Pisa, it was through him that I discovered Foucault; ever since, Arnold has been the most exemplary of mentors, interlocutors, and friends. The third life of this book was also deeply shaped by day-to-day conversations with Sabina Vaccarino Bremner, whose philosophical brilliance and generosity are for me a source of never-ending amazement, and whose insightful comments on several drafts of the manuscript helped me improve it enormously. My work on Foucault's history of truth, *parrhesia*, and genealogy, on Austin's notion of the perlocutionary, and on Cavell's conception of passionate utterance has also greatly benefited from engagement with and feedback from many extraordinary friends, colleagues, and scholars: Amy Allen, Bruno Ambroise, Valérie Aucouturier, Nancy Bauer, Miguel de Beistegui, Jocelyn Benoist, Jean-François Braunstein, Fabienne Brugère, Judith Butler, Cesar Candiotto, the late Stanley Cavell, Philippe Chevallier, Niki Kasumi Clements, Andrew Cooper, Laura Cremonesi, the late Daniel Defert, Andrea Di Gesu, Élise Domenach, Piergiorgio Donatelli, André Duarte, Stuart Elden, Marta Faustino, Thiago Fortes Ribas, Miranda Fricker, Henri-Paul Fruchaud, Isabelle Galichon, Pascale Gillot, Frédéric Gros, David Halperin, Béatrice Han-Pile, Bernard Harcourt, Stephen Houlgate, Andrew Huddleston, Orazio Irrera, Anaïs Jomat, Sandra Laugier, Guillaume le Blanc, Stephen Legg, Guy Longworth, Hans-Jürgen Lüsebrink, Nancy Luxon, Giovanni Mascaretti, Edward McGushin, Martin Mees, Richard Moran, Nicolae Morar, Johanna Oksala, David Owen, Peter Poellner, Jim Porter, Matthieu Queloz, Daniel Rodríguez-Navas, Sverre Raffnsøe, Layla Raïd, Ariane Revel, Judith Revel, Jeanne-Marie Roux, Philippe Sabot, Lorenzo Serini, Arianna Sforzini, Pedro de Souza, Ann Laura Stoler, Martina Tazzioli, Federico Testa, Tuomo Tiisala, Daniel Verginelli Galantin, Naomi Waltham-Smith, and Daniel Wyche. I am also grateful to all of my wonderful colleagues and students at the University of Saint-Louis–Brussels, the University of Warwick, and the University of Pennsylvania, as well as to the organizers, speakers, and audiences of the many venues where I had the chance to present my work on these topics: the Centre Marc Bloch in Berlin, Columbia

University, Goldsmiths University of London, NOVA University Lisbon, the Hebrew University of Jerusalem, the New School for Social Research, UC Berkeley, the University of Chicago, the University of Essex, the University of Helsinki, the University of Lille, the University of Oregon, the University of Oxford, the University of Paris 1 Panthéon-Sorbonne, the University of Paris 8 Vincennes-Saint-Denis, the University of Saarlandes, and Yale University. In addition to Kyle Wagner, I would like to express my appreciation to Stephen Twilley, Kristin Rawlings, Nathan Petrie, and Marian Rogers for their invaluable assistance at different stages of the preparation of this manuscript. Last but certainly not least, the entire manuscript benefited immensely from careful reading and insightful comments by Verena Erlenbusch-Anderson and Colin Koopman, whose scholarship on Foucault, genealogy, and critique has been a constant source of inspiration for me throughout the years.

Finally, I am forever grateful to my mother, Patrizia Luppi, and my father, Agostino Lorenzini, who have always encouraged me to find my own way and voice in this life, and whose loving support during the past thirty-six years (and counting) has made everything else possible.

Forza d'Agrò, Italy
July 2022

Notes

Introduction

1. See, e.g., Hilary Putnam, *Reason, Truth, and History* (Cambridge: Cambridge University Press, 1981), 155, or the entries on cognitive relativism and Foucault's political thought in the *Internet Encyclopedia of Philosophy* (Emrys Westacott, "Cognitive Relativism," *Internet Encyclopedia of Philosophy*, 2006, https://www.iep.utm.edu/cog-rel/; Mark G. E. Kelly, "Michel Foucault: Political Thought," *Internet Encyclopedia of Philosophy*, https://www.iep.utm.edu/fouc-pol/).

2. Lee McIntyre, *Post-Truth* (Cambridge, MA: MIT Press, 2018), 139–41. For a rebuttal to these claims, see Sergei Prozorov ("Why Is There Truth? Foucault in the Age of Post-Truth Politics," *Constellations* 26[1] [2019]: 18–30), who convincingly argues that Foucault's political history of truth is not only distinct from the disposition toward post-truth, but may actually be helpful in criticizing it. For a critique of the concept of post-truth itself, which does not seem able to adequately capture contemporary political discourses and tactics, see Quassim Cassam, "Bullshit, Post-Truth, and Propaganda," in *Political Epistemology*, edited by E. Edenberg and M. Hannon (Oxford: Oxford University Press, 2021), 49–63.

3. Michel Foucault, *The Order of Things: An Archaeology of the Human Sciences* (New York: Routledge, 1989); Foucault, *Discipline and Punish: The Birth of the Prison*, translated by A. Sheridan (New York: Vintage Books, 1995); Noam Chomsky and Michel Foucault, "Human Nature: Justice vs. Power," in *The Chomsky-Foucault Debate: On Human Nature* (New York: New Press, 1971), 16–17, 40; Foucault, "The Political Function of the Intellectual" (1976), translated by C. Gordon, *Radical Philosophy* 17 (1977): 12–14.

4. Charles Taylor, "Foucault on Freedom and Truth," *Political Theory* 12(2) (1984): 152–53.

5. Putnam, *Reason, Truth, and History*, 156, 161.

6. Miranda Fricker, *Epistemic Injustice: Power and the Ethics of Knowing* (Oxford: Oxford University Press, 2007), 3.

7. Daniel Dennett, "I Begrudge Every Hour I Have to Spend Worrying about Politics: Interview with Carole Cadwalladr," *The Guardian*, February 12, 2017, https://www.theguardian.com/science/2017/feb/12/daniel-dennett-politics-bacteria-bach-back-dawkins-trump-interview. See also Kurt Andersen ("How America Lost Its Mind," *The Atlantic*, December 28, 2017, https://www.theatlantic.com/magazine/archive/2017/09/how-america-lost-its-mind/534231/), who claims that the "suspicion of reason," which supposedly characterizes the entirety of Foucault's work, that

is, the idea that rationality is just a coercive regime of truth, or "oppression by other means," has become so embedded in American academia and culture at large that it merits recognition as one the main causes of our current misfortunes.

8. Jacques Bouveresse, *Nietzsche contre Foucault: Sur la vérité, la connaissance et le pouvoir* (Marseille: Agone, 2016).

9. Bouveresse, *Nietzsche contre Foucault*, 110–11. See Bernard Williams, *Truth and Truthfulness: An Essay in Genealogy* (Princeton, NJ: Princeton University Press, 2002), 61–62, 271–72. For an analogous claim, see also Pascal Engel, "Michel Foucault: Vérité, connaissance et éthique," in *Michel Foucault*, edited by P. Artières et al. (Paris: L'Herne, 2011), 322.

10. Bouveresse, *Nietzsche contre Foucault*, 112, 115.

11. Williams, *Truth and Truthfulness*, 61, 163.

12. On Williams's lifelong suspicion of deflationary, disquotational, and redundancy theories of truth, see Mark P. Jenkins, *Bernard Williams* (New York: Routledge, 2014), 123–24.

13. Bouveresse, *Nietzsche contre Foucault*, 109.

14. Bouveresse, *Nietzsche contre Foucault*, 62.

15. Michel Foucault, *Lectures on the Will to Know: Lectures at the Collège de France, 1970–71*, edited by D. Defert, translated by G. Burchell; series edited by A. I. Davidson (Basingstoke: Palgrave Macmillan, 2013); Foucault, "The Order of Discourse" (1971), in *Archives of Infamy: Foucault on State Power in the Lives of Ordinary Citizens*, edited by N. Luxon, translated by T. Scott-Railton (Minneapolis: University of Minnesota Press, 2019), 141–73. It is important to remember that the edition of Foucault's *Lectures on the Will to Know* was established not from tape recordings (as in the case of almost all of his other Collège de France lecture courses), but from rather schematic and often incomplete manuscripts (Daniel Defert, "Course Context," in Foucault, *Lectures on the Will to Know*, 278–80).

16. See in particular the lecture series delivered at the Université Catholique de Louvain, *Wrong-Doing, Truth-Telling* (1981), and at the University of California, Berkeley, *Discourse and Truth* (1983). See also the Collège de France lecture courses, *On the Government of the Living* (1980), *Subjectivity and Truth* (1981), *The Government of Self and Others* (1983), and *The Courage of Truth* (1984).

17. Filip Buekens, "A Truth-Minimalist Reading of Foucault," *Le Foucaldien* 7(1) (2021), https://doi.org/10.16995/lefou.7989.

18. The distinctively anti-Platonic strategy adopted by Foucault in his analyses of truth and truth-telling was emphasized early on by Thomas R. Flynn ("Foucault as Parrhesiast: His Last Course at the Collège de France [1984]," *Philosophy and Social Criticism* 12[2–3] [1987]: 213–29), who rightly argues that its result is nevertheless not "epistemic anarchy": "The proliferation of events and truths in Foucault's discourse is not without rhyme or reason. But these reasons are in the plural and the history of their appearance and demise can be charted, if not explained" (224).

19. Bouveresse, *Nietzsche contre Foucault*, 111–12.

20. Bouveresse, *Nietzsche contre Foucault*, 122.

21. Paul Horwich, *Truth* (Oxford: Oxford University Press, 1998). On this point, and consequently on the gulf that separates Heidegger's and Foucault's respective histories of truth, see Miguel de Beistegui, "The Subject of Truth: On Foucault's *Lectures on the Will to Know*," *Quadranti: Rivista Internazionale di Filosofia Contemporanea* 2(1) (2014): 88–89.

22. Bouveresse, *Nietzsche contre Foucault*, 14.

23. Michel Foucault, *On the Government of the Living: Lectures at the Collège de France, 1979–80*, edited by M. Senellart, translated by G. Burchell; series edited by A. I. Davidson (Basingstoke: Palgrave Macmillan, 2014), 93.

24. Foucault, *Lectures on the Will to Know*, 202. On this point, see also Judith Revel, *Foucault avec Merleau-Ponty: Ontologie politique, présentisme et histoire* (Paris: Vrin, 2015), 79–109.

25. Foucault, *Lectures on the Will to Know*, 217.

26. Michel Foucault, "Truth and Juridical Forms" (1973), in Foucault, *Power*, vol. 3 of *Essential Works of Foucault (1954–84)*, edited by J. D. Faubion, translated by R. Hurley et al.; series edited by P. Rabinow (New York: New Press, 2000), 2.

27. Michel Foucault, "Nietzsche, Genealogy, History" (1971), in Foucault, *Aesthetics, Method, and Epistemology*, vol. 2 of *Essential Works of Foucault (1954–84)*, edited by J. D. Faubion, translated by R. Hurley et al.; series edited by P. Rabinow (New York: New Press, 1998), 370, 372, 379 (trans. mod.). See also Foucault, "Truth and Juridical Forms," 6–7.

28. Amia Srinivasan, "Genealogy, Epistemology, and Worldmaking," *Proceedings of the Aristotelian Society* 119(2) (2019): 128.

29. Friedrich Nietzsche, *On the Genealogy of Morality*, edited by K. Ansell-Pearson, translated by C. Diethe (Cambridge: Cambridge University Press, 1997), III, §24, p. 113 (trans. mod.).

30. Nietzsche, *On the Genealogy of Morality*, III, §24, pp. 112–13. See Christopher Janaway, *Beyond Selflessness: Reading Nietzsche's "Genealogy"* (Oxford: Oxford University Press, 2007), 5–6: "Nietzsche urges us to question whether truth at all costs is something we should be pursuing. It is not that truth has no value for Nietzsche, let alone that he thinks we can have no knowledge of truths . . . , rather that philosophy's assumption of the unconditional value of truth is questionable."

31. See David Owen, *Nietzsche's Genealogy of Morality* (Stocksfield: Acumen, 2007), 126–29. As Canguilhem puts it, in our society the truth normally plays the role of a "normative pre-sup-position," because the modern, scientific regime of truth makes it almost "impossible to consider anything that is not true [from a scientific standpoint] as anything other than vain, illusory, useless" ("De la science et de la contre-science," in *Hommage à Jean Hyppolite*, edited by S. Bachelard et al. [Paris: PUF, 1971], 176).

32. Michel Foucault, *Subjectivity and Truth: Lectures at the Collège de France, 1980–81*, edited by F. Gros, translated by G. Burchell; series edited by A. I. Davidson (Basingstoke: Palgrave Macmillan, 2017), 220–21.

33. Foucault, *Subjectivity and Truth*, 221.

34. Foucault, *Subjectivity and Truth*, 221.

35. Bouveresse, for instance, attributes to Foucault the claim that "it is only because we say that you are white, and say that this statement is true, that you are white" (Bouveresse, *Nietzsche contre Foucault*, 44). But see Michel Foucault, "The Ethics of the Concern for Self as a Practice of Freedom" (1984), in Foucault, *Ethics: Subjectivity and Truth*, vol. 1 of *Essential Works of Foucault (1954–84)*, edited by P. Rabinow, translated by R. Hurley et al.; series edited by P. Rabinow (New York: New Press, 1997), 297: "There are games of truth in which truth is a construction and others in which it is not. One can have, for example, a game of truth that consists of describing things in such and such a way: a person giving an anthropological description of a society supplies

not a construction but a description, which itself has a certain number of historically changing rules, so that one can say that it is to a certain extent a construction with respect to another description. This does not mean that there's just a void, that everything is a figment of the imagination. On the basis of what can be said, for example, about this transformation of games of truth, some people conclude that I have said that nothing exists—I have been seen as saying that madness does not exist, whereas the problem is absolutely the converse: it was a question of knowing how madness, under the various definitions that have been given, was at a particular time integrated into an institutional field that constituted it as a mental illness occupying a specific place alongside other illnesses." For a convincing defense of Foucault's "tacit realism," see Carlos G. Prado, *Starting with Foucault: An Introduction to Genealogy* (Boulder: Westview Press, 2000), 145–61.

36. Foucault, *Subjectivity and Truth*, 221.

37. Foucault, *Subjectivity and Truth*, 222; see also 235–36, where he defines the move that consists in "using the criterion of verification as an explanation of existence" as a "logicist dodge [*esquive logiciste*]," and argues once more that "reality does not contain in itself the raison d'être of discourse," or at least, that "the reality at issue in the discourse cannot by itself account for the existence of the discourse that speaks of it."

38. Edward Craig, *Knowledge and the State of Nature: An Essay in Conceptual Synthesis* (Oxford: Clarendon Press, 1990); Williams, *Truth and Truthfulness*; Fricker, *Epistemic Injustice*. A genealogy is "vindicatory" when it aims to *vindicate* a belief, concept, or practice by showing that, given a set of basic human needs, its emergence was (and its continued existence is) necessary. By contrast, a genealogy is "subversive" (or "unmasking") when it aims to *criticize* a belief, concept, or practice by showing that it emerged in a contingent way or, worse, as a consequence of ignoble historical events. This distinction was coined by Williams (36–37) and has since become omnipresent in the literature; see, e.g., David Couzens Hoy, "Genealogy, Phenomenology, Critical Theory," *Journal of the Philosophy of History* 2(3) (2008): 276–94; Colin Koopman, *Genealogy as Critique: Foucault and the Problems of Modernity* (Bloomington: Indiana University Press, 2013); Srinivasan, "Genealogy, Epistemology, and Worldmaking." I will return to this in chapter 5.

39. On this point, see Matthieu Queloz, *The Practical Origins of Ideas: Genealogy as Conceptual Reverse-Engineering* (Oxford: Oxford University Press, 2021).

40. In terms of monographs, see Chloë Taylor (*The Culture of Confession from Augustine to Foucault: A Genealogy of the "Confessing Animal"* [New York: Routledge, 2009]), who offers a Foucauldian genealogy of confession and the confessing subject from antiquity to the present; Nancy Luxon (*Crisis of Authority: Politics, Trust, and Truth-Telling in Freud and Foucault* [Cambridge: Cambridge University Press, 2013]), who insightfully uses Foucault's texts and lectures on *parrhesia* to examine the relations between authority, trust, and truthfulness in contemporary democratic theory and politics; Torben B. Dyrberg (*Foucault on the Politics of* Parrhesia [Basingstoke: Palgrave Macmillan, 2014]), who discusses the relevance of Foucault's notion of *parrhesia* in ancient and modern democracies; and Paul Allen Miller (*Foucault's Seminars on Antiquity: Learning to Speak the Truth* [New York: Bloomsbury, 2021]), who provides a detailed account of Foucault's genealogy of truth-telling in his Collège de France lectures from the 1980s. For other contributions discussing Foucault's texts and lectures on *parrhesia* from the standpoint of political philosophy and/or democratic

theory, see Matthew Sharpe, "A Question of Two Truths? Remarks on *Parrhesia* and the 'Political-Philosophical' Difference," *Parrhesia* 2 (2007): 89–108; David Owen and Clare Woodford, "Foucault, Cavell, and the Government of Self and Others: On Truth-Telling, Friendship, and an Ethics of Democracy," *Iride: Filosofia e Discussione Pubblica* 66 (2012): 299–316; Nancy Luxon, "Authority, Interpretation, and the Space of the Parrhesiastic Encounter," *materiali foucaultiani* 5–6 (2014): 71–90; Johanna Oksala, "What Is Political Philosophy?," *materiali foucaultiani* 5–6 (2014): 91–112; Henrik Paul Bang, *Foucault's Political Challenge: From Hegemony to Truth* (Basingstoke: Palgrave Macmillan, 2015), 1–86; Torben B. Dyrberg, "Foucault on *Parrhesia*: The Autonomy of Politics and Democracy," *Political Theory* 44(2) (2016): 265–88; Stephen Legg, "Subjects of Truth: Resisting Governmentality in Foucault's 1980s," *Environment and Planning D: Society and Space* 37(1) (2019): 27–45; Andrea Di Gesu, "The Cynic Scandal: Parrhesia, Community, and Democracy," *Theory, Culture & Society* 39(3) (2022): 169–86. Foucault's analyses of truth-telling are also addressed by Edward F. McGushin, *Foucault's Askēsis: An Introduction to the Philosophical Life* (Evanston, IL: Northwestern University Press, 2007), Laura Cremonesi, *Foucault e il mondo antico: Spunti per una critica dell'attualità* (Pisa: ETS, 2008), and Daniele Lorenzini, *Éthique et politique de soi: Foucault, Hadot, Cavell et les techniques de l'ordinaire* (Paris: Vrin, 2015) in the context of their respective reconstructions of his later works. Finally, an interesting engagement with (and *use* of) Foucault's analyses of truth-telling and problematizations of the relation between truth, power, and conduct can be found in Paul Rabinow's later works (see, e.g., Paul Rabinow, *The Accompaniment: Assembling the Contemporary* [Chicago: University of Chicago Press, 2011]; Paul Rabinow and Anthony Stavrianakis, *Designs on the Contemporary: Anthropological Tests* [Chicago: University of Chicago Press, 2014]); I am grateful to Colin Koopman for this suggestion.

41. On this point, see Flynn, "Foucault as Parrhesiast," 226–27.

42. In his careful reconstruction of the development of Foucault's work throughout the 1970s and 1980s, even Stuart Elden (*Foucault's Last Decade* [Cambridge: Polity Press, 2016]; *Foucault: The Birth of Power* [Cambridge: Polity Press, 2017]) chooses to focus on the emergence of *Discipline and Punish* and the vicissitudes linked to the history of sexuality project, thus implicitly relegating Foucault's history of truth to the status of a secondary project. By contrast, my claim is that Foucault's history of truth defines the principal and most general project he develops during those years. See, e.g., Michel Foucault, *The History of Sexuality*, vol. 2, *The Use of Pleasure*, translated by R. Hurley (New York: Vintage Books, 1985), 11: "I seem to have gained a better perspective on the way I worked—gropingly, and by means of different successive fragments—on this project [of a history of sexuality], whose goal is a history of truth."

43. And potentially also to his archaeological writings, or more precisely, the attention he devotes to the "extralinguistic" throughout the 1960s. However, a full account of the way in which Foucault's work pre-1970 could be connected with his project of a history of truth is outside the scope of this book, which focuses instead on the form such a project takes after it is explicitly formulated in 1970. For a discussion of the problem of truth in Foucault's archaeological writings, see Gary Gutting, *Michel Foucault's Archaeology of Scientific Reason* (Cambridge: Cambridge University Press, 1989), 261–88.

44. Foucault, *Lectures on the Will to Know*; Foucault, "Nietzsche, Genealogy, History."

45. Michel Foucault, *Psychiatric Power: Lectures at the Collège de France, 1973-74*, edited by J. Lagrange, translated by G. Burchell; series edited by A. I. Davidson (Basingstoke: Palgrave Macmillan, 2006), 235-39. On Foucault's shift, in the early 1970s, from the term "dynastics" to the term "genealogy" to describe his own approach, see Stuart Elden, "From Dynastics to Genealogy," *Abolition Democracy 13/13*, 2021, http://blogs.law.columbia.edu/abolition1313/stuart-elden-from-dynastics-to-genealogy/.

46. Michel Foucault, "What Is Enlightenment?" (1984), in Foucault, *Ethics*, 315-16.

47. As convincingly argued by Bernard E. Harcourt, *Critique and Praxis: A Radical Critical Philosophy of Illusions, Values, and Action* (New York: Columbia University Press, 2020).

48. Daniele Lorenzini and Martina Tazzioli, "Critique without Ontology: Genealogy, Collective Subjects, and the Deadlocks of Evidence," *Radical Philosophy* 207 (2020): 27-28.

49. On this point, see Tommie Shelby, "Ideology, Racism, and Critical Social Theory," *The Philosophical Forum* 34(2) (2003): 170-72; Linda M. G. Zerilli, "Fact-Checking and Truth-Telling in an Age of Alternative Facts," *Le Foucaldien* 6(1) (2020), http://doi.org/10.16995/lefou.68.

50. As suggested, perhaps too hastily, by Harcourt (*Critique and Praxis*, 184-90). For a convincing characterization of Foucault as a "critical empiricist" whose work bears witness to "an attention to detail and to fact, in the midst of commitments to inquiry, and to finding out under the guidance of attitudes of curiosity and fallibility," see Colin Koopman, "Two Uses of Michel Foucault in Political Theory: Concepts and Methods in Giorgio Agamben and Ian Hacking," *Constellations* 22(4) (2015): 572, 582.

51. Michel Foucault, *About the Beginning of the Hermeneutics of the Self: Lectures at Dartmouth College, 1980*, edited by H.-P. Fruchaud and D. Lorenzini (Chicago: University of Chicago Press, 2015), 34.

52. For a very popular, recent example, see Steven Pinker, *Enlightenment Now: The Case for Reason, Science, Humanism, and Progress* (New York: Viking, 2018).

53. Michel Foucault, *The History of Sexuality*, vol. 1, *An Introduction*, translated by R. Hurley (New York: Pantheon Books, 1978), 60; Amy Allen, "Power/Knowledge/Resistance: Foucault and Epistemic Injustice," in *The Routledge Handbook of Epistemic Injustice*, edited by I. J. Kidd, J. Medina, and G. Pohlhaus, Jr. (New York: Routledge, 2017), 187.

54. Frédéric Gros aptly remarks that Foucault's refusal to address the epistemological question of the (universal, suprahistorical) criteria defining truth, or to elaborate a theory of truth, does not entail indifference on his part for the question of truth, nor an *ante litteram* endorsement of a "post-truth" attitude. If Foucault's "political history of truth" does not rely on an epistemic definition or a theory of truth, it is because it "describes the incessant struggle, the eternal battle between truths that teach us to obey, to accept reality, and those 'counter-truths' that make us resist, that lead us to transform the world and ourselves" (Frédéric Gros, "Vérités et contre-vérités," *Revue Internationale de Philosophie* 292 [2020]: 14-15).

55. See John Langshaw Austin, "Performative Utterances" (1956), in Austin, *Philosophical Papers*, edited by J. O. Urmson and G. J. Warnock (Oxford: Oxford University Press, 1979), 251: "Besides the question that has been very much studied in the past as to what a certain utterance *means*, there is a further question distinct from this as to what is the *force*, as we may call it, of the utterance"; Oswald Ducrot, *Dire et ne pas dire: Principes de sémantique linguistique* (Paris: Hermann, 1991), 285-91.

56. John Langshaw Austin, *How to Do Things with Words*, edited by J. O. Urmson and M. Sbisà (Cambridge, MA: Harvard University Press, 1975), 14, 15. The other four conditions listed by Austin are the following: "(B.1) The procedure must be executed by all participants both correctly and (B.2) completely. (Γ.1) Where, as often, the procedure is designed for use by persons having certain thoughts or feelings, or for the inauguration of certain consequential conduct on the part of any participant, then a person participating in and so invoking the procedure must in fact have those thoughts or feelings, and the participants must intend so to conduct themselves, and further (Γ.2) must actually so conduct themselves subsequently" (15).

57. Pierre Bourdieu, "Price Formation and the Anticipation of Profits" (1980), in Bourdieu, *Language and Symbolic Power*, edited by J. B. Thompson, translated by G. Raymond and M. Adamson (Cambridge: Polity Press, 1991), 72 (trans. mod.).

58. Bourdieu, "Price Formation and the Anticipation of Profits," 67.

59. Bourdieu, "Price Formation and the Anticipation of Profits," 74–75.

60. See, e.g., Pierre Bourdieu, "Authorized Language: The Social Conditions for the Effectiveness of Ritual Discourse" (1975), in Bourdieu, *Language and Symbolic Power*, 107; Bourdieu, "Price Formation and the Anticipation of Profits," 76.

61. Judith Butler, *Excitable Speech: A Politics of the Performative* (New York: Routledge, 1997), 142.

62. Jacques Derrida, "Signature Event Context," in *Margins of Philosophy*, translated by A. Bass (Chicago: University of Chicago Press, 1982), 307–30.

63. Butler, *Excitable Speech*, 145.

64. Butler, *Excitable Speech*, 145.

65. Butler, *Excitable Speech*, 142, 147.

66. Butler, *Excitable Speech*, 147, 152, 155.

67. Michel Foucault, *The Archaeology of Knowledge*, translated by A. M. Sheridan Smith (New York: Routledge, 2002).

68. Jocelyn Benoist, "Des actes de langage à l'inventaire des énoncés," *Archives de Philosophie* 79(1) (2016): 74.

69. See, e.g., Michel de Certeau, *The Capture of Speech and Other Political Writings*, edited by L. Giard, translated by T. Conley (Minneapolis: University of Minnesota Press, 1997).

70. Ludwig Wittgenstein, *Philosophical Investigations*, edited by P. M. S. Hacker and J. Schulte, translated by G. E. M. Anscombe, P. M. S. Hacker, and J. Schulte (Oxford: Wiley-Blackwell, 2009), I, §83, p. 44ᵉ.

71. Stanley Cavell, *Philosophy the Day after Tomorrow* (Cambridge, MA: Harvard University Press, 2005), 159.

72. Raoul Moati, *Derrida/Searle: Deconstruction and Ordinary Language*, translated by T. Attanucci and M. Chun (New York: Columbia University Press, 2014), 20.

73. Stanley Cavell, *A Pitch of Philosophy: Autobiographical Exercises* (Cambridge, MA: Harvard University Press, 1994), 80.

74. See Michel Foucault, "What Is Critique?," in *The Politics of Truth*, edited by S. Lotringer, translated by L. Hochroth (Los Angeles: Semiotext(e), 2007), 46–47.

Chapter 1

1. The conceptual pair *assujettissement-subjectivation* originally derives from the dual meaning of the word "subject": "subject to someone else by control and de-

pendence, and tied to one's own identity by conscience or self-knowledge" (Michel Foucault, "The Subject and Power" [1982], in Foucault, *Power*, vol. 3 of *Essential Works of Foucault [1954-84]*, edited by J. D. Faubion, translated by R. Hurley et al.; series edited by P. Rabinow [New York: New Press, 2000], 331 [trans. mod.]). Even though Foucault claims that "both meanings suggest a form of power that subjugates and makes subject to" (331), in what follows, when I talk about "subjectivation," I do not refer to an ever-increasing centering on the subject and her identity (Charles Taylor, *The Ethics of Authenticity* [Cambridge, MA: Harvard University Press, 1991], 81), nor to a movement necessarily leading to a state of subjection (Judith Butler, *The Psychic Life of Power: Theories in Subjection* [Stanford, CA: Stanford University Press, 1997], 83, 90-91; Pierre Macherey, *Le sujet des normes* [Paris: Éditions Amsterdam, 2014], 51, 55), but to a process of subject-formation that, while always taking place within a given network of power relations, is potentially capable of breaking with it and giving rise to a "subject of critique" (Daniele Lorenzini, "Foucault, Regimes of Truth, and the Making of the Subject," in *Foucault and the Making of Subjects*, edited by L. Cremonesi et al. [London: Rowman & Littlefield, 2016], 63-75). On this topic, see also Arnold I. Davidson, "Dall'assoggettamento alla soggettivazione: Michel Foucault e la storia della sessualità," *aut aut* 331 (2006): 3-10.

2. In 1983, Foucault presents the notion of problematization as the cornerstone of his lifelong project of writing the "history of thought," that is, of analyzing "the way a field of experience and a set of practices—which were accepted without any problem, which were familiar and silent, or at least beyond discussion—become an issue and raise discussions, debates, and incite new reactions, and so induce a crisis in habits, in practices, and in institutions" (Michel Foucault, *Discourse and Truth*, edited by H.-P. Fruchaud and D. Lorenzini; English edition by N. Luxon [Chicago: University of Chicago Press, 2019], 115). In other words, "problematization" is the term Foucault uses to indicate "how and why certain things, conducts, phenomena, processes"—such as madness, crime, sexuality, or truth-telling—become "a problem" in a given time and place (224). I address the problematizing dimension of Foucault's genealogies in more detail in chapter 5.

3. Michel Foucault, *Psychiatric Power: Lectures at the Collège de France, 1973-74*, edited by J. Lagrange, translated by G. Burchell; series edited by A. I. Davidson (Basingstoke: Palgrave Macmillan, 2006), 238.

4. Michel Foucault, *Lectures on the Will to Know: Lectures at the Collège de France, 1970-71*, edited by D. Defert, translated by G. Burchell; series edited by A. I. Davidson (Basingstoke: Palgrave Macmillan, 2013), 32. The distinction between *savoir* and *connaissance* is crucial to Foucault's archaeological project (see Todd May, *Between Genealogy and Epistemology: Psychology, Politics, and Knowledge in the Thought of Michel Foucault* [University Park: Penn State University Press, 1993], 28) and, as we will see, to his project of a history of truth as well. Foucault characterizes such a distinction as follows: "By *connaissance* I mean the relation of the subject to the object and the formal rules that govern it. *Savoir* refers to the conditions that are necessary in a particular period for this or that type of object to be given to *connaissance* and for this or that enunciation to be formulated" (Michel Foucault, *The Archaeology of Knowledge*, translated by A. M. Sheridan Smith [New York: Routledge, 2002], 15).

5. Foucault, *Psychiatric Power*, 235.

6. Foucault, *Psychiatric Power*, 235.

7. Foucault, *Psychiatric Power*, 235-36.

8. Michel Foucault, *Abnormal: Lectures at the Collège de France, 1974–75*, edited by V. Marchetti and A. Salomoni, translated by G. Burchell; series edited by A. I. Davidson (London: Verso, 2003).

9. Foucault, *Psychiatric Power*, 236.

10. Foucault, *Psychiatric Power*, 236.

11. Foucault, *Psychiatric Power*, 236. On the notion of spirituality, which according to Foucault should be carefully distinguished from religion, for "spirituality is something that can be found in religion but also outside of religion; that can be found in Buddhism, a religion without theology, in monotheisms, but that can also be found in Greek civilization," see also Michel Foucault, "Political Spirituality as the Will for Alterity: An Interview with the *Nouvel Observateur*," edited and translated by S. Vaccarino Bremner, *Critical Inquiry* 47(1) (2020): 123.

12. Michel Foucault, *The Hermeneutics of the Subject: Lectures at the Collège de France, 1981–82*, edited by F. Gros, translated by G. Burchell; series edited by A. I. Davidson (Basingstoke: Palgrave Macmillan, 2005), 15 (trans. mod.). The radical transformation of the subject's "mode of being," or the fact of "no longer being the subject that one had been up to that point"—of being "displaced, transformed, disrupted, to the point of renouncing [one's] own individuality, [one's] own subject position"—is also crucial in the definitions of spirituality in Michel Foucault, "The Ethics of the Concern for Self as a Practice of Freedom" (1984), in Foucault, *Ethics: Subjectivity and Truth*, vol. 1 of *Essential Works of Foucault (1954–84)*, edited by P. Rabinow, translated by R. Hurley et al.; series edited by P. Rabinow (New York: New Press, 1997), 294; and Foucault "Political Spirituality as the Will for Alterity," 124.

13. Foucault, *The Hermeneutics of the Subject*, 17 (trans. mod.).

14. Foucault, *The Hermeneutics of the Subject*, 18 (trans. mod.).

15. Foucault, *Psychiatric Power*, 236 (trans. mod.), emphasis added.

16. Foucault, *Psychiatric Power*, 236.

17. Foucault, *Psychiatric Power*, 236–37.

18. Foucault, *Psychiatric Power*, 237. In addressing alchemical practice (but this also applies to other forms of truth-event), Foucault emphasizes the importance of the opportune moment or propitious occasion—the *kairos*—for grasping the truth (237). In the second volume of his *History of Sexuality*, he argues that the *kairos* is also "one of the most important objectives, and one of the most delicate, in the art of making use of the pleasures" (*The History of Sexuality*, vol. 2, *The Use of Pleasure*, translated by R. Hurley [New York: Vintage Books, 1985], 57).

19. See Michel Foucault, *The Courage of Truth: Lectures at the Collège de France, 1983–84*, edited by F. Gros, translated by G. Burchell; series edited by A. I. Davidson (Basingstoke: Palgrave Macmillan, 2011), 15–19.

20. Foucault, *Psychiatric Power*, 237.

21. Foucault, *Psychiatric Power*, 237. Arguably, the contrast ancient-recent admits of exceptions and should not be taken too literally: Aristotle, for instance, would no doubt be part of the truth-demonstration series, while Nietzsche clearly belongs to the truth-event series. See, e.g., Foucault, *Lectures on the Will to Know*, 1–30.

22. Foucault, *Psychiatric Power*, 237.

23. Foucault, "Truth and Juridical Forms" (1973), in Foucault, *Power*, 4.

24. Foucault, "Truth and Juridical Forms," 4.

25. Foucault, *Lectures on the Will to Know*, 32.

26. Foucault, *Lectures on the Will to Know*, 32.

27. Foucault, "Truth and Juridical Forms," 15.

28. Foucault, *Psychiatric Power*, 238 (trans. mod.).

29. Foucault, *Psychiatric Power*, 238.

30. Foucault, *Psychiatric Power*, 247.

31. Foucault, *Psychiatric Power*, 247.

32. See also Foucault, "Political Spirituality as the Will for Alterity," 129–30, emphasis added: "Ultimately, what is Western science, if not an experience in which a pure, fixed subject of rationality is *constituted*, capable of mastering a discourse that can be proven from start to finish, or a world that can be tested from start to finish? . . . Truth is nothing but an episode in the history of *spirituality*."

33. Michel Foucault, "À propos de la généalogie de l'éthique: Un aperçu du travail en cours" (1984), in Foucault, *Dits et écrits II, 1976–88*, edited by D. Defert and F. Ewald (Paris: Gallimard, 2001), 1449. See also Michel Foucault, "On the Genealogy of Ethics: An Overview of Work in Progress" (1983), in Foucault, *Ethics*, 278–79; Foucault, "Débat au Département de Français de l'Université de Californie à Berkeley," in *Qu'est-ce que la critique?* suivi de *La culture de soi*, edited by H.-P. Fruchaud and D. Lorenzini (Paris: Vrin, 2015), 175. Foucault's interpretation of Descartes is, however, far more complex than it first appears; on this point, see Daniele Lorenzini, "Philosophical Discourse and Ascetic Practice: On Foucault's Readings of Descartes' *Meditations*," *Theory, Culture & Society*, 2021, https://doi.org/10.1177%2F0263276420980510.

34. See already Foucault, *Lectures on the Will to Know*, 31–32.

35. This first appearance of the term "genealogy" to describe Foucault's own approach shows that, from the beginning, archaeology and genealogy constitute for him two *complementary* tasks rather than two *alternate* approaches (allegedly focused, respectively, on discursive practices and systems of power/knowledge). On this point, see also Michel Foucault, "What Is Enlightenment?" (1984), in Foucault, *Ethics*, 315–16; Foucault, *The History of Sexuality*, vol. 2, *The Use of Pleasure*, 11–12.

36. Foucault, *Psychiatric Power*, 238.

37. Foucault, *Psychiatric Power*, 238–39 (trans. mod.). For an argument that goes in the same direction (but relies on Canguilhem's work), see Étienne Balibar ("'Being in the True?' Science and Truth in the Philosophy of Georges Canguilhem" [1993], translated by A. Fan, *Décalages* 2[2] [2016], https://core.ac.uk/download/pdf/215496915.pdf), who claims that "*if science is not everything*, . . . it may nevertheless be said that virtually *nothing is external to it*, insofar as it can *exteriorize everything*, including its own activity" (15).

38. Michel Foucault, *Discipline and Punish: The Birth of the Prison*, translated by A. Sheridan (New York: Vintage Books, 1995), 23. On the concept of regime of truth in Foucault's work, see Philippe Chevallier, *Michel Foucault et le christianisme* (Lyon: ENS Éditions, 2011), 91–108; Chevallier, "Vers l'éthique: La notion de 'régime de vérité' dans le cours *Du gouvernement des vivants*," in *Michel Foucault: Éthique et vérité (1980–1984)*, edited by Daniele Lorenzini, Ariane Revel, and Arianna Sforzini (Paris: Vrin, 2013), 53–65; Daniele Lorenzini, "What Is a 'Regime of Truth'?," *Le Foucaldien* 1(1) (2015), http://doi.org/10.16995/lefou.2.

39. See Michel Foucault, *"Society Must Be Defended": Lectures at the Collège de France, 1975–76*, edited by M. Bertani and A. Fontana, translated by D. Macey; series edited by A. I. Davidson (New York: Picador, 2003), 164; Foucault, *The Birth of Biopolitics: Lectures at the Collège de France, 1978–79*, edited by M. Senellart, translated by G. Burchell; series edited by A. I. Davidson (Basingstoke: Palgrave Macmillan, 2008), 18.

40. Michel Foucault, "The Political Function of the Intellectual" (1976), translated by C. Gordon, *Radical Philosophy* 17 (1977): 13 (trans. mod.).

41. Foucault, "The Political Function of the Intellectual," 13.

42. Foucault, "The Political Function of the Intellectual," 13.

43. Friedrich Nietzsche, *Daybreak: Thoughts on the Prejudices of Morality*, edited by M. Clark and B. Leiter, translated by R. J. Hollingdale (Cambridge: Cambridge University Press, 1997), II, §102, p. 59.

44. See, e.g., Foucault, "Truth and Juridical Forms," 6–15. In *Beyond Good and Evil*, Nietzsche criticizes one of the fundamental "prejudices by which metaphysicians of all ages can be recognized," that is, the belief in the purity of origin: "Things of the highest value must have another, separate origin *of their own*—they cannot be derived from this ephemeral, seductive, deceptive, lowly world, from this mad chaos of confusion and desire. Look instead to the lap of being, the everlasting, the hidden God, the 'thing-in-itself'—*this* is where their ground must be, and nowhere else!" (*Beyond Good and Evil*, edited by R.-P. Horstmann and J. Norman, translated by J. Norman [Cambridge: Cambridge University Press, 2002], §2, p. 6). For a convincing account of Nietzsche's subversive genealogy of morality, see Jesse J. Prinz, *The Emotional Construction of Morals* (Oxford: Oxford University Press, 2007), 215–43. For a helpful characterization of it in terms of "pragmatic genealogy," see Bernard Reginster, "What Is Nietzsche's Genealogical Critique of Morality?," *Inquiry: An Interdisciplinary Journal of Philosophy*, 2020, https://doi.org/10.1080/0020174X.2020.1762727.

45. Foucault, "The Political Function of the Intellectual," 14 (trans. mod.).

46. Foucault, "The Political Function of the Intellectual," 14. For an interesting discussion of Foucault's politics of truth that puts it in conversation with Gilles Deleuze's and Alain Badiou's respective accounts of truth, resistance, and militancy, see Iain MacKenzie, *Resistance and the Politics of Truth: Foucault, Deleuze, Badiou* (Bielefeld: Transcript, 2018).

47. Michel Foucault, *On the Government of the Living: Lectures at the Collège de France, 1979–80*, edited by M. Senellart, translated by G. Burchell; series edited by A. I. Davidson (Basingstoke: Palgrave Macmillan, 2014), 7. Foucault coins the word "alethurgy" by drawing from the Greek adjective *alethourges*, which the grammarian Heraclitus used (albeit only once) to refer to the truthful person—someone who speaks the truth, or better, who "realizes" the truth. It is noteworthy that, in the lecture on April 22, 1981, of his Louvain series, *Wrong-Doing, Truth-Telling*, when he introduces the notion of "alethurgy" in the context of his analysis of the chariot race described in book 23 of Homer's *Iliad*, Foucault no longer refers to Heraclitus, but points to the notion of "liturgy," no doubt in order to emphasize the ritual dimension of the manifestation of truth at issue there. Indeed, according to him, that race aimed "to manifest a truth that [was] already recognized"; it was therefore nothing else than a "liturgy of truth"—an "alethurgy," precisely, that is, "a ritual procedure for bringing forth *alethes*: that which is true" (*Wrong-Doing, Truth-Telling: The Function of Avowal in Justice*, edited by F. Brion and B. E. Harcourt, translated by S. W. Sawyer [Chicago: University of Chicago Press, 2014], 39).

48. On this point, see Daniele Lorenzini, "Anarcheology and the Emergence of the Alethurgic Subject in Foucault's *On the Government of the Living*," *Foucault Studies* ("Foucault Lectures" series) 3(1) (2020): 53–70.

49. See Michel Foucault, "What Is Critique?," in *The Politics of Truth*, edited by S. Lotringer, translated by L. Hochroth (Los Angeles: Semiotext(e), 2007), 41–81;

Foucault, *Security, Territory, Population: Lectures at the Collège de France, 1977–78*, edited by M. Senellart, translated by G. Burchell; series edited by A. I. Davidson (Basingstoke: Palgrave Macmillan, 2009).

50. The project of a genealogy of the modern subject, which underpins Foucault's 1980 lecture course at the Collège de France, *On the Government of the Living*, as well as his series of lectures at the Université Catholique de Louvain, *Wrong-Doing, Truth-Telling*, is formulated with unparalleled clarity in his lectures at Berkeley and Dartmouth College in the fall of 1980. See Michel Foucault, *About the Beginning of the Hermeneutics of the Self: Lectures at Dartmouth College, 1980*, edited by H.-P. Fruchaud and D. Lorenzini (Chicago: University of Chicago Press, 2015), 21.

51. Foucault, "Truth and Juridical Forms," 13; Foucault, *The History of Sexuality*, vol. 1, *An Introduction*, translated by R. Hurley (New York: Pantheon Books, 1978), 60; Foucault, *About the Beginning of the Hermeneutics of the Self*, 76. On the notion of a "politics of ourselves," see Daniele Lorenzini, "Genealogia della verità e politica di noi stessi," in *Foucault e le genealogie del dir-vero*, edited by L. Cremonesi et al. (Naples: Cronopio, 2014), 145–62.

52. Foucault, *On the Government of the Living*, 4–5. Foucault emphasizes again, albeit in a slightly different way, the necessity to remove the "utilitarian and economic postulate" in his 1981 lecture course at the Collège de France, *Subjectivity and Truth*: "When one considers the considerable deployment of the game of true and false and how little actual, effective, and useful truth humanity has been able to get from this game, when one compares what costs, what economic, political, social, human costs it needed, what sacrifices and wars even in the strict sense of the term these games of veridiction, of the true and false, called for, and when one sees what the economic or political benefit has been of the truth found through this game of true and false, the difference is such that one can say that on the scale of human history the game of veridiction has cost much more than it has yielded" (*Subjectivity and Truth: Lectures at the Collège de France, 1980–81*, edited by F. Gros, translated by G. Burchell; series edited by A. I. Davidson [Basingstoke: Palgrave Macmillan, 2017], 238).

53. Foucault, *On the Government of the Living*, 5.

54. Foucault, *On the Government of the Living*, 6.

55. Foucault, *On the Government of the Living*, 6. Other rituals of manifestation of the truth that sustain the exercise of power include, e.g., religious confession, medical, psychiatric, and juridical examination, or demographic and statistical assessments of different aspects of a population.

56. Foucault, *On the Government of the Living*, 7, 75.

57. Foucault, *On the Government of the Living*, 7. See also Foucault, *Subjectivity and Truth*, 238 (trans. mod.): "After all, science is only one of the possible games of true and false. You know indeed that without doubt the game of truth and falsity peculiar to science cannot be defined in its unity, and that it is not possible to speak of 'science' in the singular, but that one should speak of different so-called scientific games of true and false in terms of borders that are always both difficult to establish and changing."

58. Foucault, *On the Government of the Living*, 12.

59. The topic of the government of human beings and the notion of an "art of governing" had already been introduced by Foucault in 1975, in the context of an analysis of disciplinary power and its normalizing function (Foucault, *Abnormal*, 48–49).

60. Foucault, *About the Beginning of the Hermeneutics of the Self*, 26.

61. See Foucault, *About the Beginning of the Hermeneutics of the Self*, 25–26: "The

contact point, where the way individuals are driven by others is tied to the way they conduct themselves, is what we can call, I think, government. Governing people, in the broad meaning of the word, is not a way to force people to do what the governor wants; it is always a versatile equilibrium, with complementarity and conflicts between techniques which assure coercion and processes through which the self is constructed or modified by himself."

62. See Foucault's definition of critique as "the art of not being governed quite so much" in Foucault, "What Is Critique?," 45. On this topic, see also Daniele Lorenzini, "From Counter-Conduct to Critical Attitude: Michel Foucault and the Art of Not Being Governed Quite So Much," *Foucault Studies* 21 (2016): 7-21.

63. Foucault, *On the Government of the Living*, 11.

64. Foucault, *On the Government of the Living*, 17.

65. Foucault, *On the Government of the Living*, 7.

66. Foucault, *On the Government of the Living*, 17.

67. Foucault, *On the Government of the Living*, 23.

68. Foucault, *On the Government of the Living*, 37.

69. Foucault, *On the Government of the Living*, 48. On this point, see Daniele Lorenzini, "Alèthurgie oculaire et littérature de témoignage: De Sophocle à Soljenitsyne," *Revue Internationale de Philosophie* 292 (2020): 17-23.

70. Foucault, *On the Government of the Living*, 41-42, 48.

71. Foucault, *On the Government of the Living*, 73.

72. Foucault, *On the Government of the Living*, 49 (trans. mod.).

73. Foucault, *On the Government of the Living*, 52, 80.

74. Foucault, *On the Government of the Living*, 75.

75. Foucault, *On the Government of the Living*, 75.

76. On this point, see Bernard E. Harcourt, "Introducing *On the Government of the Living*," *Foucault 13/13*, 2016, http://blogs.law.columbia.edu/foucault1313/2016/02/07/introducing-on-the-government-of-the-living/.

77. See Foucault, *Security, Territory, Population*, 193.

78. Foucault, *On the Government of the Living*, 81.

79. Foucault, *The History of Sexuality*, vol. 1, *An Introduction*, 59.

80. Foucault, *The History of Sexuality*, vol. 1, *An Introduction*, 60.

81. Foucault, *The History of Sexuality*, vol. 1, *An Introduction*, 60.

82. In his 1974-75 lecture course, *Abnormal*, Foucault had already traced a schematic genealogy of the rituals of confession from early Christianity to the nineteenth century, including in the medical and psychiatric fields; see Foucault, *Abnormal*, 171-258.

83. Foucault, *The History of Sexuality*, vol. 1, *An Introduction*, 63 (trans. mod.).

84. Foucault, *The History of Sexuality*, vol. 1, *An Introduction*, 64 (trans. mod.).

85. Foucault, *The History of Sexuality*, vol. 1, *An Introduction*, 64-65. On the constitution of sexology and scientific lexicography as "confessional sciences," see Stephen Turton, "The Confessional Sciences: Scientific Lexicography and Sexology in the *Oxford English Dictionary*," *Language & History*, 2020, https://doi.org/10.1080/17597536.2020.1755204.

86. Foucault, *The Hermeneutics of the Subject*, 16.

87. Foucault, *On the Government of the Living*, 311. These same three forms of self-alethurgy (preparation for baptism, canonical penance, and spiritual direction) constitute the subject matter of the first chapter of the fourth volume of Foucault's *History*

of Sexuality, published posthumously as *Confessions of the Flesh*; see Michel Foucault, *The History of Sexuality*, vol. 4, *Confessions of the Flesh*, edited by F. Gros, translated by R. Hurley (New York: Pantheon Books, 2021).

88. Foucault, *On the Government of the Living*, 311.

89. Foucault, *On the Government of the Living*, 82, emphasis added.

90. Foucault, *On the Government of the Living*, 82.

91. Foucault, *On the Government of the Living*, 81.

92. Foucault, *On the Government of the Living*, 82.

Chapter 2

1. It is "paradoxical" too, since it is actually constituted by two different regimes: the regime of faith and the regime of confession (Michel Foucault, *On the Government of the Living: Lectures at the Collège de France, 1979–80*, edited by M. Senellart, translated by G. Burchell; series edited by A. I. Davidson [Basingstoke: Palgrave Macmillan, 2014], 82–84).

2. Foucault, *On the Government of the Living*, 93.

3. Foucault, *On the Government of the Living*, 11.

4. Miranda Fricker, "Feminism in Epistemology: Pluralism without Postmodernism," in *The Cambridge Companion to Feminism in Philosophy*, edited by M. Fricker and J. Hornsby (Cambridge: Cambridge University Press, 2000), 154. For a rebuttal to these claims, see Daniele Lorenzini, "Reason versus Power: Genealogy, Critique, and Epistemic Injustice," *The Monist* 105(4) (2022): 541–57.

5. Foucault, *On the Government of the Living*, 93–94.

6. Foucault, *On the Government of the Living*, 95.

7. Foucault, *On the Government of the Living*, 95.

8. Foucault, *On the Government of the Living*, 99–100.

9. Foucault, *On the Government of the Living*, 95.

10. Foucault, *On the Government of the Living*, 95.

11. Jacques Bouveresse, *Nietzsche contre Foucault: Sur la vérité, la connaissance et le pouvoir* (Marseille: Agone, 2016), 6, 9.

12. See Spinoza's LXXVI letter to Albert Burgh (Baruch Spinoza, *The Correspondence of Spinoza* [New York: Lincoln MacVeagh/The Dial Press, 1928], 352): "The truth reveals itself and the false [*est enim verum index sui, et falsi*]."

13. Foucault, *On the Government of the Living*, 96. See Michel Foucault, "The Ethics of the Concern for Self as a Practice of Freedom" (1984), in Foucault, *Ethics: Subjectivity and Truth*, vol. 1 of *Essential Works of Foucault (1954–84)*, edited by P. Rabinow, translated by R. Hurley et al.; series edited by P. Rabinow (New York: New Press, 1997), 297: "When I say 'game [of truth],' I mean a set of rules by which truth is produced." See also "Foucault" (1984), in Foucault, *Aesthetics, Method, and Epistemology*, vol. 2 of *Essential Works of Foucault (1954–84)*, edited by J. D. Faubion, translated by R. Hurley et al.; series edited by P. Rabinow (New York: New Press, 1998), 460 (trans. mod.): "['Games of truth' indicate] not the discovery of true things, but the rules according to which what a subject can say about certain things pertains to the question of true and false."

14. Foucault, *On the Government of the Living*, 96 (trans. mod.).

15. Foucault, *On the Government of the Living*, 96–97.

16. Foucault, *On the Government of the Living*, 97.

17. Foucault, *On the Government of the Living*, 97.

18. Foucault, *On the Government of the Living*, 97.

19. Foucault, *On the Government of the Living*, 95–96. Here, as well as in countless other passages throughout his work, Foucault is thinking of the first rule of Descartes's method, the *règle de l'évidence*, which consists in never accepting "anything as true that I did not *incontrovertibly* [*évidemment*] know to be so" (René Descartes, *A Discourse on the Method*, translated by I. Maclean [Oxford: Oxford University Press, 2006], 17). The French term *évidence* clearly cannot be translated into English as "evidence," but I find Graham Burchell's choice to translate it as "self-evidence" to be equally unsatisfactory. I will translate it as "obviousness" instead.

20. Thus also making us realize that "there are many other ways of binding the individual to the manifestation of truth, and of binding her to the manifestation of truth by other acts, with other forms of bond, according to other obligations and with other effects than those defined in science, for example, by the self-indexation of truth" (Foucault, *On the Government of the Living*, 99 [trans. mod.]). Think, for instance, of religious confession or juridical avowal.

21. Philippe Chevallier, *Michel Foucault et le christianisme* (Lyon: ENS Éditions, 2011), 93–94.

22. Chevallier, *Michel Foucault et le christianisme*, 94.

23. Michel Foucault, "The Order of Discourse" (1971), in *Archives of Infamy: Foucault on State Power in the Lives of Ordinary Citizens*, edited by N. Luxon, translated by T. Scott-Railton (Minneapolis: University of Minnesota Press, 2019), 145 (trans. mod.); see also 153–54: "Within its limits, each discipline recognizes true and false propositions; . . . but . . . a proposition must fulfill complex and weighty requirements to be able to belong to the ensemble of a discipline; before being called true or false, it must be, as Monsieur Canguilhem would say, 'in the truth' [*'dans le vrai'*]."

24. See, e.g., Michel Foucault, *Lectures on the Will to Know: Lectures at the Collège de France, 1970–71*, edited by D. Defert, translated by G. Burchell; series edited by A. I. Davidson (Basingstoke: Palgrave Macmillan, 2013), 2: "*The game* I would like to play . . . will involve seeing whether the will to truth exercises a role of exclusion in relation to discourse—to some extent, and I mean only to some extent—analogous to the possible role played by the contrast between madness and reason, or by the system of prohibitions. In other words, it will involve seeing whether the will to truth is not as profoundly historical as any other system of exclusion; whether it is not as arbitrary in its roots as they are; whether it is not as modifiable as they are in the course of history; whether like them it is not dependent upon and constantly reactivated by a whole institutional network; and whether it does not form a system of constraint which is exercised not only on other discourses, but on a whole series of other practices. In short, it is a matter of seeing what real struggles and relations of domination are involved in the will to truth."

25. Frantz Fanon, *Decolonizing Madness: The Psychiatric Writings of Frantz Fanon*, edited by N. Gibson, translated by L. Damon (Basingstoke: Palgrave Macmillan, 2014), 87.

26. On this point, see Daniele Lorenzini and Martina Tazzioli, "Confessional Subjects and Conducts of Non-Truth: Foucault, Fanon, and the Making of the Subject," *Theory, Culture & Society* 35(1) (2018): 71–90.

27. Fanon, *Decolonizing Madness*, 88.

28. Fanon, *Decolonizing Madness*, 87.

29. This distinction also underpins Foucault's definition of science as a "family of games of truth all of which obey the same regime, although they do not obey the same grammar, and this very specific, very particular regime of truth is a regime in which the power of the truth is organized in a way such that constraint is assured by truth itself" (Foucault, *On the Government of the Living*, 99 [trans. mod.]). Note that, in his *Philosophical Investigations*, Wittgenstein speaks of "family resemblances" to indicate the relation that different language games have with each other; indeed, according to him, "language" is actually a family of language games with different "affinities" between them. See Ludwig Wittgenstein, *Philosophical Investigations*, edited by P. M. S. Hacker and J. Schulte, translated by G. E. M. Anscombe, P. M. S. Hacker, and J. Schulte (Oxford: Wiley-Blackwell, 2009), I, §§65–67, pp. 35ᵉ–36ᵉ, and §108, p. 51ᵉ.

30. See Foucault, "The Ethics of the Concern for Self," 296, emphasis added: "When I talk about power relations and games of truth, I am absolutely not saying that games of truth are just concealed power relations—that would be a horrible exaggeration. My problem, as I have already said, is to understand how truth games are set up and how they are *connected with* power relations."

31. Contra Chevallier, who claims that, in 1980, Foucault's position consists in arguing that "the formal rules of scientific statements, which assure the systematicity of their propositions," are "outside of any 'regime'" (Chevallier, *Michel Foucault et le christianisme*, 94–95).

32. American Psychiatric Association, *Diagnostic and Statistical Manual of Mental Disorders: Fifth Edition (DSM-5)* (Washington, DC: American Psychiatric Publishing, 2013), 451.

33. See, e.g., Kevan Wylie et al., "Good Practice Guidelines for the Assessment and Treatment of Adults with Gender Dysphoria," *Sexual and Relationship Therapy* 29(2) (2014): 154–214.

34. On this point, see Judith Butler, *Giving an Account of Oneself* (New York: Fordham University Press, 2005), 22–23.

35. Foucault, *On the Government of the Living*, 98. On Descartes's *Meditations* and the "violent" exclusion of madness in the path of the Cartesian doubt, see Michel Foucault, *History of Madness*, translated by J. Murphy and J. Khalfa (New York: Routledge, 2006), 44–47. See also Foucault, "My Body, This Paper, This Fire" (1972), in Foucault, *History of Madness*, 550–74; Foucault, "Reply to Derrida" (1972), in Foucault, *History of Madness*, 575–90.

36. Foucault, *On the Government of the Living*, 98.

37. Foucault, *On the Government of the Living*, 98.

38. Foucault, *On the Government of the Living*, 97 (trans. mod.).

39. Foucault, *On the Government of the Living*, 97.

40. Foucault, *On the Government of the Living*, 97–98 (trans. mod.).

41. Foucault, *On the Government of the Living*, 98.

42. Foucault famously defines "ethics" as the domain pertaining to the "forms of moral subjectivation," that is, the ways in which "one ought to form oneself as an ethical subject acting in reference to the prescriptive elements that make up [a given] code" (*The History of Sexuality*, vol. 2, *The Use of Pleasure*, translated by R. Hurley [New York: Vintage Books, 1985], 26, 29). Analogously, within a given regime of truth, the subject forms herself in response to the prescriptive elements that make up such regime—namely, by accepting or rejecting the "you have to" of the truth and acting accordingly.

43. Foucault, *On the Government of the Living*, 76.

44. Foucault, *On the Government of the Living*, 76-77 (trans. mod.).

45. Foucault, *On the Government of the Living*, 77 (trans. mod.).

46. On Foucault's recurrent critique of the notion of ideology throughout the 1970s and 1980s, see Orazio Irrera, "Foucault e la questione dell'ideologia," *materiali foucaultiani* 7-8 (2015): 149-72; Irrera, "Foucault and the Refusal of Ideology," in *Foucault and the Making of Subjects*, edited by L. Cremonesi et al. (London: Rowman & Littlefield, 2016), 111-27; Orazio Irrera and Pierre Macherey, "Michel Foucault et les critiques de l'idéologie," *Methodos: Savoirs et textes* 16 (2016), https://doi.org/10 .4000/methodos.4667. Foucault develops a critique of the traditional understanding of ideology as false consciousness, or as a discourse opposed to science, already in his 1969 lecture course at the University of Vincennes (*La sexualité: Cours donné à l'université de Clermont-Ferrand [1964]* suivi de *Le discours de la sexualité: Cours donné à l'université de Vincennes [1969]*, edited by C.-O. Doron [Paris: EHESS-Gallimard-Seuil, 2018], 129-33).

47. Foucault, *On the Government of the Living*, 75.

48. Foucault, *On the Government of the Living*, 100.

49. Foucault, *On the Government of the Living*, 100 (trans. mod.).

50. Foucault, *On the Government of the Living*, 101 (trans. mod.).

51. Michel Foucault, "What Is Critique?," in *The Politics of Truth*, edited by S. Lotringer, translated by L. Hochroth (Los Angeles: Semiotext(e), 2007), 41-81.

52. Foucault, *On the Government of the Living*, 77-78.

53. Foucault, *On the Government of the Living*, 77-78.

54. Foucault, "What Is Critique?," 45.

55. Foucault, *On the Government of the Living*, 78-79 (trans. mod.). See Paul Feyerabend, *Against Method: Outline of an Anarchist Theory of Knowledge* (London: New Left Books, 1975).

56. Foucault, *On the Government of the Living*, 100.

57. Foucault, *On the Government of the Living*, 101, emphasis added.

58. See Jeremy Carrette ("'Spiritual Gymnastics': Reflections on Michel Foucault's *On the Government of the Living* 1980 Collège de France Lectures," *Foucault Studies* 20 [2015]: 281), who argues that, in *On the Government of the Living*, "Foucault consciously moves back to the methods of archaeology, to a discursive mode rather than continuing the genealogical—body and pastoral power—question in relation to Christianity." That this kind of investigation is genealogical is rightly emphasized, e.g., by Jean-Michel Landry, "Confession, Obedience, and Subjectivity: Michel Foucault's Unpublished Lectures *On the Government of the Living*," *Telos* 146 (2009): 111-23. For some interesting remarks on the kind of genealogy that Foucault practices in *On the Government of the Living*, see Colin Gordon, "The Christian Art of Being Governed," *Foucault Studies* 20 (2015): 256-57.

59. I am grateful to Verena Erlenbusch-Anderson for pressing me on this point.

60. Foucault, *On the Government of the Living*, 77.

61. Foucault, *On the Government of the Living*, 77.

62. Michel Foucault, "Questions of Method [Round Table of 20 May 1978]" (1980), in Foucault, *Power*, vol. 3 of *Essential Works of Foucault (1954-84)*, edited by J. D. Faubion, translated by R. Hurley et al.; series edited by P. Rabinow (New York: New Press, 2000), 230, 233 (trans. mod.).

63. Foucault, *On the Government of the Living*, 99 (trans. mod.). On the many ways in which Foucault and Wittgenstein can be fruitfully put in conversation with each other, see Frédéric Gros and Arnold I. Davidson, *Foucault, Wittgenstein: De possibles rencontres* (Paris: Kimé, 2011); Pascale Gillot and Daniele Lorenzini, *Foucault/Wittgenstein: Subjectivité, politique, éthique* (Paris: CNRS Éditions, 2016).

64. Wittgenstein, *Philosophical Investigations*, I, §116, p. 53ᵉ; Wittgenstein, *Tractatus Logico-Philosophicus*, translated by D. F. Pears and B. F. McGuinness (New York: Routledge, 2001), prop. 5.6, p. 68. Foucault explicitly acknowledges his debt to this Wittgensteinian insight: "People have begun to realize—one thinks of logicians above all, students of Bertrand Russell and Ludwig Wittgenstein—that language can be analyzed in its formal properties only if one takes its concrete functioning into account. . . . In this context, what I am doing is situated in the general anonymity of all the investigations currently revolving around language—that is, not only the language that enables us to say things, but the discourses that have been said" ("On the Ways of Writing History" [1967], in Foucault, *Aesthetics, Method, and Epistemology*, 290 [trans. mod.]). See also Michel Foucault, "The Analytic Philosophy of Politics" (1978), translated by G. Mascaretti, *Foucault Studies* 24 (2018): 192–93.

65. Pierre Hadot, *Wittgenstein et les limites du langage* (Paris: Vrin, 2004), 33.

66. Ludwig Wittgenstein, *On Certainty*, edited by G. E. M. Anscombe and G. H. von Wright, translated by D. Paul and G. E. M. Anscombe (Oxford: Basil Blackwell, 1969), §94, p. 15ᵉ. On this point, see Sandra Laugier, *Wittgenstein: Les sens de l'usage* (Paris: Vrin, 2009).

67. Wittgenstein, *Philosophical Investigations*, I, §654, p. 175ᵉ.

68. Hadot, *Wittgenstein et les limites du langage*, 79.

69. Richard Rorty makes a similar point in advancing a Wittgensteinian distinction between "sentences" and "vocabularies": he claims that "to say that truth is not out there is simply to say that where there are no sentences there is no truth, that sentences are elements of human languages, and that human languages are human creations" (*Contingency, Irony, and Solidarity* [Cambridge: Cambridge University Press, 1989], 5). I am grateful to Colin Koopman for this suggestion.

70. Wittgenstein, *Philosophical Investigations*, I, §23, p. 15ᵉ.

71. Hadot, *Wittgenstein et les limites du langage*, 73. Importantly, these rules do not need to be explicitly formulated, as one can learn a language game "purely practically, without learning any explicit rules" (Wittgenstein, *On Certainty*, §95, p. 15ᵉ). The same can be said for the rules that Foucault refers to in his definition of games of truth (see, e.g., Foucault, "Foucault," 460). On this point, see Tuomo Tiisala, "Overcoming 'the Present Limits of the Necessary': Foucault's Conception of a Critique," *Southern Journal of Philosophy* 55 (2017): 21.

72. Wittgenstein, *Philosophical Investigations*, I, §23, pp. 14ᵉ–15ᵉ.

73. Think, for instance, of the "primitive language" described by Wittgenstein at the beginning of his *Philosophical Investigations* (I, §2, p. 3ᵉ), or the language games that we use to talk about art, which are indexed to practical aims and aesthetics values, respectively.

74. Foucault, *On the Government of the Living*, 7.

75. Michel Foucault, "Le discours ne doit pas être pris comme . . ." (1976), in Foucault, *Dits et écrits II, 1976–88*, edited by D. Defert and F. Ewald (Paris: Gallimard, 2001), 123–24; Foucault, "La vérité et les formes juridiques" (1973), in Foucault, *Dits et écrits I, 1954–75*, edited by D. Defert and F. Ewald (Paris: Gallimard, 2001), 1499.

76. Foucault, "La vérité et les formes juridiques," 1499. This criticism is certainly unfair, at least to Austin, who focuses precisely on *"the statement's anchoring in reality itself"* by analyzing the ways in which human beings ordinarily speak (Jocelyn Benoist, "Des actes de langage à l'inventaire des énoncés," *Archives de Philosophie* 79[1] [2016]: 63–64). As I argue below, however, when he refers to "a more real historical context," Foucault is no doubt thinking more specifically of power relations and processes of subject-constitution.

77. Foucault, "The Analytic Philosophy of Politics," 192–93. On Foucault's project of an "analytic philosophy of politics," see Daniele Lorenzini, *Éthique et politique de soi: Foucault, Hadot, Cavell et les techniques de l'ordinaire* (Paris: Vrin, 2015), 19–88.

78. Foucault, "The Analytic Philosophy of Politics," 192–93. On the analogy between Foucault's concept of game of power and Wittgenstein's concept of language game, see Arnold I. Davidson, "Structures and Strategies of Discourse: Remarks toward a History of Foucault's Philosophy of Language," in *Foucault and His Interlocutors*, edited by Arnold I. Davidson (Chicago: University of Chicago Press, 1997), 4.

79. Foucault, "The Analytic Philosophy of Politics," 192 (trans. mod.).

80. Wittgenstein, *Philosophical Investigations*, I, §126, p. 55^e, and §129, p. 56^e.

81. Wittgenstein, *Philosophical Investigations*, I, §124, p. 55^e.

82. Michel Foucault, *The History of Sexuality*, vol. 1, *An Introduction*, translated by R. Hurley (New York: Pantheon Books, 1978), 86.

83. Foucault, "The Analytic Philosophy of Politics," 192.

84. This is the path followed by Bernard Harcourt (*Critique and Praxis: A Radical Critical Philosophy of Illusions, Values, and Action* [New York: Columbia University Press, 2020]), who elaborates a critical theory and praxis that rely on the values of compassion, equality, solidarity, autonomy, and social justice, while doing away with the reference to truth.

85. Foucault, "The Analytic Philosophy of Politics," 192–94. On the concept of counter-conduct, see Daniele Lorenzini, "From Counter-Conduct to Critical Attitude: Michel Foucault and the Art of Not Being Governed Quite So Much," *Foucault Studies* 21 (2016): 7–21.

86. In Alain Badiou et al., "Philosophie et vérité" (1965), in Foucault, *Dits et écrits I, 1954–75*, 476–92 (transcript of the TV broadcast), Canguilhem argues that "philosophy is not a kind of speculation whose value can be measured in terms of truth and falsity"; however, "the fact that philosophy cannot be said to be true does not entail that it is a purely verbal or gratuitous game": "The value of philosophy is something other than the value of truth," which Canguilhem considers suitable only for scientific knowledge. See also Georges Canguilhem, "De la science et de la contre-science," in *Hommage à Jean Hyppolite*, edited by S. Bachelard et al. (Paris: PUF, 1971), 176–78. On this point, see Daniele Lorenzini, "Para acabar con la verdad-demostración: Bachelard, Canguilhem, Foucault y la historia de los 'regímenes de verdad,'" *Laguna: Revista de Filosofía* 26 (2010): 23–26.

87. Michel Foucault, *Subjectivity and Truth: Lectures at the Collège de France, 1980–81*, edited by F. Gros, translated by G. Burchell; series edited by A. I. Davidson (Basingstoke: Palgrave Macmillan, 2017), 10–11.

88. Foucault, *Subjectivity and Truth*, 10 (trans. mod.).

89. Foucault, *Subjectivity and Truth*, 10–11.

90. Foucault, *Subjectivity and Truth*, 11 (trans. mod.).

91. Foucault, *Subjectivity and Truth*, 10–11 (trans. mod.).

92. Foucault, *Subjectivity and Truth*, 11.

93. Foucault, *Subjectivity and Truth*, 12 (trans. mod.), emphasis added.

94. Foucault, *Subjectivity and Truth*, 12–13 (trans. mod.).

95. Foucault, *Subjectivity and Truth*, 13. See also Foucault, "Foucault," 459–61.

96. Michel Foucault, *The Hermeneutics of the Subject: Lectures at the Collège de France, 1981–82*, edited by F. Gros, translated by G. Burchell; series edited by A. I. Davidson (Basingstoke: Palgrave Macmillan, 2005), 15–19.

97. Michel Foucault, *The Government of Self and Others: Lectures at the Collège de France, 1982–83*, edited by F. Gros, translated by G. Burchell; series edited by A. I. Davidson (Basingstoke: Palgrave Macmillan, 2010), 4–5.

98. Foucault, *The Government of Self and Others*, 42 (trans. mod.).

99. Foucault, *The Government of Self and Others*, 45. See also Michel Foucault, *The Courage of Truth: Lectures at the Collège de France, 1983–84*, edited by F. Gros, translated by G. Burchell; series edited by A. I. Davidson (Basingstoke: Palgrave Macmillan, 2011), 8: "It seems to me that by examining the notion of *parrhesia* we can see how the analysis of modes of veridiction, the study of techniques of governmentality, and the identification of forms of practice of the self interweave. Connecting together modes of veridiction, techniques of governmentality, and practices of the self is basically what I have always been trying to do."

100. Foucault, *The Courage of Truth*, 2–3 (trans. mod.).

101. Foucault, *The Courage of Truth*, 3.

102. Foucault, *On the Government of the Living*, 100.

103. For a detailed reconstruction, see Daniele Lorenzini, "'El cinismo hace de la vida una *alethurgie*': Apuntes para una relectura del recorrido filosófico del último Michel Foucault," *Laguna: Revista de Filosofía* 23 (2008): 63–90.

104. Foucault, *The Hermeneutics of the Subject*, 14–15.

105. Foucault, *The Hermeneutics of the Subject*, 16.

106. See, e.g., Foucault, *On the Government of the Living*, 193–313; Foucault, *About the Beginning of the Hermeneutics of the Self: Lectures at Dartmouth College, 1980*, edited by H.-P. Fruchaud and D. Lorenzini (Chicago: University of Chicago Press, 2015), 56–76.

107. For an analysis that adopts this perspective and focuses on the emergence and transformation of the concept of desire, from ancient Greco-Roman philosophy to early Christian texts and ultimately to contemporary neoliberal governmentality, see Daniele Lorenzini, "The Emergence of Desire: Notes toward a Political History of the Will," *Critical Inquiry* 45(2) (2019): 448–70.

108. Michel Foucault, *Discourse and Truth*, edited by H.-P. Fruchaud and D. Lorenzini; English edition by N. Luxon (Chicago: University of Chicago Press, 2019), 42.

Chapter 3

1. Stanley Cavell, *Philosophy the Day after Tomorrow* (Cambridge, MA: Harvard University Press, 2005), 17.

2. Cavell, *Philosophy the Day after Tomorrow*, 186–87.

3. John Langshaw Austin, *How to Do Things with Words*, edited by J. O. Urmson and M. Sbisà (Cambridge, MA: Harvard University Press, 1975), 103.

4. See, e.g., John R. Searle, "Austin on Locutionary and Illocutionary Acts," *Philosophical Review* 77(4) (1968): 405–24; Lynd W. Forguson, "Locutionary and Illo-

cutionary Acts," in *Essays on J. L. Austin*, edited by I. Berlin et al. (Oxford: Oxford University Press, 1973), 160–86.

5. Cavell, *Philosophy the Day after Tomorrow*, 7–27, 155–91. See, e.g., Layla Raïd, "Énoncés passionnés et performatifs selon Stanley Cavell," *Revue Internationale de Philosophie* 256 (2011): 151–65; Daniele Lorenzini, "Performative, Passionate, and Parrhesiastic Utterance: On Cavell, Foucault, and Truth as an Ethical Force," *Critical Inquiry* 41(2) (2015): 254–68; David Kaufmann, "A Plea for Perlocutions," *Conversations: The Journal of Cavellian Studies* 4 (2016): 43–60; Sandra Laugier and Daniele Lorenzini, *Perlocutoire: Normativités et performativités du langage ordinaire* (Paris: Mare & Martin, 2021); Laugier and Lorenzini, "The Perlocutionary and the Illocutionary," Special issue, *Inquiry: An Interdisciplinary Journal of Philosophy* (forthcoming).

6. Cavell, *Philosophy the Day after Tomorrow*, 5.

7. Cavell, *Philosophy the Day after Tomorrow*, 5. For an analysis of hate speech as illocutionary act and the explicit broadening of Austin's notion of "performativity," see Judith Butler, *Excitable Speech: A Politics of the Performative* (New York: Routledge, 1997).

8. Austin, *How to Do Things with Words*, 102–3. For a critical discussion of the ways in which the distinction between the illocutionary and the perlocutionary has been characterized in the literature on speech acts, see Daniele Lorenzini, "From Recognition to Acknowledgment: Rethinking the Perlocutionary," *Inquiry: An Interdisciplinary Journal of Philosophy*, 2020, https://doi.org/10.1080/0020174X.2020.1712231.

9. Austin, *How to Do Things with Words*, 109, 121.

10. See Cavell, *Philosophy the Day after Tomorrow*, 169.

11. Austin, *How to Do Things with Words*, 101.

12. Cavell, *Philosophy the Day after Tomorrow*, 169.

13. Stanley Cavell, *In Quest of the Ordinary: Lines of Skepticism and Romanticism* (Chicago: University of Chicago Press, 1988), 141.

14. There are at least two places in which Foucault, albeit very briefly, *does* offer a philosophical definition and discussion of *parrhesia*: the second hour of the lecture on January 12, 1983, of his course at the Collège de France, *The Government of Self and Others* (*The Government of Self and Others: Lectures at the Collège de France, 1982–83*, edited by F. Gros, translated by G. Burchell; series edited by A. I. Davidson [Basingstoke: Palgrave Macmillan, 2010], 61–70), and the lecture on October 24, 1983, of his series of lectures at the University of California, Berkeley, *Discourse and Truth* (*Discourse and Truth*, edited by H.-P. Fruchaud and D. Lorenzini; English edition by N. Luxon [Chicago: University of Chicago Press, 2019], 39–46). However, Foucault never published anything on *parrhesia*, and the attention he devotes to this notion in most of his lectures and writings from 1982–84, albeit genealogically motivated, primarily takes the form of a historical examination of the meanings and uses of *parrhesia* in antiquity.

15. Cavell, *Philosophy the Day after Tomorrow*, 11, 15. On the theme of the voice in opera, see Stanley Cavell, *A Pitch of Philosophy: Autobiographical Exercises* (Cambridge, MA: Harvard University Press, 1994), 129–69.

16. Cavell, *Philosophy the Day after Tomorrow*, 15, emphasis added.

17. Alfred Jules Ayer, *Language, Truth, and Logic* (London: Gollancz, 1936), 107–9.

18. Ayer, *Language, Truth, and Logic*, 108.

19. Cavell, *Philosophy the Day after Tomorrow*, 16; see also 160–61.

20. Austin, *How to Do Things with Words*, 6.

21. Cavell, *Philosophy the Day after Tomorrow*, 17.

22. Cavell, *Philosophy the Day after Tomorrow*, 17.

23. Cavell, *Philosophy the Day after Tomorrow*, 156.

24. Cavell, *Philosophy the Day after Tomorrow*, 159.

25. Cavell, *Philosophy the Day after Tomorrow*, 159; see also 163, 170.

26. I should add that Austin's and Cavell's remarks on the relation between the *felicity conditions* of performative utterances and the *truth conditions* of constative utterances—"for a certain performative utterance to be happy, certain statements have to be true" (Austin, *How to Do Things with Words*, 45; Cavell, *Philosophy the Day after Tomorrow*, 166)—are not relevant to the specific issue I want to address here.

27. Even though, as I mentioned above, he does come close to such a definition a couple of times. See Foucault, *The Government of Self and Others*, 61–70; Foucault, *Discourse and Truth*, 39–46.

28. Foucault, *Discourse and Truth*, 40, 45–46.

29. Foucault, *The Government of Self and Others*, 47 (trans. mod.).

30. Plutarch, *Lives*, vol. 6, translated by B. Perrin (Cambridge, MA: Harvard University Press, 1961), 11–12. I am quoting Foucault's own translation of the text, based on the French translation realized by Bernard Latzarus for the Classiques Garnier edition of Plutarch's *Parallel Lives*; see Foucault, *The Government of Self and Others*, 48–49.

31. Foucault, *The Government of Self and Others*, 49.

32. Foucault, *The Government of Self and Others*, 50.

33. See Michel Foucault, *The Hermeneutics of the Subject: Lectures at the Collège de France, 1981–82*, edited by F. Gros, translated by G. Burchell; series edited by A. I. Davidson (Basingstoke: Palgrave Macmillan, 2005), 137, 164, 241–42, 366–68, 371–91, 395–409. On this topic, see Daniele Lorenzini, *Éthique et politique de soi: Foucault, Hadot, Cavell et les techniques de l'ordinaire* (Paris: Vrin, 2015), 166–71.

34. See Michel Foucault, "*Parrēsia*: Lecture at the University of Grenoble (May 18, 1982)," translated by G. Burchell, in Foucault, *Discourse and Truth*, 30–33; Foucault, *The Hermeneutics of the Subject*, 401–7.

35. Seneca, *Epistles*, vol. 2, translated by R. M. Gummere (Cambridge, MA: Harvard University Press, 1989), Letter 75, pp. 137, 139. Here again I am quoting Foucault's own translation of the text, based on the French translation realized by Henri Noblot for the Belles Lettres edition of Seneca's *Letters to Lucilius*; see Foucault, "*Parrēsia*," 30–31.

36. Foucault, *The Government of Self and Others*, 51.

37. Foucault, *The Government of Self and Others*, 52.

38. Foucault, *The Government of Self and Others*, 52. On this point, see Nancy Luxon, "Truthfulness, Risk, and Trust in the Late Lectures of Michel Foucault," *Inquiry: An Interdisciplinary Journal of Philosophy* 47(5) (2004): 465–66.

39. Foucault, *The Government of Self and Others*, 55–56.

40. Foucault, *The Government of Self and Others*, 56.

41. Foucault, *The Government of Self and Others*, 56.

42. Foucault, *The Government of Self and Others*, 56.

43. Foucault, *The Government of Self and Others*, 61.

44. Arnold I. Davidson, "Structures and Strategies of Discourse: Remarks toward a History of Foucault's Philosophy of Language," in *Foucault and His Interlocutors*, edited by A. I. Davidson (Chicago: University of Chicago Press, 1997), 1–17; David-

son, *The Emergence of Sexuality: Historical Epistemology and the Formation of Concepts* (Cambridge, MA: Harvard University Press, 2001), 178-91; Davidson, "Introduction," in Foucault, *"Society Must Be Defended": Lectures at the Collège de France, 1975-76*, edited by M. Bertani and A. Fontana, translated by D. Macey; series edited by A. I. Davidson (New York: Picador, 2003), xv-xxiii.

45. Foucault, unpublished letter to Daniel Defert (1967), quoted in Michel Foucault, *Dits et écrits I, 1954-75*, edited by D. Defert and F. Ewald (Paris: Gallimard, 2001), 40.

46. Michel Foucault, "Structuralism and Literary Analysis," translated by S. Taylor and J. Schroeder, *Critical Inquiry* 45(2) (2019): 543 (trans. mod.). As Sandra Laugier aptly remarks, building on Cavell's reading of Wittgenstein's later philosophy, "We should not only be concerned with the analysis, the (empirical) content, and the logical structure of statements; we should be concerned with what we say, with the *we* and the *saying*: we should ask ourselves what we do with our language, that is, how our actions in such and such a situation are part of what we say" ("Stanley Cavell: Les voix du langage ordinaire," in *Lectures de Wittgenstein*, edited by C. Chauviré and S. Plaud [Paris: Ellipses, 2012], 378).

47. Foucault, "Structuralism and Literary Analysis," 542 (trans. mod.). On the notion of extralinguistic in Foucault's lectures and writings from the 1960s, see Azucena G. Blanco, "Foucault on Raymond Roussel: The Extralinguistic outside of Literature," *Theory, Culture & Society*, 2020, https://doi.org/10.1177/0263276420950458.

48. Michel Foucault, "Le discours ne doit pas être pris comme . . ." (1976), in Foucault, *Dits et écrits II, 1976-88*, edited by D. Defert and F. Ewald (Paris: Gallimard, 2001), 123-24. See also Michel Foucault, "Truth and Juridical Forms" (1973), in Foucault, *Power*, vol. 3 of *Essential Works of Foucault (1954-84)*, edited by J. D. Faubion, translated by R. Hurley et al.; series edited by P. Rabinow (New York: New Press, 2000), 2-3.

49. On this point, see Jocelyn Benoist ("Des actes de langage à l'inventaire des énoncés," *Archives de Philosophie* 79[1] [2016]), who argues that, while clearly drawing from the Anglo-American philosophy of language, Foucault actually turned its main postulate upside down: according to him, it is not true that, "in order to speak [*tenir un discours*], one *first* has to perform speech acts," because "such 'acts,' like every other aspect of language, are only possible—because effective—within discourse [*discours*]." In other words, if the analysis of speech acts allows us to isolate certain "typical forms of speech," what Foucault (at least in the 1960s) is interested in is rather "the singularity of what is actually said as a *real singularity*—that of the utterance—and not as an ideal singularity (even though, just as in the theory of speech acts, such singularity is anchored in reality)" (72-73, 78).

50. Cavell, *Philosophy the Day after Tomorrow*, 18; see also 177.

51. Foucault only mentions female parrhesiasts twice: when he discusses the confrontation between Electra and Clytemnestra in Euripides's *Electra*, and when he analyzes Creusa's speech in Euripides's *Ion*. See Foucault, *The Government of Self and Others*, 134-45; Foucault, *Discourse and Truth*, 74-76, 85, 92-99. For a different analysis of a historical example of a female parrhesiast (Hypatia), see Stefania Ferrando, *Michel Foucault, la politica presa a rovescio: La pratica antica della verità nei corsi al Collège de France* (Milan: Franco Angeli, 2012), 230-50. For a critique of Foucault's "gendered reading of truth-telling" and his "typically masculine understanding" of it, as well as the elaboration of an alternate reading based on the figure of Creusa in

the *Ion*, see Lida Maxwell, "The Politics and Gender of Truth-Telling in Foucault's Lectures on *Parrhesia*," *Contemporary Political Theory* 18 (2019): 22–42.

52. Cavell, *Philosophy the Day after Tomorrow*, 18.

53. Cavell, *Philosophy the Day after Tomorrow*, 172.

54. Cavell, *Philosophy the Day after Tomorrow*, 18; see also 180.

55. Foucault, *The Government of Self and Others*, 62.

56. Nancy Bauer, "How to Do Things with Pornography," in *Reading Cavell*, edited by A. Crary and S. Shieh (New York: Routledge, 2006), 71.

57. Jennifer Hornsby, "Illocution and Its Significance," in *Foundations of Speech Act Theory: Philosophical and Linguistic Perspectives*, edited by S. L. Tsohatzidis (New York: Routledge, 1994), 194.

58. Cavell, *Philosophy the Day after Tomorrow*, 172.

59. Foucault, *The Government of Self and Others*, 65 (trans. mod.).

60. Foucault, *The Government of Self and Others*, 63. On the fundamental role that social authority plays in Austin's definition of performative utterance, see Benoist, "Des actes de langage," 61.

61. Foucault, *The Government of Self and Others*, 65. This is clearly stipulated by Austin when he draws his list of necessary conditions for the happy functioning of performative utterances (*How to Do Things with Words*, 14–15). However, Austin's focus on "convention," here and more generally in his way of differentiating the illocutionary from the perlocutionary (see, e.g., 103, 105, 121), has been criticized by many scholars, who have emphasized that a great number of illocutionary acts are performed without the need for the speaker to conform to any established conventional procedure. On this point, see, e.g., Peter Frederick Strawson, "Intention and Convention in Speech Acts," *Philosophical Review* 73(4) (1964): 443–45.

62. Foucault, *The Government of Self and Others*, 65 (trans. mod.).

63. Foucault, *The Government of Self and Others*, 66 (trans. mod.).

64. Cavell, *Philosophy the Day after Tomorrow*, 19; see also 185. This "uncanny resonance between Foucault's discussion of *parrhesia* . . . and Cavell's treatment of the illocution/perlocution distinction in Austin" is emphasized also by Aletta J. Norval, "Moral Perfectionism and Democratic Responsiveness: Reading Cavell with Foucault," *Ethics & Global Politics* 4(4) (2011): 220–21.

65. Pierre Bourdieu, "Price Formation and the Anticipation of Profits" (1980), in Bourdieu, *Language and Symbolic Power*, edited by J. B. Thompson, translated by G. Raymond and M. Adamson (Cambridge: Polity Press, 1991), 76, emphasis added.

66. Pierre Bourdieu, "Authorized Language: The Social Conditions for the Effectiveness of Ritual Discourse" (1975), in Bourdieu, *Language and Symbolic Power*, 107 (trans. mod.).

67. See Foucault, *The Government of Self and Others*, 124–25.

68. Foucault, *The Government of Self and Others*, 133.

69. Dianna Taylor, *Sexual Violence and Humiliation: A Foucauldian-Feminist Perspective* (New York: Routledge, 2020), 70.

70. In his analysis of the Christian practice of *exagoreusis*, Foucault emphasizes a similar condition: the monk who confesses by exhaustively verbalizing his thoughts must do so, not only out loud, but also necessarily in the presence of another person (his spiritual director, another monk, even a stranger). In other words, if the monk verbalizes his thoughts alone, speaking only to himself, he does not *actually* confess. See Michel Foucault, *About the Beginning of the Hermeneutics of the Self: Lectures at*

Dartmouth College, 1980, edited by H.-P. Fruchaud and D. Lorenzini (Chicago: University of Chicago Press, 2015), 71–72. However, unlike the case of *parrhesia*, here the other person has no reason to feel questioned or challenged by the monk's confession. Thus, confession secures obedience rather than prompting resistance.

71. Cavell, *Philosophy the Day after Tomorrow*, 18; see also 181.

72. The two, however, are undoubtedly linked. See, e.g., Stanley Cavell, *Cities of Words: Pedagogical Letters on a Register of the Moral Life* (Cambridge, MA: Harvard University Press, 2004), 142: "That my actions are part of the life form of talkers (as Wittgenstein characterizes the human, at *Investigations* §174) makes them *open to criticism*. That I am open to, perhaps responsive to, the criticism of being insensitive, cruel, petty, clumsy, narrow-minded, self-absorbed, cold, hard, heedless, reckless . . . is as much a mystery as my being open to the charge of being imprudent or undutiful or unfair. That we are not transparent to ourselves means that such criticism demands confrontation and conversation. The mystery is not that we are impure but that we can be moved to change by speech, and (hence) by silence."

73. Foucault, *The Government of Self and Others*, 56, 62.

74. Foucault, *The Government of Self and Others*, 62–63.

75. See Taylor, *Sexual Violence and Humiliation*, 70–71.

76. Pierre Hadot, "Spiritual Exercises" (1977), in *Philosophy as a Way of Life: Spiritual Exercises from Socrates to Foucault*, edited by A. I. Davidson, translated by M. Chase (Oxford: Blackwell, 1995), 91.

77. See Foucault, *The Government of Self and Others*, 63: "Even when the situation is not as extreme as this [Foucault is referring here to the confrontation between Plato and Dionysius], even when it does not involve a tyrant with the power of life and death over the person who speaks, what defines the parrhesiastic statement, what precisely makes the statement of its truth in the form of *parrhesia* something absolutely unique among other forms of utterance and other formulations of the truth, is that *parrhesia* opens up a risk."

78. Foucault, *Discourse and Truth*, 43.

79. Foucault, *The Government of Self and Others*, 66.

80. Michel Foucault, *The Courage of Truth: Lectures at the Collège de France, 1983–84*, edited by F. Gros, translated by G. Burchell; series edited by A. I. Davidson (Basingstoke: Palgrave Macmillan, 2011), 11–12 (trans. mod.).

81. On this topic, see Alison Ross, "Why Is 'Speaking the Truth' Fearless? 'Danger' and 'Truth' in Foucault's Discussion of *Parrhesia*," *Parrhesia* 4 (2008): 62–75.

82. Foucault, *The Government of Self and Others*, 63; see above, pp. 15–23.

83. Foucault, *The Government of Self and Others*, 63.

84. Foucault, *The Government of Self and Others*, 63.

85. Foucault, *The Government of Self and Others*, 63.

86. See above, pp. 20–21, 39–41.

87. On this notion and the different meanings that Foucault attributes to it, see Foucault, *Discourse and Truth*, 232–33n20.

88. See Foucault, *The Government of Self and Others*, 162–63: "The servant arrives before Pentheus and says to him: I would like to know whether I should report this news (concerning the excesses of the Bacchae) quite frankly (*parrhesia*) or whether I must watch my words. . . . To which Pentheus replies: 'You may speak: you have nothing to fear from me. One should not be angry with he who does his duty.' And in fact it is the Bacchae who are punished. . . . This is what could be called, if you

like, the parrhesiastic pact: if he wishes to govern properly, the one with power must accept that those who are weaker tell him the truth, even the unpleasant truth." See also Foucault, *"Parrēsia,"* 8–9; Foucault, *Discourse and Truth*, 73–74.

89. Foucault, *Discourse and Truth*, 76.

90. Foucault, *The Courage of Truth*, 12–13 (trans. mod.).

91. Foucault, *The Courage of Truth*, 13 (trans. mod.).

92. Aristotle, *Nicomachean Ethics*, translated by W. D. Ross, revised by J. O. Urmson, in *The Complete Works of Aristotle: The Revised Oxford Translation*, edited by J. Barnes (Princeton, NJ: Princeton University Press, 1984), 1124b26–29, 2:1775. See Foucault, *The Courage of Truth*, 12.

93. It is precisely in these terms that Foucault interprets the dialogue between Diogenes and Alexander in his 1983 lectures at Berkeley (Foucault, *Discourse and Truth*, 174–81).

94. Dio Chrysostom, "The Fourth Discourse on Kingship," translated by J. W. Cohoon, in *Dio Chrysostom* (Cambridge, MA: Harvard University Press, 1932), 1:169–233.

95. The pact that Socrates, Nicias, and Laches stipulate in Plato's *Laches*, for instance, is explicit. See Foucault, *The Courage of Truth*, 122, 128, 141–44.

96. Cavell, *Philosophy the Day after Tomorrow*, 19; see also 184.

97. Stanley Cavell, *Pursuits of Happiness: The Hollywood Comedy of Remarriage* (Cambridge, MA: Harvard University Press, 1981), 1–2, 87.

98. Cavell, *Pursuits of Happiness*, 87–88.

99. On this point, see Lorenzini, "From Recognition to Acknowledgment."

100. Foucault, *The Government of Self and Others*, 53 (trans. mod.).

101. Foucault, *The Hermeneutics of the Subject*, 405.

102. Paul Allen Miller, *Foucault's Seminars on Antiquity: Learning to Speak the Truth* (New York: Bloomsbury, 2021), 95.

103. Miller, *Foucault's Seminars on Antiquity*, 96.

104. Miller, *Foucault's Seminars on Antiquity*, 96.

105. Arthur E. Walzer, *"Parrēsia,* Foucault, and the Classical Rhetorical Tradition," *Rhetoric Society Quarterly* 43(1) (2013): 1–21.

106. On the many delicate problems that one faces in addressing the question of the relations between rhetoric and *parrhesia*, see Pat J. Gehrke et al., "Forum on Arthur Walzer's *'Parrēsia,* Foucault, and the Classical Rhetorical Tradition,'" *Rhetoric Society Quarterly* 43(4) (2013): 355–81. Pat Gehrke's response to Walzer is particularly convincing in showing that, at least within the context of Athenian democracy, "when speaking as *parrhesiastes* [one] does not speak as rhetor or via the *technē* of rhetoric," and that more generally the ancient Greeks understood and used the two terms— *parrhesia* and rhetoric—to denote two *different* verbal activities (357).

107. Foucault, *The Hermeneutics of the Subject*, 135–36.

108. See Foucault, *The Hermeneutics of the Subject*, 381: "Rhetoric is first of all defined as a technique whose methods obviously do not aim to establish a truth; rhetoric is defined as an art of persuading those to whom one is speaking, whether one wishes to convince them of a truth or a lie, a nontruth. Aristotle's definition in the *Rhetoric* is clear: it is the ability to find that which is capable of persuading. The question of the content and the question of the truth of the discourse delivered do not arise." See also Foucault, *The Government of Self and Others*, 53, 304–5.

109. On Plato's and Aristotle's "exclusion" of the Sophists and of sophisms as one of the defining moments in the "institutionalization" of philosophy, see Michel Fou-

cault, *Lectures on the Will to Know: Lectures at the Collège de France, 1970–71,* edited by D. Defert, translated by G. Burchell; series edited by A. I. Davidson (Basingstoke: Palgrave Macmillan, 2013), 31–68.

110. Foucault, *The Hermeneutics of the Subject,* 348 (trans. mod.).

111. Foucault, *The Hermeneutics of the Subject,* 368 (trans. mod.).

112. Foucault, *The Hermeneutics of the Subject,* 368.

113. Foucault, *The Hermeneutics of the Subject,* 368; on *kairos,* see 384.

114. This characterization of *parrhesia* as both a technique and an ethics marks a significant shift from what Foucault argued in his 1980 lectures at Berkeley and Dartmouth College. There, Foucault—who still had not "discovered" *parrhesia*—claims that the spiritual director's discourse possesses a *rhetorical quality*: the truth that this discourse is supposed to convey is obtained by a "rhetorical explanation of what is good for anyone who wants to approach the life of a sage." In other words, the master's discourse is characterized by a "persuasive rhetoric," and Foucault goes so far as to claim that all ancient technologies of the self are closely connected, not only with the art of memory (mnemotechnics), but also with the art of persuasion (rhetoric). See Foucault, *About the Beginning of the Hermeneutics of the Self,* 36–38.

115. Foucault, *The Hermeneutics of the Subject,* 373; see also 385–86: "In a word, let's say then that speaking freely, *parrhesia,* is in its very structure completely different from and opposed to rhetoric. Of course, as I was saying at the start, this opposition is not of exactly the same type as that between speaking freely and flattery.... In its structure, in its game, the discourse of *parrhesia* is completely different from rhetoric. This does not mean that, in the tactic of *parrhesia* itself, in order to obtain one's intended outcome, it may not be necessary from time to time to call upon some elements and procedures belonging to rhetoric. Let's say that *parrhesia* is fundamentally freed from the rules of rhetoric, that it takes rhetoric up obliquely and only uses it if it needs to." This idea is surprisingly close to Habermas's remarks on the relations between philosophy and rhetoric—and to his conclusion according to which philosophy must make use of rhetoric as a means that allows it to bridge the gap between its own specialized language and ordinary language. See Jürgen Habermas, *The Philosophical Discourse of Modernity: Twelve Lectures,* translated by F. Lawrence (Cambridge: Polity Press, 1990), 209.

116. Foucault, *The Hermeneutics of the Subject,* 382.

117. Foucault, *The Government of Self and Others,* 53.

118. Foucault, *The Government of Self and Others,* 53.

119. Foucault, *The Government of Self and Others,* 54, emphasis added.

120. Foucault, *"Parrēsia,"* 34.

121. Foucault, *The Government of Self and Others,* 54. In 1984, Foucault does refer to Socratic irony as one of the forms taken by the "courage of truth," even though he carefully avoids using the word *parrhesia* (*The Courage of Truth,* 233–34). In his book on the philosophy and history of sincerity, Andrea Tagliapietra argues that irony pursues the same strategic objective as *parrhesia,* and that "*parrhesia* and irony are therefore two different *tactics* within the same *strategy*": "irony does indirectly and prudently what *parrhesia* does directly and courageously" (*La virtù crudele: Filosofia e storia della sincerità* [Turin: Einaudi, 2003], 76–77).

122. Foucault, *The Government of Self and Others,* 314.

123. Foucault, *The Government of Self and Others,* 314.

124. Foucault, *The Government of Self and Others,* 314 (trans. mod.).

125. Foucault, *The Government of Self and Others,* 314–15.

126. Foucault, *The Government of Self and Others*, 315.

127. Foucault, *Discourse and Truth*, 41-42.

128. Foucault, *The Courage of Truth*, 13.

129. Foucault, *The Courage of Truth*, 13.

130. See Foucault, *The Courage of Truth*, 13-14.

131. Foucault, *The Courage of Truth*, 14 (trans. mod.).

132. The claim that Foucault is unable to convincingly distinguish *parrhesia* from rhetoric, such that he just ends up uncritically endorsing Plato's views about the relations between philosophy, politics, and rhetoric (see Geoffrey Bennington, "The Truth about *Parrhesia*: Philosophy, Rhetoric, and Politics in Late Foucault," in *Foucault/Derrida Fifty Years Later: The Futures of Genealogy, Deconstruction, and Politics*, edited by O. Custer, P. Deutscher, and S. Haddad [New York: Columbia University Press, 2016], 205-20), is therefore to be rejected.

133. See, e.g., Habermas, *The Philosophical Discourse of Modernity*, 279; Thomas Biebricher, "Habermas, Foucault, and Nietzsche: A Double Misunderstanding," *Foucault Studies* 3 (2005): 18.

134. One of the most common criticisms of Foucault's analysis of *parrhesia* is that he chooses to translate the latter as "truth-telling," while being aware that this term—at least in its etymology—does not contain any explicit reference to truth (*Discourse and Truth*, 39-40). *Parrhesia* literally means "to say everything," and originally indicates "the freedom of the private [Athenian] citizen to say what he believes, in the way he wishes, and against whom he wants to" (Giuseppe Scarpat, *Parrhesia: Storia del termine e delle sue traduzioni in latino* [Brescia: Paideia, 1964], 29). The notion of truth, however, is clearly encompassed within *parrhesia*'s semantic horizon. As Giuseppe Scarpat aptly argues, "truth is the essential element of *parrhesia*," and at the time of Diogenes of Sinope "truth, freedom, and *parrhesia* are almost synonymous: they are indissoluble virtues, the very substance of philosophy" (46, 67-68). Similarly, Ineke Sluiter and Ralph Rosen explain that *parrhesia* "always involves frankness and the full disclosure of one's thoughts," and that consequently it is "linked in an interesting way with truth: the parrhesiast must necessarily believe in the truth of what he is saying, or at least in the fact that to the best of his knowledge what he is saying is true" ("General Introduction," in *Free Speech in Classical Antiquity*, edited by I. Sluiter and R. M. Rosen [Leiden and Boston: Brill, 2004], 6-7).

Chapter 4

1. Michel Foucault, *The Courage of Truth: Lectures at the Collège de France, 1983-84*, edited by F. Gros, translated by G. Burchell; series edited by A. I. Davidson (Basingstoke: Palgrave Macmillan, 2011), 3.

2. Michel Foucault, *On the Government of the Living: Lectures at the Collège de France, 1979-80*, edited by M. Senellart, translated by G. Burchell; series edited by A. I. Davidson (Basingstoke: Palgrave Macmillan, 2014), 7.

3. Foucault, *On the Government of the Living*, 7.

4. See Michel Foucault, *The Government of Self and Others: Lectures at the Collège de France, 1982-83*, edited by F. Gros, translated by G. Burchell; series edited by A. I. Davidson (Basingstoke: Palgrave Macmillan, 2010), 314; Foucault, *Discourse and Truth*, edited by H.-P. Fruchaud and D. Lorenzini; English edition by N. Luxon (Chicago: University of Chicago Press, 2019), 41.

5. See above, p. 150, note 35.

6. See above, p. 150, note 35.

7. Michel Foucault, *"Parrēsia*: Lecture at the University of Grenoble (May 18, 1982)," translated by G. Burchell, in Foucault, *Discourse and Truth*, edited by H.-P. Fruchaud and D. Lorenzini; English edition by N. Luxon (Chicago: University of Chicago Press, 2019), 30.

8. Foucault, *"Parrēsia,"* 31 (trans. mod.).

9. Foucault, *"Parrēsia,"* 31–32 (trans. mod.). See also Michel Foucault, *The Hermeneutics of the Subject: Lectures at the Collège de France, 1981–82*, edited by F. Gros, translated by G. Burchell; series edited by A. I. Davidson (Basingstoke: Palgrave Macmillan, 2005), 405–7.

10. See, e.g., Foucault, *Discourse and Truth*, 142–49; Foucault, *The Courage of Truth*, 83–85, 141–153.

11. Foucault, *The Government of Self and Others*, 63 (trans. mod.).

12. Foucault, *The Government of Self and Others*, 64.

13. Foucault, *The Government of Self and Others*, 64.

14. John Langshaw Austin, *How to Do Things with Words*, edited by J. O. Urmson and M. Sbisà (Cambridge, MA: Harvard University Press, 1975), 39–40. However, Austin rightly argues that insincerities do not render the performance of these acts "void": an insincere promise is still a promise, although clearly defective or "unhappy," as Austin puts it (39).

15. Austin, *How to Do Things with Words*, 15.

16. Stanley Cavell, *Philosophy the Day after Tomorrow* (Cambridge, MA: Harvard University Press, 2005), 19; see also 181–82.

17. Foucault, *The Courage of Truth*, 310 (trans. mod.).

18. Foucault, *The Hermeneutics of the Subject*, 16; Foucault, *The Government of Self and Others*, 68 (trans. mod.).

19. Foucault, *The Government of Self and Others*, 64–65 (trans. mod.); see also 67: "There is *parrhesia* from the moment Plato actually accepts the risk of being exiled, killed, sold, etcetera, in telling the truth. So *parrhesia* is really that by which the subject binds himself to the statement, to the enunciation, and to the consequences of this statement and enunciation."

20. Foucault, *The Government of Self and Others*, 66 (trans. mod.), 68. This is not what Foucault thought at the beginning of his explorations of *parrhesia*: in May 1982, at the University of Grenoble, he suggested that *parrhesia* should be analyzed in terms "of what is now called a pragmatics of discourse," as "the set of characteristics that grounds and renders effective the discourse of the other in the practice of care of self." If the latter, in antiquity, required the spiritual director's discourse in order to be effectively carried out, then *parrhesia* is what characterized such a discourse "considered as act, as action on myself" (*"Parrēsia,"* 15). See also Michel Foucault, *Speaking the Truth about Oneself: Lectures at Victoria University, Toronto, 1982*, edited by H.-P. Fruchaud and D. Lorenzini; English edition by D. L. Wyche (Chicago: University of Chicago Press, 2021), 172–73, 218–22.

21. Foucault, *The Government of Self and Others*, 67–68 (trans. mod.).

22. See Michel Foucault, "Structuralism and Literary Analysis," translated by S. Taylor and J. Schroeder, *Critical Inquiry* 45(2) (2019): 542–44.

23. Foucault, *The Government of Self and Others*, 68.

24. Foucault, *The Government of Self and Others*, 68.

25. Austin, *How to Do Things with Words*, 145. See also Austin, "Performative Utterances" (1956), in Austin, *Philosophical Papers*, edited by J. O. Urmson and G. J. Warnock (Oxford: Oxford University Press, 1979), 250–51.

26. Bruno Ambroise, "From J. L. Austin to Charles Travis: A Pragmatic Account of Truth?," *HAL*, December 10, 2013, https://halshs.archives-ouvertes.fr/halshs -00916223, 10.

27. It is not reducible to them, however, because for Austin truth is at bottom a dimension of assessment: it is a question of *judgment*—of situated individuals deciding whether a state of affairs, in given circumstances, can properly be "designated by a sentence having a certain meaning" (Ambroise, "From J. L. Austin to Charles Travis," 13). On this point, see John Langshaw Austin, "Truth," *Proceedings of the Aristotelian Society*, suppl. vol. 24 (1950): 111–28; Austin, "Unfair to Facts" (1954), in Austin, *Philosophical Papers*, 154–74.

28. Austin, *How to Do Things with Words*, 3.

29. Recent scholarship on pragmatic and moral encroachment concurs in arguing that epistemic statuses often depend on pragmatic as well as ethico-political factors. See, e.g., Jeremy Fantl and Matthew McGrath, "On Pragmatic Encroachment in Epistemology," *Philosophy and Phenomenological Research* 75(3) (2007): 558–89; James Fritz, "Pragmatic Encroachment and Moral Encroachment," *Pacific Philosophical Quarterly* 98(S1) (2017): 643–61; Sarah Moss, "Moral Encroachment," *Proceedings of the Aristotelian Society* 118(2) (2018): 177–205. However, a full-fledged discussion of *parrhesia* in terms of pragmatic, moral, and political encroachment is beyond my aims here.

30. I am grateful to Daniel Verginelli Galantin for suggesting this analogy to me.

31. Foucault, *The Government of Self and Others*, 176.

32. Foucault, *Speaking the Truth about Oneself*, 172–73.

33. For an analysis of *parrhesia* in the field of literature, see Azucena G. Blanco, "Toward a Politics of Literature in the Late Foucault: Parrhesia and Mimesis," *Revue Internationale de Philosophie* 292 (2020): 29–38; Daniele Lorenzini, "Alèthurgie oculaire et littérature de témoignage: De Sophocle à Soljenitsyne," *Revue Internationale de Philosophie* 292 (2020): 17–28.

34. On the notion of "perlocutionary responsibility," see Daniele Lorenzini, "From Recognition to Acknowledgment: Rethinking the Perlocutionary," *Inquiry: An Interdisciplinary Journal of Philosophy*, 2020, https://doi.org/10.1080/0020174X.2020 .1712231.

35. Similarly, Cavell argues that two of the conditions for the felicity of passionate utterance are that "the one singled out must respond now and here" and "respond in kind, that is to say, be moved to respond, or else resist the demand" (*Philosophy the Day after Tomorrow*, 19; see also 181–82).

36. Foucault, *The Government of Self and Others*, 62.

37. Michel Foucault, *Psychiatric Power: Lectures at the Collège de France, 1973–74*, edited by J. Lagrange, translated by G. Burchell; series edited by A. I. Davidson (Basingstoke: Palgrave Macmillan, 2006), 237.

38. See Foucault, "*Parrēsia*," 32 (trans. mod.): "There is a reciprocal opening of two partners when the one who guides the other implicates himself in what he says, not just in order to affirm that he is exactly true to the truth of what he says, but that he himself strives to arrive at it." This remark makes it possible to establish a fruitful connection between *parrhesia* and moral perfectionism as Cavell defines it; on this

topic, see David Owen, "Perfectionism, Parrhesia, and the Care of the Self: Foucault and Cavell on Ethics and Politics," in *The Claim to Community: Essays on Stanley Cavell and Political Philosophy*, edited by A. Norris (Stanford, CA: Stanford University Press, 2006), 143-47; Daniele Lorenzini, "Must We Do What We Say? Truth, Responsibility, and the Ordinary in Ancient and Modern Perfectionism," *European Journal of Pragmatism and American Philosophy* 2 (2010): 18-23.

39. Cavell, *Philosophy the Day after Tomorrow*, 182. On this point, see Aletta J. Norval, "Moral Perfectionism and Democratic Responsiveness: Reading Cavell with Foucault," *Ethics & Global Politics* 4(4) (2011): 213-15; David Owen and Clare Woodford, "Foucault, Cavell, and the Government of Self and Others: On Truth-Telling, Friendship, and an Ethics of Democracy," *Iride: Filosofia e Discussione Pubblica* 66 (2012): 307-11. For an analysis of the theme of education (and its relations with democracy and care of the self) in Foucault's study of *parrhesia*, see Michael A. Peters, "Truth-Telling as an Educational Practice of the Self: Foucault, *Parrhesia*, and the Ethics of Subjectivity," *Oxford Review of Education* 29 (2003): 207-24.

40. See, e.g., Stanley Cavell, *Pursuits of Happiness: The Hollywood Comedy of Remarriage* (Cambridge, MA: Harvard University Press, 1981), 1-42, 86-89; Cavell, *Cities of Words: Pedagogical Letters on a Register of the Moral Life* (Cambridge, MA: Harvard University Press, 2004), 38-48. On this topic, see Daniele Lorenzini, *Éthique et politique de soi: Foucault, Hadot, Cavell et les techniques de l'ordinaire* (Paris: Vrin, 2015), 162-66.

41. Cavell, *Philosophy the Day after Tomorrow*, 121-22.

42. Cavell, *Philosophy the Day after Tomorrow*, 122.

43. Michel Foucault, "The Analytic Philosophy of Politics" (1978), translated by G. Mascaretti, *Foucault Studies* 24 (2018): 189.

44. See Foucault, *Discourse and Truth*, 63.

45. Stanley Cavell, *Conditions Handsome and Unhandsome: The Constitution of Emersonian Perfectionism* (Chicago: University of Chicago Press, 1991), 6-7; Cavell, *Cities of Words*, 445-47.

46. Foucault, *The Government of Self and Others*, 312.

47. Foucault, *The Government of Self and Others*, 313.

48. See Foucault, *The Government of Self and Others*, 313-15.

49. Andrea Tagliapietra, *La virtù crudele: Filosofia e storia della sincerità* (Turin: Einaudi, 2003). In this book, Tagliapietra largely draws from the outline advanced by Vladimir Jankélévitch in the second volume of his *Traité des vertus* (*Traité des vertus II: Les vertus et l'amour*, vol. 1 [Paris: Flammarion, 1986], 181-284).

50. Tagliapietra, *La virtù crudele*, viii-ix, 3, 29. For an analogous definition of sincerity as truthfulness, see Lionel Trilling, *Sincerity and Authenticity* (Cambridge, MA: Harvard University Press, 1972), 2; Bernard Williams, *Truth and Truthfulness: An Essay in Genealogy* (Princeton, NJ: Princeton University Press, 2002), 71: "A sincere assertion will be one made by someone who himself believes that P."

51. Tagliapietra, *La virtù crudele*, 6.

52. Tagliapietra, *La virtù crudele*, ix, 29-30.

53. As Tagliapietra himself argues, "Truthfulness as a mere pragmatics of truthtelling acquires moral value, thus becoming the first form of veracity . . . , when it intercepts the sphere of courage and the sovereign exercise of freedom"; consequently, in his view, "truthfulness as veracity alludes to the Greek meaning of *parrhesia*" (*La virtù crudele*, 35).

54. Tagliapietra, *La virtù crudele*, ix, 44.

55. See Tagliapietra, *La virtù crudele*, x: "Being sincere with oneself means to 'become what one is,' [fulfilling] that inner agreement which forces us—as a moral duty as well as an indispensable requirement of our 'I' and our individual personality—to be authentic, to actualize ourselves, to recognize ourselves and to be recognized by others for what we *truly* are." See also Trilling, *Sincerity and Authenticity*, 4–6, 11.

56. Tagliapietra, *La virtù crudele*, xi.

57. Authenticity, understood as "a deep truth to be discovered and that constitutes the foundation, the base, the ground of our subjectivity," is according to Foucault one of the three fundamental features that characterize the modern "model" of Western subjectivity. To this model, he explicitly opposes the Greek idea of *bios*, which "is not defined by a relation to a hidden authenticity that has to be discovered," but is "the indefinite search, or the finite search in the very form of existence, for an end that one both does and does not reach" (Michel Foucault, *Subjectivity and Truth: Lectures at the Collège de France, 1980–81*, edited by F. Gros, translated by G. Burchell; series edited by A. I. Davidson [Basingstoke: Palgrave Macmillan, 2017], 253–54).

58. Michel Foucault, *About the Beginning of the Hermeneutics of the Self: Lectures at Dartmouth College, 1980*, edited by H.-P. Fruchaud and D. Lorenzini (Chicago: University of Chicago Press, 2015), 75–76. For a helpful problematization of Foucault's approach to Greco-Roman accounts and experiences of the self, see James I. Porter, "Living on the Edge: Self and World *in extremis* in Roman Philosophy," *Classical Antiquity* 39(2) (2020): 225–83.

59. See Charles Taylor, *The Ethics of Authenticity* (Cambridge, MA: Harvard University Press, 1991), 15–17, 25–29. On the "ambiguous" invention of authenticity in the eighteenth century (especially in Rousseau and Diderot), and on the ethical and social dangers associated with it, see Williams, *Truth and Truthfulness*, 172–205.

60. Michel Foucault, "Débat au Département de Français de l'Université de Californie à Berkeley," in *Qu'est-ce que la critique? suivi de La culture de soi*, edited by H.-P. Fruchaud and D. Lorenzini (Paris: Vrin, 2015), 155–56; Foucault, "On the Genealogy of Ethics: An Overview of Work in Progress" (1983), in Foucault, *Ethics: Subjectivity and Truth*, vol. 1 of *Essential Works of Foucault (1954–84)*, edited by P. Rabinow, translated by R. Hurley et al.; series edited by P. Rabinow (New York: New Press, 1997), 271; Foucault, "À propos de la généalogie de l'éthique: Un aperçu du travail en cours" (1984), in Foucault, *Dits et écrits II, 1976–88*, edited by D. Defert and F. Ewald (Paris: Gallimard, 2001), 1443. Thus, Tagliapietra's reference to Foucault's "*ethics of aesthetics*" to illustrate the shift from sincerity to authenticity, that is, "from an ethical to an aesthetic dimension, from a deontology to an ontology of the present" (*La virtù crudele*, 49), indicates a deep misunderstanding of Foucault's thought.

61. Tagliapietra, *La virtù crudele*, part II.

62. Alain Lhomme, "Les métamorphoses d'une vertu," in *La sincérité: L'insolence du cœur*, edited by C. Baron and C. Doroszczuk (Paris: Autrement, 1995), 22.

63. Lhomme, "Les métamorphoses d'une vertu," 22.

64. On this point, see Daniele Lorenzini, "Genealogia della verità e politica di noi stessi," in *Foucault e le genealogie del dir-vero*, edited by L. Cremonesi et al. (Naples: Cronopio, 2014), 145–62.

65. Michel Foucault, *Wrong-Doing, Truth-Telling: The Function of Avowal in Justice*, edited by F. Brion and B. E. Harcourt, translated by S. W. Sawyer (Chicago: University of Chicago Press, 2014), 18. For a thorough engagement with this analysis, see Judith

Butler, "Wrong-Doing, Truth-Telling: The Case of Sexual Avowal," in *Foucault and the Making of Subjects*, edited by L. Cremonesi et al. (London: Rowman & Littlefield, 2016), 77–93.

66. Foucault, *Wrong-Doing, Truth-Telling*, 14.

67. Foucault, *Wrong-Doing, Truth-Telling*, 15 (trans. mod.).

68. Foucault, *Wrong-Doing, Truth-Telling*, 15.

69. Foucault, *Wrong-Doing, Truth-Telling*, 16 (trans. mod.).

70. Foucault, *Wrong-Doing, Truth-Telling*, 17. As Butler aptly argues, "Telling the truth about oneself comes at a price, and the price of that telling is the suspension of a critical relation to the truth regime in which one lives": indeed, by avowing and telling the truth about ourselves, "we conform to a criterion of truth, and we accept that criterion as binding upon us" (*Giving an Account of Oneself* [New York: Fordham University Press, 2005], 121–22).

71. Foucault, *Wrong-Doing, Truth-Telling*, 17.

72. Foucault, *Wrong-Doing, Truth-Telling*, 17 (trans. mod.).

73. Foucault, *The Courage of Truth*, 217.

74. Frédéric Gros, "Verità, soggettività, filosofia nell'ultimo Foucault," in *Foucault, oggi*, edited by M. Galzigna (Milan: Feltrinelli, 2008), 298.

75. For a recent account of Foucault's study of Cynic truth-telling (or truth-*living*) in terms of "parrhesiastic performativity," see Andrea Di Gesu, "The Cynic Scandal: Parrhesia, Community, and Democracy," *Theory, Culture & Society* 39(3) (2022): 169–86.

76. Cavell, *Philosophy the Day after Tomorrow*, 173. Oswald Ducrot also remarks that speech is but one of the possible means for the production of perlocutionary effects (*Dire et ne pas dire: Principes de sémantique linguistique* [Paris: Hermann, 1991], 281).

77. Cavell, *Philosophy the Day after Tomorrow*, 173.

78. Sandra Laugier, *Wittgenstein: Les sens de l'usage* (Paris: Vrin, 2009), 287.

79. Foucault, *The Government of Self and Others*, 320.

80. Foucault *On the Government of the Living*, 7.

81. Foucault, *The Courage of Truth*, 283–87; Stanley Cavell, *This New Yet Unapproachable America: Lectures after Emerson after Wittgenstein* (Chicago: University of Chicago Press, 2013), 47, emphasis added.

82. Foucault, *The Courage of Truth*, 172.

83. On this point, see Daniele Lorenzini, "Éthique et politique de nous-mêmes: À partir de Michel Foucault et Stanley Cavell," in *Michel Foucault: Éthique et vérité (1980–1984)*, edited by Daniele Lorenzini, Ariane Revel, and Arianna Sforzini (Paris: Vrin, 2013), 248–52.

84. Foucault, *Discourse and Truth*, 49, 165.

85. Foucault, *Discourse and Truth*, 169–81. For a detailed analysis of these parrhesiastic practices, see also Kristen Kennedy, "Cynic Rhetoric: The Ethics and Tactics of Resistance," *Rhetoric Review* 18(1) (1999): 32–42.

86. According to Foucault, the Cynic provocative dialogue resembles "a fight, a battle, a war, with peaks of great aggression and some moments of peaceful calm, of nice exchanges" (Foucault, *Discourse and Truth*, 178); see also 181.

87. Foucault, *The Courage of Truth*, 163, emphasis added.

88. It is worth noting that the expression "true life" (*alethes bios* or *alethinos bios*) is extremely rare in Greek texts from the Classical and Hellenistic periods. It can be

found, as Foucault scrupulously remarks (*The Courage of Truth*, 221-25), in Plato's *Theætetus* (176a), *Critias* (121b), and *Seventh Letter* (327d), whereas it appears only once in the Cynic corpus, in the twenty-eighth epistle of Pseudo-Diogenes of Sinope—a text Foucault does not refer to. It is therefore possible that Foucault derives the idea of analyzing the *bios kunikos* as a "true life" from Donald Dudley's book on Cynicism: in addressing Diogenes's *parrhesia*, Dudley describes his philosophical mission in terms of "a thoroughgoing onslaught on convention, custom, and tradition in all aspects," whose aim is "to convert men to *a truer way of life*, not, like Socrates, by dialectic, nor by allegory, as did Antisthenes, but by the practical example of his daily life" (*A History of Cynicism: From Diogenes to the 6th Century A.D.* [London: Bristol Classical Press, 1937], 28, emphasis added).

89. Foucault, *The Courage of Truth*, 253.

90. Foucault, *The Courage of Truth*, 255.

91. Foucault, *The Courage of Truth*, 258.

92. Foucault, *The Courage of Truth*, 265.

93. Foucault, *The Courage of Truth*, 280.

94. See Foucault, *The Courage of Truth*, 310 (trans. mod.): "The Cynic is therefore like the visible statue of the truth. Stripped of all vain ornament, of everything that would be, as it were, the equivalent of rhetoric for the body, he appeared at the same time in full, blooming health: the very being of the true, rendered visible through the body."

95. See Diogenes Laertius, *Lives of Eminent Philosophers*, translated by R. D. Hicks, vol. 2 (London and New York: William Heinemann and G.P. Putnam's Sons, 1925), VI 69, p. 71 (trans. mod.): "It was [Diogenes's] habit to do everything in public, the works of Demeter and of Aphrodite alike. He used to draw out the following arguments: 'If it is not absurd to eat breakfast, then it is not absurd to eat breakfast in the market place either; but to eat breakfast is not absurd, therefore it is not absurd to eat breakfast in the market place.' While masturbating in public, he said he wished 'it were as easy to banish hunger by rubbing the belly.'"

96. See, e.g., Foucault, *The Courage of Truth*, 300-302; see also 280.

97. This is of course not the case for political *parrhesia* in Athenian democracy; see, e.g., Foucault, *The Government of Self and Others*, 174-84; Foucault, *Discourse and Truth*, 103-14. For a detailed analysis of political *parrhesia* in democratic Athens, see Ryan K. Balot, "Free Speech, Courage, and Democratic Deliberation," in *Free Speech in Classical Antiquity*, edited by I. Sluiter and R. M. Rosen (Leiden and Boston: Brill, 2004), 233-59; Arlene Saxonhouse, *Free Speech and Democracy in Ancient Athens* (Cambridge: Cambridge University Press, 2006), 85-178.

98. Even though they both consist in "questions and answers," in his 1983 lectures at Berkeley Foucault emphasizes several important differences between Socrates's and Diogenes's "parrhesiastic games" (*Discourse and Truth*, 175-81).

99. Foucault, *The Courage of Truth*, 284-85.

100. Dio Chrysostom, "The Eighth Discourse: Diogenes or On Virtue," translated by J. W. Cohoon, in *Dio Chrysostom* (Cambridge, MA: Harvard University Press, 1932), 1:397-99 (trans. mod.). See also Foucault, *The Courage of Truth*, 283.

101. On this point, see Lorenzini, *Éthique et politique de soi*, 261-62.

102. Foucault, *The Courage of Truth*, 283 (trans. mod.).

103. Foucault, *The Courage of Truth*, 256.

104. On this point, see Marie-Odile Goulet-Cazé, "Michel Foucault et sa vision

du cynisme dans *Le courage de la vérité*," in Lorenzini, Revel, and Sforzini, *Michel Foucault*, 114.

105. Foucault, *The Courage of Truth*, 265 (trans. mod.).

106. Michel Foucault, "What Is Enlightenment?" (1984), in Foucault, *Ethics: Subjectivity and Truth*, vol. 1 of *Essential Works of Foucault (1954–84)*, edited by P. Rabinow, translated by R. Hurley et al.; series edited by P. Rabinow (New York: New Press, 1997), 315.

107. Foucault, *The Courage of Truth*, 270.

108. Foucault, *The Courage of Truth*, 284.

109. Foucault, *The Courage of Truth*, 174, 179.

110. Foucault, *The Courage of Truth*, 180.

111. See Foucault, *The Courage of Truth*, 181–83.

112. See Foucault, *The Courage of Truth*, 183–86. In his 1982 lecture series at Victoria University, Toronto, Foucault explains that "after having studied the historical problem of subjectivity through the problem of madness, crime, sex," he would like "to study the problem of revolutionary subjectivity," thereby addressing revolution "as a subjective experience, as a type of subjectivity" (*Speaking the Truth about Oneself*, 73). Hence, Foucault explicitly establishes a link between the theme of social and political revolution and his (relatively recent) interest in the techniques of the self (231), thus anticipating his analysis of philosophical militancy in *The Courage of Truth* and making clear that political concerns remain crucial for him until the end of his life.

113. Foucault, *The Courage of Truth*, 188 (trans. mod.).

114. Foucault, *The Courage of Truth*, 184.

115. Foucault, *The Government of Self and Others*, 309.

116. Foucault, *The Government of Self and Others*, 309–10.

Chapter 5

1. Stanley Cavell, *In Quest of the Ordinary: Lines of Skepticism and Romanticism* (Chicago: University of Chicago Press, 1988), 141.

2. Important work on this topic, putting the two traditions in conversation, has been done by Colin Koopman, *Genealogy as Critique: Foucault and the Problems of Modernity* (Bloomington: Indiana University Press, 2013); Koopman, "Conceptual Analysis for Genealogical Philosophy: How to Study the History of Practices after Foucault and Wittgenstein," *Southern Journal of Philosophy* 55(S1) (2017): 103–21; Catarina Dutilh Novaes, "Conceptual Genealogy for Analytic Philosophy," in *Beyond the Analytic-Continental Divide: Pluralist Philosophy in the Twenty-First Century*, edited by J. A. Bell, A. Cutrofello, and P. M. Livingston (New York: Routledge, 2015), 75–11; Dutilh Novaes, "Carnap Meets Foucault: Conceptual Engineering and Genealogical Investigations," *Inquiry: An Interdisciplinary Journal of Philosophy*, 2020, https://doi .org/10.1080/0020174X.2020.1860122; Amia Srinivasan, "Genealogy, Epistemology, and Worldmaking," *Proceedings of the Aristotelian Society* 119(2) (2019): 127–56; Matthieu Queloz, *The Practical Origins of Ideas: Genealogy as Conceptual Reverse-Engineering* (Oxford: Oxford University Press, 2021).

3. Martin Kusch and Robin McKenna, "The Genealogical Method in Epistemology," *Synthese* 197(3) (2020): 1057–76. See Edward Craig, *Knowledge and the State of Nature: An Essay in Conceptual Synthesis* (Oxford: Clarendon Press, 1990); Bernard Williams, *Truth and Truthfulness: An Essay in Genealogy* (Princeton, NJ: Princeton

University Press, 2002); Miranda Fricker, *Epistemic Injustice: Power and the Ethics of Knowing* (Oxford: Oxford University Press, 2007); Fricker, "Scepticism and the Genealogy of Knowledge: Situating Epistemology in Time," *Philosophical Papers* 37(1) (2008): 27–50. For insightful discussion of these three authors' respective uses of "pragmatic genealogy," that is, "partly fictional, partly historical narratives" that examine "what might have driven us to develop certain ideas in order to discover what these ideas do for us," see Queloz, *The Practical Origins of Ideas*, 2.

4. See, e.g., Rudi Visker, *Michel Foucault: Genealogy as Critique*, translated by C. Turner (London: Verso, 1995); Raymond Geuss, "Genealogy as Critique," *European Journal of Philosophy* 10(2) (2002): 209–15; Martin Saar, *Genealogie als Kritik: Geschichte und Theorie des Subjekts nach Nietzsche und Foucault* (Frankfurt am Main: Campus, 2007); Koopman, *Genealogy as Critique*.

5. Srinivasan, "Genealogy, Epistemology, and Worldmaking."

6. The vindicatory-subversive distinction was coined by Williams (*Truth and Truthfulness*) and then widely used in the literature (see, e.g., David Couzens Hoy, "Genealogy, Phenomenology, Critical Theory," *Journal of the Philosophy of History* 2[3] [2008]: 276–94; Koopman, *Genealogy as Critique*; Srinivasan, "Genealogy, Epistemology, and Worldmaking").

7. Koopman, *Genealogy as Critique*; Amy Allen, *The End of Progress: Decolonizing the Normative Foundations of Critical Theory* (New York: Columbia University Press, 2016). The possibilizing aspect of Foucauldian genealogy can be found, in slightly different forms, in other genealogies as well, for instance in Beauvoir's genealogy of morality in *The Second Sex* (Sabina Vaccarino Bremner, "On Moral Unintelligibility: Beauvoir's Genealogy of Morality in *The Second Sex*," *The Monist* 105[4] [2022]: 521–40). Yet not all subversive genealogies, that is, not all genealogies that show that things could and/or should be otherwise, aim to open up a contingent space of possibilities (Amy Allen, "Dripping with Blood and Dirt from Head to Toe: Marx's Genealogy of Capitalism in *Capital*, Volume 1," *The Monist* 105[4] [2022]: 470–86).

8. Michel Foucault, "What Is Critique?," in *The Politics of Truth*, edited by S. Lotringer, translated by L. Hochroth (Los Angeles: Semiotext(e), 2007), 41–81; Foucault, *Security, Territory, Population: Lectures at the Collège de France, 1977–78*, edited by M. Senellart, translated by G. Burchell; series edited by A. I. Davidson (Basingstoke: Palgrave Macmillan, 2009). On this point, see Daniele Lorenzini, "From Counter-Conduct to Critical Attitude: Michel Foucault and the Art of Not Being Governed Quite So Much," *Foucault Studies* 21 (2016): 7–21.

9. Michel Foucault, *Discourse and Truth*, edited by H.-P. Fruchaud and D. Lorenzini; English edition by N. Luxon (Chicago: University of Chicago Press, 2019), 63.

10. Michel Foucault, "What Is Enlightenment?" (1984), in Foucault, *Ethics: Subjectivity and Truth*, vol. 1 of *Essential Works of Foucault (1954–84)*, edited by P. Rabinow, translated by R. Hurley et al.; series edited by P. Rabinow (New York: New Press, 1997), 315–16, emphasis added.

11. On this point, see Arnold I. Davidson, "In Praise of Counter-Conduct," *History of the Human Sciences* 24(4) (2011): 25–41.

12. Michel Foucault, "Polemics, Politics, and Problematizations: An Interview with Michel Foucault" (1984), in Foucault, *Ethics*, 114, emphasis added.

13. On disciplinary control and punishment, see Michel Foucault, *Discipline and Punish: The Birth of the Prison*, translated by A. Sheridan (New York: Vintage Books, 1995); Foucault, *The Punitive Society: Lectures at the Collège de France, 1972–73*, edited

by B. E. Harcourt, translated by G. Burchell; series edited by A. I. Davidson (Basingstoke: Palgrave Macmillan, 2015). On sexuality, see Michel Foucault, *The History of Sexuality,* vol. 1, *An Introduction,* translated by R. Hurley (New York: Pantheon Books, 1978); Foucault, *The History of Sexuality,* vol. 2, *The Use of Pleasure,* translated by R. Hurley (New York: Vintage Books, 1985); Foucault, *The History of Sexuality,* vol. 3, *The Care of the Self,* translated by R. Hurley (New York: Pantheon Books, 1986); Foucault, *The History of Sexuality,* vol. 4, *Confessions of the Flesh,* edited by F. Gros, translated by R. Hurley (New York: Pantheon Books, 2021). On truth and truth-telling, see Michel Foucault, *Lectures on the Will to Know: Lectures at the Collège de France, 1970–71,* edited by D. Defert, translated by G. Burchell; series edited by A. I. Davidson (Basingstoke: Palgrave Macmillan, 2013); Foucault, *Wrong-Doing, Truth-Telling: The Function of Avowal in Justice,* edited by F. Brion and B. E. Harcourt, translated by S. W. Sawyer (Chicago: University of Chicago Press, 2014).

14. See, e.g., Charles Taylor, "Foucault on Freedom and Truth," *Political Theory* 12(2) (1984): 152–83.

15. Nancy Fraser, "Foucault on Modern Power: Empirical Insights and Normative Confusions," *Praxis International* 3 (1981): 272–87; Fraser, "Michel Foucault: A 'Young Conservative'?," *Ethics* 96(1) (1985): 165–84; Jürgen Habermas, "Modernity versus Postmodernity," translated by S. Benhabib, *New German Critique* 22 (1981): 3–14; Habermas, *The Philosophical Discourse of Modernity: Twelve Lectures,* translated by F. Lawrence (Cambridge: Polity Press, 1990).

16. Rahel Jaeggi, "Rethinking Ideology," in *New Waves in Political Philosophy,* edited by B. de Bruin and C. F. Zurn (Basingstoke: Palgrave Macmillan, 2009), 73.

17. Contrary to what Habermas thinks: "[Foucault] contrasts his critique of power with the 'analysis of truth' in such a fashion that the former becomes deprived of the normative benchmarks that it would have to borrow from the latter" (Jürgen Habermas, "Taking Aim at the Heart of the Present," in *Foucault: A Critical Reader,* edited by D. C. Hoy [Malden, MA: Blackwell, 1986], 108 [trans. mod.]).

18. See Amy Allen, "Discourse, Power, and Subjectivation: The Foucault/Habermas Debate Reconsidered," *Philosophical Forum* 40 (2009): 1–28; James Schmidt, "Foucault, Habermas, and the Debate That Never Was," *Persistent Enlightenment,* 2013, https://persistentenlightenment.com/2013/07/17/debate1/.

19. Habermas, *The Philosophical Discourse of Modernity,* 275–76.

20. Habermas, *The Philosophical Discourse of Modernity,* 279.

21. Habermas, *The Philosophical Discourse of Modernity,* 279, 281. Earlier in the book, Habermas addresses an analogous criticism to Nietzsche, who "owes his concept of modernity, developed in terms of his theory of power, to an unmasking critique of reason that sets itself outside the horizon of reason" (96). For a response to Habermas's criticisms of Nietzsche, see Raymond Geuss, "Nietzsche and Genealogy," *European Journal of Philosophy* 2(3) (1994): 274–92; for a critical discussion of Habermas's reading of both Nietzsche and Foucault, see Thomas Biebricher, "Habermas, Foucault, and Nietzsche: A Double Misunderstanding," *Foucault Studies* 3 (2005): 1–26.

22. Habermas, *The Philosophical Discourse of Modernity,* 283.

23. Fraser, "Foucault on Modern Power," 283. See also Fraser, "Michel Foucault."

24. See, e.g., Thomas McCarthy, "The Critique of Impure Reason: Foucault and the Frankfurt School," in *Critique and Power: Recasting the Foucault/Habermas Debate,* edited by Michael Kelly (Cambridge, MA: MIT Press, 1994), 243–82.

25. See, e.g., Wendy Brown, "Genealogical Politics," in *The Later Foucault,* ed-

ited by J. Moss, 33–49 (London: Sage Publishing, 1998); James H. Tully, "To Think and Act Differently: Foucault's Four Reciprocal Objections to Habermas' Theory," in *Foucault contra Habermas: Recasting the Dialogue between Genealogy and Critical Theory*, edited by S. Ashenden and D. Owen (London: Sage Publishing, 1999), 90–142; Béatrice Han-Pile, "Foucault, Normativity, and Critique as a Practice of the Self," *Continental Philosophy Review* 49(1) (2016): 85–101; Mark G. E. Kelly, *For Foucault: Against Normative Political Theory* (New York: SUNY Press, 2018). For a recent defense of Foucauldian genealogy as a *"reparatively concerned* exercise" without normative ambitions, see Bonnie Sheehey, "Reparative Critique, Care, and the Normativity of Foucauldian Genealogy," *Angelaki: Journal of Theoretical Humanities* 25(5) (2020): 67–82.

26. See, e.g., Michael Kelly, "Foucault, Habermas, and the Self-Referentiality of Critique," in Kelly, *Critique and Power*, 365–400; Paul Patton, "Foucault's Subject of Power," *Political Theory Newsletter* 6(1) (1994): 60–71; Johanna Oksala, *Foucault on Freedom* (Cambridge: Cambridge University Press, 2005); Amy Allen, *The Politics of Our Selves: Power, Autonomy, and Gender in Contemporary Critical Theory* (New York: Columbia University Press, 2008); Allen, "Discourse, Power, and Subjectivation"; Tuomo Tiisala, "Overcoming 'the Present Limits of the Necessary': Foucault's Conception of a Critique," *Southern Journal of Philosophy* 55 (2017): 7–24; Giovanni Mascaretti, "Foucault, Normativity, and Freedom: A Reappraisal," *Foucault Studies* 27 (2019): 23–47.

27. See, e.g., Thomas R. Flynn, "Foucault and the Politics of Postmodernity," *Noûs* 23(2) (1989): 187–98; Bent Flyvbjerg, "Habermas and Foucault: Thinkers for Civil Society," *British Journal of Sociology* 49(2) (1998): 210–33; Samantha Ashenden and David Owen, "Introduction: Foucault, Habermas, and the Politics of Critique," in Ashenden and Owen, *Foucault contra Habermas*, 1–20; Judith Butler, "What Is Critique? An Essay on Foucault's Virtue," in *The Judith Butler Reader*, edited by S. Salih and J. Butler (Malden, MA: Blackwell, 2004), 302–22.

28. See, e.g., Axel Honneth, *The Critique of Power: Reflective Stages in a Critical Social Theory*, translated by K. Baynes (Cambridge, MA: MIT Press, 1991); Matthew King, "Clarifying the Foucault-Habermas Debate: Morality, Ethics, and 'Normative Foundations,'" *Philosophy & Social Criticism* 35(3) (2009): 287–314; Koopman, *Genealogy as Critique*.

29. Flyvbjerg ("Habermas and Foucault"), David Owen ("Orientation and Enlightenment: An Essay on Critique and Genealogy," in Ashenden and Owen, *Foucault contra Habermas*, 21–44), Martin Saar ("Genealogy and Subjectivity," *European Journal of Philosophy* 10[2] [2002]: 231–45), Mark Bevir ("What Is Genealogy?," *Journal of the Philosophy of History* 2[3] [2008]: 263–75), King ("Clarifying the Foucault-Habermas Debate"), and Srinivasan ("Genealogy, Epistemology, and Worldmaking") all make this point, in one form or another.

30. Hoy, "Genealogy, Phenomenology, Critical Theory," 282–83. See also Jesse J. Prinz, "History as Genealogy: Interrogating Liberalism through Philosophy's Past" (unpublished manuscript, 2018), 25.

31. See, respectively, Axel Honneth, "Reconstructive Social Critique with a Genealogical Reservation: On the Idea of Critique in the Frankfurt School," *Graduate Faculty Philosophy Journal* 22(2) (2001): 7; and Colin Koopman, "Genealogical Pragmatism: How History Matters for Foucault and Dewey," *Journal of the Philosophy of History* 5(3) (2011): 545.

32. Allen, *The End of Progress*, 195; David Owen, "Criticism and Captivity: On Genealogy and Critical Theory," *European Journal of Philosophy* 10(2) (2002): 216; Saar, "Genealogy and Subjectivity," 217. Without mentioning their genealogical dimension, Nancy Luxon ("Ethics and Subjectivity: Practices of Self-Governance in the Late Lectures of Michel Foucault," *Political Theory* 36[3] [2008]: 377–402; *Crisis of Authority: Politics, Trust, and Truth-Telling in Freud and Foucault* [Cambridge: Cambridge University Press, 2013], 187–96) defends the compelling idea that Foucault's analyses of ancient *parrhesia* offer a "model of ethical self-governance" that could still be helpful for us today. Even if this were true, however, the question remains of whether or not they are also able to instill a commitment to this model.

33. Koopman, *Genealogy as Critique*, 18, 60.

34. Koopman, "Genealogical Pragmatism," 533–46. On this point, see also Verena Erlenbusch-Anderson, *Genealogies of Terrorism: Revolution, State Violence, Empire* (New York: Columbia University Press, 2018), 163–68.

35. Koopman, *Genealogy as Critique*, 85, 164–65. See Foucault, "What Is Enlightenment?," 319, emphasis added: "The critical ontology of ourselves . . . must be conceived as an attitude, an *ethos*, a philosophical life in which the critique of what we are is at one and the same time the historical analysis of the limits imposed on us and *an experiment* with the possibility of going beyond them [*de leur franchissement possible*]." On this point, see also Hoy, "Genealogy, Phenomenology, Critical Theory," 294: "Genealogy's ability to unmask power relations is . . . an effective means for writing the kind of critical history that can lead to experimentation and transformation."

36. Koopman claims that problematization also characterizes Foucault's philosophical project *as a whole*: "The primary task of philosophy is what [Foucault] called 'problematization,' which involves the critical-historical work of clarifying the problems at the heart of practices and projects we otherwise would take as unproblematic" ("Genealogical Pragmatism," 533–34). Even though it does constitute a crucial aspect of Foucault's work, I would like to suggest that problematization is merely a preparatory step toward his conception of the main goal of philosophy, not the primary task per se, namely, to instill in his audience a sense of ethico-political commitment to the concrete elaboration of alternate ways of thinking and being.

37. See Foucault, "What Is Critique?," 47–50.

38. Foucault, "What Is Critique?," 44, 67.

39. Foucault, "What Is Critique?," 47 (trans. mod.), 67.

40. Foucault, *Discourse and Truth*, 46.

41. Foucault, *Discourse and Truth*, 43.

42. Michel Foucault, *The Government of Self and Others: Lectures at the Collège de France, 1982–83*, edited by F. Gros, translated by G. Burchell; series edited by A. I. Davidson (Basingstoke: Palgrave Macmillan, 2010), 350; Foucault, *Discourse and Truth*, 63. Foucault no doubt had methodological reasons to consistently refer to "our" society—a tendency for which he has rightfully been criticized (see, e.g., Ann Laura Stoler, *Race and the Education of Desire: Foucault's "History of Sexuality" and the Colonial Order of Things* [Durham, NC: Duke University Press, 1996]). Yet, as Martin Saar aptly argues, "all genealogies have in common a structural reflexivity, a self-implication in the fact that whoever enacts a genealogical criticism does this by criticizing aspects and elements . . . of his or her own culture or background. . . . Genealogical criticism is therefore always self-criticism" ("Genealogy and Subjectivity," 236).

43. With the exception of Andreas Folkers, who, however, reduces Foucault's gene-

alogy of critique to its mere problematizing dimension and thus misses its specificity: "Genealogy is not only a means of exercising critique, but also a way to reflect on critique," that is, a "critique of critique" that "contributes to and expands the current problematizations of critique" ("Daring the Truth: Foucault, Parrhesia, and the Genealogy of Critique," *Theory, Culture & Society* 33[1] [2016]: 4, 18).

44. Foucault, *Security, Territory, Population*, 201.

45. Foucault, *The History of Sexuality*, vol. 4, *Confessions of the Flesh*, 147; Peter Brown, "The Notion of Virginity in the Early Church," in *Christian Spirituality: Origins to the Twelfth Century*, edited by B. McGinn, J. Meyendorff, and J. Leclercq (New York: Crossroad, 1985), 430. On this point, see Daniele Lorenzini, "The Emergence of Desire: Notes toward a Political History of the Will," *Critical Inquiry* 45(2) (2019): 448–70. On Foucault's genealogy of the subject of desire and its contemporary political implications, see Miguel de Beistegui, *The Government of Desire: A Genealogy of the Liberal Subject* (Chicago: University of Chicago Press, 2018).

46. Foucault, *Security, Territory, Population*, 204–14. See also Foucault, "What Is Critique?," 45–47; Michel Foucault, *The Courage of Truth: Lectures at the Collège de France, 1983–84*, edited by F. Gros, translated by G. Burchell; series edited by A. I. Davidson (Basingstoke: Palgrave Macmillan, 2011), 182–83.

47. Michel Foucault, *Abnormal: Lectures at the Collège de France, 1974–75*, edited by V. Marchetti and A. Salomoni, translated by G. Burchell; series edited by A. I. Davidson (London: Verso, 2003), 212–27. On this point, see Mark D. Jordan, *Convulsing Bodies: Religion and Resistance in Foucault* (Stanford, CA: Stanford University Press, 2014).

48. Michel Foucault, *Penal Theories and Institutions: Lectures at the Collège de France, 1971–72*, edited by B. E. Harcourt, translated by G. Burchell; series edited by A. I. Davidson (Basingstoke: Palgrave Macmillan, 2019).

49. Michel Foucault, *Psychiatric Power: Lectures at the Collège de France, 1973–74*, edited by J. Lagrange, translated by G. Burchell; series edited by A. I. Davidson (Basingstoke: Palgrave Macmillan, 2006).

50. Foucault, *The Courage of Truth*, 183–89.

51. Michel Foucault, "Introduction," in *Herculine Barbin: Being the Recently Discovered Memoirs of a Nineteenth-Century French Hermaphrodite*, translated by R. McDougall (New York: Vintage Books, 1980), vii, xiii. For a detailed analysis of genealogy in Foucault's *Herculine Barbin*, see Colin Koopman, "Critique without Judgment in Political Theory: Politicization in Foucault's Historical Genealogy of Herculine Barbin," *Contemporary Political Theory* 18(4) (2018): 477–97.

52. Michel Foucault, "Un plaisir si simple" (1979), in Foucault, *Dits et écrits II, 1976–88*, edited by D. Defert and F. Ewald (Paris: Gallimard, 2001), 777–79; Foucault, "Conversation avec Werner Schroeter" (1982), in Foucault, *Dits et écrits II*, 1070–79. On this point, see Davidson, "In Praise of Counter-Conduct," 38. For additional examples of strategies of resistance to biopolitical regulation, see Banu Bargu, *Starve and Immolate: The Politics of Human Weapons* (New York: Columbia University Press, 2014), 61–62.

53. See, e.g., Michel Foucault, *About the Beginning of the Hermeneutics of the Self: Lectures at Dartmouth College, 1980*, edited by H.-P. Fruchaud and D. Lorenzini (Chicago: University of Chicago Press, 2015), 21; Foucault, *The Government of Self and Others*, 42; Foucault, *The Courage of Truth*, 2–3.

54. Étienne Balibar interprets some of these critical attitudes squarely as parrhe-siastic scenes connected to each other by a certain "family resemblance" ("Sulle par-rhèsia(e) di Foucault," *materiali foucaultiani* 11-12 [2017]: 66-67).

55. Foucault, *The History of Sexuality*, vol. 1, *An Introduction*, 95.

56. Foucault, *The History of Sexuality*, vol. 1, *An Introduction*, 95 (trans. mod.). On the connection between the subversion of values and the debunking of the self, see Martin Saar, "Understanding Genealogy: History, Power, and the Self," *Journal of the Philosophy of History* 2(3) (2008): 295-314; and Prinz, "History as Genealogy."

57. Michel Foucault, "Politics and Ethics: An Interview," translated by C. Porter, in *The Foucault Reader*, edited by P. Rabinow (New York: Pantheon Books, 1984), 374.

58. See, e.g., Kelly, "Foucault, Habermas, and the Self-Referentiality of Critique"; James Schmidt and Thomas E. Wartenberg, "Foucault's Enlightenment: Critique, Revolution, and the Fashioning of the Self," in Kelly, *Critique and Power*, 283-314.

59. Foucault, "What Is Enlightenment?," 315-16, emphasis added. A few lines be-low, Foucault adds that, in order not to "settle for the affirmation or the empty dream of freedom," the historico-critical attitude he is advocating "must also be an experi-mental one," that is, it must, "on the one hand, open up a realm of historical inquiry and, on the other, put itself to the test of reality, of contemporary reality, both to grasp *the points where change is possible and desirable*, and to determine the precise form this change should take" (316, emphasis added). On this point, see also Michel Foucault, "Structuralism and Post-Structuralism" (1983), in Foucault, *Aesthetics, Method, and Epistemology*, vol. 2 of *Essential Works of Foucault (1954-84)*, edited by J. D. Faubion, translated by R. Hurley et al.; series edited by P. Rabinow (New York: New Press, 1998), 449-50.

60. Importantly, this genealogy is not vindicatory, because it (also) shows that critique, far from being universal and ahistorical, cannot exist unless embodied in a series of concrete and historically situated discourses and practices. The very na-ture of Foucauldian genealogy entails that nothing is in principle exempt from it: freedom, autonomy, and critique itself are all genealogizable. Thus, the genealogy of the critical attitude possesses a *subversive* dimension, insofar as it does not "search for some 'immobile form' [of critique] that has developed throughout history," but reveals that "there is no essence or original unity [of critique] to be discovered" (Da-vidson, "Archaeology, Genealogy, Ethics," in Hoy, *Foucault*, 224). Consequently, it also encompasses a *problematizing* dimension, for it is a "critique of critique" (Amy Allen, "Foucault and Enlightenment: A Critical Reappraisal," *Constellations* 10[2] [2003]: 180-98; Folkers, "Daring the Truth"), or a "metacritique" (Sabina Vaccarino Bremner, "Anthropology as Critique: Foucault, Kant, and the Metacritical Tradition," *British Journal for the History of Philosophy* 28[2] [2020]: 336-58), that is, a critical investigation of the conditions of possibility of the practical exercise of the concept of critique itself.

61. Michel Foucault, "On the Genealogy of Ethics: An Overview of Work in Pro-gress" (1983), in Foucault, *Ethics*, 256, emphasis added. See also Foucault, "The Ethics of the Concern for Self as a Practice of Freedom" (1984), in Foucault, *Ethics*, 291-92. In the *Genealogy*, Nietzsche also claims that (Christian) morality is dangerous, not harm-ful (Friedrich Nietzsche, *On the Genealogy of Morality*, edited by K. Ansell-Pearson, translated by C. Diethe [Cambridge: Cambridge University Press, 1997], Preface, §6, p. 8). On this point, see Bernard Reginster, "What Is Nietzsche's Genealogical Cri-

tique of Morality?," *Inquiry: An Interdisciplinary Journal of Philosophy*, 2020, https://doi.org/10.1080/0020174X.2020.1762727, 20–22.

62. Michel Foucault, *Remarks on Marx: Conversations with Duccio Trombadori*, translated by R. J. Goldstein and J. Cascaito (New York: Semiotext(e), 1991), 174 (trans. mod.).

63. Foucault, *Remarks on Marx*, 174 (trans. mod.).

64. Walter Benjamin, "On the Concept of History" and "Paralipomena to 'On the Concept of History'" (1942), in *Selected Writings*, vol. 4, *1938–40*, edited by H. Eiland and M.W. Jennings (Cambridge, MA: Harvard University Press, 2006), 396.

65. On this point, see Michael Löwy, *Walter Benjamin, avertissement d'incendie: Une lecture des thèses "Sur le concept d'histoire"* (Paris: Éditions de l'éclat, 2018), 158.

66. Benjamin, "On the Concept of History" and "Paralipomena," 391, 394–95, 396. For a recent, poignant critique of the notion of historical progress inspired (at least in part) by Benjamin's insights, see Joan Wallach Scott, *On the Judgment of History* (New York: Columbia University Press, 2020).

67. Michel Foucault, "La torture, c'est la raison" (1977), in Foucault, *Dits et écrits II*, 390–91.

68. Foucault, "La torture, c'est la raison," 391.

69. Benjamin, "On the Concept of History" and "Paralipomena," 390. Benjamin's conception of the proletarian revolution is nevertheless different from Marx's. Indeed, for him, such a revolution can only "redeem" the past by *interrupting* historical evolution rather than by *completing* it: "Classless society is not the final goal of historical progress but its frequently miscarried, ultimately [*endlich*] achieved interruption" (402).

70. On this point, see Daniele Lorenzini, "Benjamin/Foucault: Histoire, discontinuité, événement," *Phantasia* 7 (2018), https://popups.uliege.be/0774-7136/index.php?id=903.

71. Eli Friedlander, *Walter Benjamin: A Philosophical Portrait* (Cambridge, MA: Harvard University Press, 2012), 168; Michel Foucault, "The Lives of Infamous Men" (1977), translated by P. Foss and M. Morris, in *Power, Truth, Strategy*, edited by M. Morris and P. Patton (Sydney: Feral Publications, 1979), 76–91.

72. For one of Foucault's clearest criticisms of the idea of the "ideology of the return" and of "a historicism that calls on the past to resolve the questions of the present," see Michel Foucault, "Space, Knowledge, and Power" (1982), in Foucault, *Power*, vol. 3 of *Essential Works of Foucault (1954–84)*, edited by J. D. Faubion, translated by R. Hurley et al.; series edited by P. Rabinow (New York: New Press, 2000), 359.

73. See, e.g., Michel Foucault, "A Preface to Transgression" (1963), in Foucault, *Language, Counter-Memory, Practice: Selected Essays and Interviews*, edited by D. F. Bouchard, translated by D. F. Bouchard and S. Simon (Ithaca, NY: Cornell University Press, 1977), 29–52; Foucault, *Remarks on Marx*, 32–42.

74. Hilary Putnam, "Literature, Science, and Reflection," *New Literary History* 7(3) (1976): 483–91.

75. See Foucault, "The Lives of Infamous Men," 79. This is why Zachary Simpson's reading of *parrhesia* as "the constructive telling of fictions to both oneself and others that would produce the effects of truth" ("The Truths We Tell Ourselves: Foucault on Parrhesia," *Foucault Studies* 13 [2012]: 100) misses the point of Foucault's genealogy of truth-telling and the critical attitude.

76. See Butler, "What Is Critique?."

77. Foucault, "Polemics, Politics, and Problematizations," 114–15 (trans. mod.), emphasis added. On this point, see Judith Revel, *Foucault avec Merleau-Ponty: Ontologie politique, présentisme et histoire* (Paris: Vrin, 2015), 53.

78. David Couzens Hoy, "Genealogy, Phenomenology, Critical Theory," *Journal of the Philosophy of History* 2(3) (2008): 294.

79. José Medina hints at this crucial aspect of Foucauldian genealogy when he describes it as a "guerrilla pluralism" that allows us to "become part of multiple communities of resistance—past, present, and future ones—which, without being unified, intersect and overlap in complex ways, creating frictions of all sorts" ("Toward a Foucauldian Epistemology of Resistance: Counter-Memory, Epistemic Friction, and *Guerrilla* Pluralism," *Foucault Studies* 12 [2011]: 12, 29). What he does not seem to realize, however, is that the we-making dimension of Foucauldian genealogy, along with the distinction between games and regimes of truth I addressed in chapter 2, is sufficient to guarantee that our epistemic, ethical, and political practices do not dissolve into chaos (Medina, *The Epistemology of Resistance: Gender and Racial Oppression, Epistemic Injustice, and Resistant Imaginations* [Oxford: Oxford University Press, 2013], 297). On this topic, see Daniele Lorenzini, "Reason versus Power: Genealogy, Critique, and Epistemic Injustice," *The Monist* 105(4) (2022): 541–57.

80. Jaeggi, "Rethinking Ideology," 73; Koopman "Genealogical Pragmatism," 561.

81. On this point, see Robert Guay, "Genealogy as Immanent Critique: Working from the Inside," in *The Edinburgh Critical History of Nineteenth-Century Philosophy*, edited by A. Stone (Edinburgh: Edinburgh University Press, 2011), 168–86.

82. Foucault, *Remarks on Marx*, 40–41. On Foucault's engagement in the GIP, see Perry Zurn and Andrew Dilts, eds., *Active Intolerance: Michel Foucault, the Prisons Information Group, and the Future of Abolition* (Basingstoke: Palgrave Macmillan, 2016); Kevin Thompson and Perry Zurn, *Intolerable: Writings from Michel Foucault and the Prisons Information Group (1970–80)*, translated by P. Zurn and E. Beranek (Minneapolis: University of Minnesota Press, 2021).

83. Foucault, *Remarks on Marx*, 36 (trans. mod.).

84. Michel Foucault, "Foucault étudie la raison d'État" (1979), in Foucault, *Dits et écrits II*, 805.

85. Foucault, *Remarks on Marx*, 38–39 (trans. mod.), 42.

86. Erlenbusch-Anderson, *Genealogies of Terrorism*, 178. Recent examples of Foucauldian critical inquiries that derive their normativity from the practices of those who are concretely fighting include Ladelle McWhorter, *Bodies and Pleasures: Foucault and the Politics of Sexual Normalization* (Bloomington: Indiana University Press, 1999); and Erlenbusch-Anderson, *Genealogies of Terrorism*.

87. Foucault, "On the Genealogy of Ethics," 256.

88. On this point, see Saar, "Genealogy and Subjectivity," 234.

89. Actually, the genealogy of the critical attitude shows us that, in a sense, the question "Why resist?" is not altogether relevant, because resistance is *always already in place*: people are already resisting, and have been resisting throughout history, against the governmental apparatuses and regimes of truth in which they are enmeshed.

90. See, e.g., Foucault, "Structuralism and Post-Structuralism," 450; Foucault, *About the Beginning of the Hermeneutics of the Self*, 137–38.

Conclusion

1. Albeit from a different perspective, Philip Kitcher addresses the same dilemma and, after "scrutinizing both the claim that science has enlightened us and that that is a wonderful thing, and the counterclaim that the 'progress' of science is antithetical to human well-being," he persuasively concludes that "both views are unwarranted" and that we need to "elaborate and defend the integration of *the value of knowledge* with *moral and political values*" (*Science, Truth, and Democracy* [Oxford: Oxford University Press, 2001], xiii, emphasis added).

2. See Daniele Lorenzini and Martina Tazzioli, "Critique without Ontology: Genealogy, Collective Subjects, and the Deadlocks of Evidence," *Radical Philosophy* 207 (2020): 27-39.

3. On the importance of developing a "non-foundational understanding of truth" that would allow us to "fight the rise of untruth in politics without either succumbing to a naïve positivism or ceding ground to science denialism," see Frieder Vogelmann, "Lonely and Beyond Truth? Two Objections to Bernard Harcourt's *Critique & Praxis*," *British Journal of Sociology* 72(3) (2021): 855.

4. Michel Foucault, *About the Beginning of the Hermeneutics of the Self: Lectures at Dartmouth College, 1980*, edited by H.-P. Fruchaud and D. Lorenzini (Chicago: University of Chicago Press, 2015), 127.

5. This is the main insight that Foucault shares with state of nature genealogists, including Craig, Williams, and Fricker, who justify the emergence of shared games of truth (namely, those focused on testimonial practices and information pooling) by relying on the definition of a series of basic human needs. On this point, see Matthieu Queloz, *The Practical Origins of Ideas: Genealogy as Conceptual Reverse-Engineering* (Oxford: Oxford University Press, 2021).

6. See Michel Foucault, "Truth and Power" (1977), in Foucault, *Power*, vol. 3 of *Essential Works of Foucault (1954-84)*, edited by J. D. Faubion, translated by R. Hurley et al.; series edited by P. Rabinow (New York: New Press, 2000), 133: "The political question, to sum up, is not error, illusion, alienated consciousness, or ideology; it is truth itself. Hence the importance of Nietzsche."

7. Colin Koopman, "Critique in Truth: Bernard Harcourt's *Critique & Practice*," *Foucault Studies* 30 (2021): 110.

8. This argument draws from Amy Allen's convincing defense of contextualism about normative justification against the threat of first-order moral relativism—a defense that relies precisely on the distinction between metanormative or second-order and substantive or first-order normative levels, which according to her is implicit "in the work of Butler, Adorno, and Foucault" (*The End of Progress: Decolonizing the Normative Foundations of Critical Theory* [New York: Columbia University Press, 2016], 212).

9. See Miranda Fricker, *Epistemic Injustice: Power and the Ethics of Knowing* (Oxford: Oxford University Press, 2007), 3.

10. Bernard E. Harcourt, *Critique and Praxis: A Radical Critical Philosophy of Illusions, Values, and Action* (New York: Columbia University Press, 2020), 187.

11. Harcourt, *Critique and Praxis*, 184-85.

12. Michel Foucault, "What Is Critique?," in *The Politics of Truth*, edited by S. Lotringer, translated by L. Hochroth (Los Angeles: Semiotext(e), 2007), 45.

13. As Habermas does in his theory of communicative action (see *The Theory of*

Communicative Action, vol. 1, *Reason and the Rationalization to Society*, translated by T. McCarthy [Boston: Beacon Press, 1984], 273–337).

14. Michel Foucault, "Politics and Ethics: An Interview," translated by C. Porter, in *The Foucault Reader*, edited by P. Rabinow, 373–80 (New York: Pantheon Books, 1984), 374 (trans. mod.).

15. Amy Allen, *The Politics of Our Selves: Power, Autonomy, and Gender in Contemporary Critical Theory* (New York: Columbia University Press, 2008), 11.

16. Wendy Brown, *States of Injury: Power and Freedom in Late Modernity* (Princeton, NJ: Princeton University Press, 1995), 64, emphasis added. For an alternate view, see Miguel de Beistegui, *The Government of Desire: A Genealogy of the Liberal Subject* (Chicago: University of Chicago Press, 2018); Daniele Lorenzini, "The Emergence of Desire: Notes toward a Political History of the Will," *Critical Inquiry* 45(2) (2019): 448–70.

17. Foucault, "What Is Critique?," 47 (trans. mod.).

18. Michel Foucault, *On the Government of the Living: Lectures at the Collège de France, 1979–80*, edited by M. Senellart, translated by G. Burchell; series edited by A. I. Davidson (Basingstoke: Palgrave Macmillan, 2014), 78–79 (trans. mod.).

Bibliography

Allen, Amy. "Foucault and Enlightenment: A Critical Reappraisal." *Constellations* 10(2) (2003): 180–98.

———. *The Politics of Our Selves: Power, Autonomy, and Gender in Contemporary Critical Theory.* New York: Columbia University Press, 2008.

———. "Discourse, Power, and Subjectivation: The Foucault/Habermas Debate Reconsidered." *Philosophical Forum* 40 (2009): 1–28.

———. *The End of Progress: Decolonizing the Normative Foundations of Critical Theory.* New York: Columbia University Press, 2016.

———. "Power/Knowledge/Resistance: Foucault and Epistemic Injustice." In *The Routledge Handbook of Epistemic Injustice,* edited by I. J. Kidd, J. Medina, and G. Pohlhaus, Jr., 187–94. New York: Routledge, 2017.

———. "Dripping with Blood and Dirt from Head to Toe: Marx's Genealogy of Capitalism in *Capital,* Volume 1." *The Monist* 105(4) (2022): 470–86.

Ambroise, Bruno. "From J. L. Austin to Charles Travis: A Pragmatic Account of Truth?" *HAL,* December 10, 2013. https://halshs.archives-ouvertes.fr/halshs -00916223.

American Psychiatric Association. *Diagnostic and Statistical Manual of Mental Disorders: Fifth Edition (DSM-5).* Washington, DC: American Psychiatric Publishing, 2013.

Andersen, Kurt. "How America Lost Its Mind." *The Atlantic,* December 28, 2017. https://www.theatlantic.com/magazine/archive/2017/09/how-america-lost -its-mind/534231/.

Aristotle. *Nicomachean Ethics.* Translated by W. D. Ross, revised by J. O. Urmson. In *The Complete Works of Aristotle: The Revised Oxford Translation,* edited by J. Barnes, 2:1729–1867. Princeton, NJ: Princeton University Press, 1984.

Ashenden, Samantha, and David Owen, eds. *Foucault contra Habermas: Recasting the Dialogue between Genealogy and Critical Theory.* London: Sage Publishing, 1999.

———. "Introduction: Foucault, Habermas, and the Politics of Critique." In Ashenden and Owen, *Foucault contra Habermas,* 1–20.

Austin, John Langshaw. "Truth." *Proceedings of the Aristotelian Society,* suppl. vol. 24 (1950): 111–28.

———. "Unfair to Facts" (1954). In Austin, *Philosophical Papers,* 154–74.

———. "Performative Utterances" (1956). In Austin, *Philosophical Papers,* 233–52.

———. *How to Do Things with Words.* Edited by J. O. Urmson and M. Sbisà. Cambridge, MA: Harvard University Press, 1975. Originally published posthumously in 1962.

———. *Philosophical Papers.* Edited by J. O. Urmson and G. J. Warnock. Oxford: Oxford University Press, 1979.

Ayer, Alfred Jules. *Language, Truth, and Logic.* London: Gollancz, 1936.

Badiou, Alain, et al. "Philosophie et vérité" (1965). In Foucault, *Dits et écrits I, 1954–75,* 476–92.

Balibar, Étienne. "'Being in the True?' Science and Truth in the Philosophy of Georges Canguilhem" (1993). Translated by A. Fan. *Décalages* 2(2) (2016). https://core.ac.uk/download/pdf/215496915.pdf.

———. "Sulle *parrhèsia(e)* di Foucault." *materiali foucaultiani* 11–12 (2017): 63–81.

Balot, Ryan K. "Free Speech, Courage, and Democratic Deliberation." In *Free Speech in Classical Antiquity,* edited by I. Sluiter and R. M. Rosen, 233–59. Leiden and Boston: Brill, 2004.

Bang, Henrik Paul. *Foucault's Political Challenge: From Hegemony to Truth.* Basingstoke: Palgrave Macmillan, 2015.

Bargu, Banu. *Starve and Immolate: The Politics of Human Weapons.* New York: Columbia University Press, 2014.

Bauer, Nancy. "How to Do Things with Pornography." In *Reading Cavell,* edited by A. Crary and S. Shieh, 68–97. New York: Routledge, 2006.

Beistegui, Miguel de. "The Subject of Truth: On Foucault's *Lectures on the Will to Know.*" *Quadranti: Rivista Internazionale di Filosofia Contemporanea* 2(1) (2014): 80–99.

———. *The Government of Desire: A Genealogy of the Liberal Subject.* Chicago: University of Chicago Press, 2018.

Benjamin, Walter. "On the Concept of History" and "Paralipomena to 'On the Concept of History'" (1942). In *Selected Writings,* vol. 4, *1938–40,* edited by H. Eiland and M.W. Jennings, 389–411. Cambridge, MA: Harvard University Press, 2006.

Bennington, Geoffrey. "The Truth about *Parrhesia*: Philosophy, Rhetoric, and Politics in Late Foucault." In *Foucault/Derrida Fifty Years Later: The Futures of Genealogy, Deconstruction, and Politics,* edited by O. Custer, P. Deutscher, and S. Haddad, 205–20. New York: Columbia University Press, 2016.

Benoist, Jocelyn. "Des actes de langage à l'inventaire des énoncés." *Archives de Philosophie* 79(1) (2016): 55–78.

Bevir, Mark. 2008. "What Is Genealogy?" *Journal of the Philosophy of History* 2(3) (2008): 263–75.

Biebricher, Thomas. 2005. "Habermas, Foucault, and Nietzsche: A Double Misunderstanding." *Foucault Studies* 3 (2005): 1–26.

Blanco, Azucena G. "Foucault on Raymond Roussel: The Extralinguistic outside of Literature." *Theory, Culture & Society,* 2020. https://doi.org/10.1177/02632764 20950458.

———. "Towards a Politics of Literature in Late Foucault: *Parrhesia* and Mimesis." *Revue Internationale de Philosophie* 292 (2020): 29–38.

Bourdieu, Pierre. "Authorized Language: The Social Conditions for the Effectiveness of Ritual Discourse" (1975). In Bourdieu, *Language and Symbolic Power,* 107–16.

———. "Price Formation and the Anticipation of Profits" (1980). In Bourdieu, *Language and Symbolic Power*, 66–89.

———. *Language and Symbolic Power*. Edited by J. B. Thompson. Translated by G. Raymond and M. Adamson. Cambridge: Polity Press, 1991.

Bouveresse, Jacques. *Nietzsche contre Foucault: Sur la vérité, la connaissance et le pouvoir*. Marseille: Agone, 2016.

Brown, Peter. "The Notion of Virginity in the Early Church." In *Christian Spirituality: Origins to the Twelfth Century*, edited by B. McGinn, J. Meyendorff, and J. Leclercq, 427–33. New York: Crossroad, 1985.

Brown, Wendy. *States of Injury: Power and Freedom in Late Modernity*. Princeton, NJ: Princeton University Press, 1995.

———. "Genealogical Politics." In *The Later Foucault*, edited by J. Moss, 33–49. London: Sage Publishing, 1998.

Buekens, Filip. "A Truth-Minimalist Reading of Foucault." *Le Foucaldien* 7(1) (2021). https://doi.org/10.16995/lefou.7989.

Butler, Judith. *Excitable Speech: A Politics of the Performative*. New York: Routledge, 1997.

———. *The Psychic Life of Power: Theories in Subjection*. Stanford, CA: Stanford University Press, 1997.

———. "What Is Critique? An Essay on Foucault's Virtue." In *The Judith Butler Reader*, edited by S. Salih and J. Butler, 302–22. Malden, MA: Blackwell, 2004.

———. *Giving an Account of Oneself*. New York: Fordham University Press, 2005.

———. "Wrong-Doing, Truth-Telling: The Case of Sexual Avowal." In *Foucault and the Making of Subjects*, edited by L. Cremonesi et al., 77–93. London: Rowman & Littlefield, 2016.

Canguilhem, Georges. "De la science et de la contre-science." In *Hommage à Jean Hyppolite*, edited by S. Bachelard et al., 173–80. Paris: PUF, 1971.

Carrette, Jeremy. "'Spiritual Gymnastics': Reflections on Michel Foucault's *On the Government of the Living* 1980 Collège de France Lectures." *Foucault Studies* 20 (2015): 277–90.

Cassam, Quassim. "Bullshit, Post-Truth, and Propaganda." In *Political Epistemology*, edited by E. Edenberg and M. Hannon, 49–63. Oxford: Oxford University Press, 2021.

Cavell, Stanley. *Pursuits of Happiness: The Hollywood Comedy of Remarriage*. Cambridge, MA: Harvard University Press, 1981.

———. *In Quest of the Ordinary: Lines of Skepticism and Romanticism*. Chicago: University of Chicago Press, 1988.

———. *Conditions Handsome and Unhandsome: The Constitution of Emersonian Perfectionism*. Chicago: University of Chicago Press, 1991.

———. *A Pitch of Philosophy: Autobiographical Exercises*. Cambridge, MA: Harvard University Press, 1994.

———. *Cities of Words: Pedagogical Letters on a Register of the Moral Life*. Cambridge, MA: Harvard University Press, 2004.

———. *Philosophy the Day after Tomorrow*. Cambridge, MA: Harvard University Press, 2005.

———. *This New Yet Unapproachable America: Lectures after Emerson after Wittgenstein*. Chicago: University of Chicago Press, 2013.

Certeau, Michel de. *The Capture of Speech and Other Political Writings*. Edited by

L. Giard. Translated by T. Conley. Minneapolis: University of Minnesota Press, 1997. Originally published in 1994.

Chevallier, Philippe. *Michel Foucault et le christianisme*. Lyon: ENS Éditions, 2011.

———. "Vers l'éthique: La notion de 'régime de vérité' dans le cours *Du gouvernement des vivants*." In Lorenzini, Revel, and Sforzini, *Michel Foucault*, 53–65.

Chomsky, Noam, and Michel Foucault. "Human Nature: Justice vs. Power." In *The Chomsky-Foucault Debate: On Human Nature*, 1–67. New York: New Press, 1971.

Craig, Edward. *Knowledge and the State of Nature: An Essay in Conceptual Synthesis*. Oxford: Clarendon Press, 1990.

Cremonesi, Laura. *Foucault e il mondo antico: Spunti per una critica dell'attualità*. Pisa: ETS, 2008.

Davidson, Arnold I. "Archaeology, Genealogy, Ethics." In Hoy, *Foucault*, 221–33.

———. "Structures and Strategies of Discourse: Remarks towards a History of Foucault's Philosophy of Language." In *Foucault and His Interlocutors*, edited by A. I. Davidson, 1–17. Chicago: University of Chicago Press, 1997.

———. *The Emergence of Sexuality: Historical Epistemology and the Formation of Concepts*. Cambridge, MA: Harvard University Press, 2001.

———. "Introduction." In Foucault, *"Society Must Be Defended,"* xv–xxiii.

———. "Dall'assoggettamento alla soggettivazione: Michel Foucault e la storia della sessualità." *aut aut* 331 (2006): 3–10.

———. "In Praise of Counter-Conduct." *History of the Human Sciences* 24(4) (2011): 25–41.

Defert, Daniel. "Course Context." In Foucault, *Lectures on the Will to Know*, 262–86.

Dennett, Daniel. "I Begrudge Every Hour I Have to Spend Worrying about Politics: Interview with Carole Cadwalladr." *The Guardian*, February 12, 2017. https://www.theguardian.com/science/2017/feb/12/daniel-dennett-politics-bacteria-bach-back-dawkins-trump-interview.

Derrida, Jacques. "Signature Event Context." In *Margins of Philosophy*, translated by A. Bass, 307–30. Chicago: University of Chicago Press, 1982. Originally published in 1972.

Descartes, René. *A Discourse on the Method*. Translated by I. Maclean. Oxford: Oxford University Press, 2006. Originally published in 1637.

Di Gesu, Andrea. "The Cynic Scandal: Parrhesia, Community, and Democracy." *Theory, Culture & Society* 39(3) (2022): 169–86.

Dio Chrysostom. "The Eighth Discourse: Diogenes or On Virtue." Translated by J. W. Cohoon. In *Dio Chrysostom*, 1:376–99. Cambridge, MA: Harvard University Press, 1932.

———. "The Fourth Discourse on Kingship." Translated by J. W. Cohoon. In *Dio Chrysostom*, 1:169–233. Cambridge, MA: Harvard University Press, 1932.

Diogenes Laertius. *Lives of Eminent Philosophers*. Translated by R. D. Hicks. Vol. 2. London and New York: William Heinemann and G.P. Putnam's Sons, 1925.

Ducrot, Oswald. *Dire et ne pas dire: Principes de sémantique linguistique*. Paris: Hermann, 1991. Originally published in 1972.

Dudley, Donald R. *A History of Cynicism: From Diogenes to the 6th Century A.D.* London: Bristol Classical Press, 1937.

Dutilh Novaes, Catarina. "Conceptual Genealogy for Analytic Philosophy." In *Beyond the Analytic-Continental Divide: Pluralist Philosophy in the Twenty-First*

Century, edited by J. A. Bell, A. Cutrofello, and P. M. Livingston, 75–110. New York: Routledge, 2015.

———. "Carnap Meets Foucault: Conceptual Engineering and Genealogical Investigations." *Inquiry: An Interdisciplinary Journal of Philosophy*, 2020. https://doi.org/10.1080/0020174X.2020.1860122.

Dyrberg, Torben B. *Foucault on the Politics of* Parrhesia. Basingstoke: Palgrave Macmillan, 2014.

———. "Foucault on *Parrhesia*: The Autonomy of Politics and Democracy." *Political Theory* 44(2) (2016): 265–88.

Elden, Stuart. *Foucault's Last Decade*. Cambridge: Polity Press, 2016.

———. *Foucault: The Birth of Power*. Cambridge: Polity Press, 2017.

———. "From Dynastics to Genealogy." *Abolition Democracy 13/13*, 2021. http://blogs.law.columbia.edu/abolition1313/stuart-elden-from-dynastics-to-genealogy/.

Engel, Pascal. "Michel Foucault: Vérité, connaissance et éthique." In *Michel Foucault*, edited by P. Artières et al., 319–26. Paris: L'Herne, 2011.

Erlenbusch-Anderson, Verena. *Genealogies of Terrorism: Revolution, State Violence, Empire*. New York: Columbia University Press, 2018.

———. "Historicizing White Supremacist Terrorism with Ida B. Wells." *Political Theory* 50(2) (2022): 275–304.

Fanon, Frantz. *Decolonizing Madness: The Psychiatric Writings of Frantz Fanon*. Edited by N. Gibson. Translated by L. Damon. Basingstoke: Palgrave Macmillan, 2014.

Fantl, Jeremy, and Matthew McGrath. "On Pragmatic Encroachment in Epistemology." *Philosophy and Phenomenological Research* 75(3) (2007): 558–89.

Ferrando, Stefania. *Michel Foucault, la politica presa a rovescio: La pratica antica della verità nei corsi al Collège de France*. Milan: Franco Angeli, 2012.

Feyerabend, Paul. *Against Method: Outline of an Anarchist Theory of Knowledge*. London: New Left Books, 1975.

Flynn, Thomas R. "Foucault as Parrhesiast: His Last Course at the Collège de France (1984)." *Philosophy and Social Criticism* 12(2–3) (1987): 213–29.

———. "Foucault and the Politics of Postmodernity." *Noûs* 23(2) (1989): 187–98.

Flyvbjerg, Bent. "Habermas and Foucault: Thinkers for Civil Society." *British Journal of Sociology* 49(2) (1998): 210–33.

Folkers, Andreas. "Daring the Truth: Foucault, Parrhesia, and the Genealogy of Critique." *Theory, Culture & Society* 33(1) (2016): 3–28.

Forguson, Lynd W. "Locutionary and Illocutionary Acts." In *Essays on J. L. Austin*, edited by I. Berlin et al., 160–86. Oxford: Oxford University Press, 1973.

Foucault, Michel. "A Preface to Transgression" (1963). In Foucault, *Language, Counter-Memory, Practice: Selected Essays and Interviews*, edited by D. F. Bouchard, translated by D. F. Bouchard and S. Simon, 29–52. Ithaca, NY: Cornell University Press, 1977.

———. "On the Ways of Writing History" (1967). In Foucault, *Aesthetics, Method, and Epistemology*, 279–95.

———. "Nietzsche, Genealogy, History" (1971). In Foucault, *Aesthetics, Method, and Epistemology*, 369–91.

———. "The Order of Discourse" (1971). In *Archives of Infamy: Foucault on State*

Power in the Lives of Ordinary Citizens, edited by N. Luxon, translated by T. Scott-Railton, 141–73. Minneapolis: University of Minnesota Press, 2019.

——. "My Body, This Paper, This Fire" (1972). In Foucault, *History of Madness,* 550–74.

——. "Reply to Derrida" (1972). In Foucault, *History of Madness,* 575–90.

——. "La vérité et les formes juridiques" (1973). In Foucault, *Dits et écrits I,* 1406–1514.

——. "Truth and Juridical Forms" (1973). In Foucault, *Power,* 1–89.

——. "Le discours ne doit pas être pris comme . . ." (1976). In Foucault, *Dits et écrits II,* 123–24.

——. "The Political Function of the Intellectual" (1976). Translated by C. Gordon. *Radical Philosophy* 17 (1977): 12–14.

——. "La torture, c'est la raison" (1977). In Foucault, *Dits et écrits II,* 390–98.

——. "The Lives of Infamous Men" (1977). Translated by P. Foss and M. Morris. In *Power, Truth, Strategy,* edited by M. Morris and P. Patton, 76–91. Sydney: Feral Publications, 1979.

——. "Truth and Power" (1977). In Foucault, *Power,* 111–33.

——. "The Analytic Philosophy of Politics" (1978). Translated by G. Mascaretti. *Foucault Studies* 24 (2018): 188–200.

——. *The History of Sexuality,* vol. 1, *An Introduction.* Translated by R. Hurley. New York: Pantheon Books, 1978. Originally published as *Histoire de la sexualité I: La volonté de savoir,* 1976.

——. "Foucault étudie la raison d'État" (1979). In Foucault, *Dits et écrits II,* 801–5.

——. "Un plaisir si simple" (1979). In Foucault, *Dits et écrits II,* 777–79.

——. "Introduction." In *Herculine Barbin: Being the Recently Discovered Memoirs of a Nineteenth-Century French Hermaphrodite,* translated by R. McDougall, vii–xvii. New York: Vintage Books, 1980.

——. "Questions of Method [Round Table of 20 May 1978]" (1980). In Foucault, *Power,* 223–38.

——. "Conversation avec Werner Schroeter" (1982). In Foucault, *Dits et écrits II,* 1070–79.

——. "*Parrēsia*: Lecture at the University of Grenoble (May 18, 1982)." Translated by G. Burchell. In Foucault, *Discourse and Truth,* 1–38.

——. "Space, Knowledge, and Power" (1982). In Foucault, *Power,* 349–64.

——. "The Subject and Power" (1982). In Foucault, *Power,* 326–48.

——. "On the Genealogy of Ethics: An Overview of Work in Progress" (1983). In Foucault, *Ethics,* 253–80.

——. "Structuralism and Post-Structuralism" (1983). In Foucault, *Aesthetics, Method, and Epistemology,* 433–58.

——. "À propos de la généalogie de l'éthique: Un aperçu du travail en cours" (1984). In Foucault, *Dits et écrits II,* 1428–50.

——. "The Ethics of the Concern for Self as a Practice of Freedom" (1984). In Foucault, *Ethics,* 281–301.

——. "Foucault" (1984). In Foucault, *Aesthetics, Method, and Epistemology,* 459–63.

——. "Polemics, Politics, and Problematizations: An Interview with Michel Foucault" (1984). In Foucault, *Ethics,* 111–19.

———. "Politics and Ethics: An Interview." Translated by C. Porter. In *The Foucault Reader*, edited by P. Rabinow, 373–80. New York: Pantheon Books, 1984.

———. "What Is Enlightenment?" (1984). In Foucault, *Ethics*, 303–19.

———. *The History of Sexuality*, vol. 2, *The Use of Pleasure*. Translated by R. Hurley. New York: Vintage Books, 1985. Originally published as *Histoire de la sexualité* II: *L'usage des plaisirs*, 1984.

———. *The History of Sexuality*, vol. 3, *The Care of the Self*. Translated by R. Hurley. New York: Pantheon Books, 1986. Originally published as *Histoire de la sexualité* III: *Le souci de soi*, 1984.

———. *The Order of Things: An Archaeology of the Human Sciences*. New York: Routledge, 1989. Originally published as *Les mots et les choses: Une archéologie des sciences humaines*, 1966.

———. *Remarks on Marx: Conversations with Duccio Trombadori*. Translated by R. J. Goldstein and J. Cascaito. New York: Semiotext(e), 1991. Originally published as *Conversazione con Michel Foucault*, 1980.

———. *Discipline and Punish: The Birth of the Prison*. Translated by A. Sheridan. New York: Vintage Books, 1995. Originally published as *Surveiller et punir: Naissance de la prison*, 1975.

———. *Ethics: Subjectivity and Truth*. Vol. 1 of *Essential Works of Foucault (1954–84)*. Edited by P. Rabinow. Translated by R. Hurley et al. Series edited by P. Rabinow. New York: New Press, 1997.

———. *Aesthetics, Method, and Epistemology*. Vol. 2 of *Essential Works of Foucault (1954–84)*. Edited by J. D. Faubion. Translated by R. Hurley et al. Series edited by P. Rabinow. New York: New Press, 1998.

———. *Power*. Vol. 3 of *Essential Works of Foucault (1954–84)*. Edited by J. D. Faubion. Translated by R. Hurley et al. Series edited by P. Rabinow. New York: New Press, 2000.

———. *Dits et écrits I, 1954–75*. Edited by D. Defert and F. Ewald. Paris: Gallimard, 2001.

———. *Dits et écrits II, 1976–88*. Edited by D. Defert and F. Ewald. Paris: Gallimard, 2001.

———. *The Archaeology of Knowledge*. Translated by A. M. Sheridan Smith. New York: Routledge, 2002. Originally published in 1969.

———. *Abnormal: Lectures at the Collège de France, 1974–75*. Edited by V. Marchetti and A. Salomoni. Translated by G. Burchell. Series edited by A. I. Davidson. London: Verso, 2003. Originally presented orally as *Les anormaux*, 1975.

———. *"Society Must Be Defended": Lectures at the Collège de France, 1975–76*. Edited by M. Bertani and A. Fontana. Translated by D. Macey. Series edited by A. I. Davidson. New York: Picador, 2003. Originally presented orally as *"Il faut défendre la société,"* 1976.

———. *The Hermeneutics of the Subject: Lectures at the Collège de France, 1981–82*. Edited by F. Gros. Translated by G. Burchell. Series edited by A. I. Davidson. Basingstoke: Palgrave Macmillan, 2005. Originally presented orally as *L'herméneutique du sujet*, 1982.

———. *History of Madness*. Translated by J. Murphy and J. Khalfa. New York: Routledge, 2006. Originally published as *Histoire de la folie à l'âge classique*, 1972 (2nd ed.).

———. *Psychiatric Power: Lectures at the Collège de France, 1973–74*. Edited by J. Lagrange. Translated by G. Burchell. Series edited by A. I. Davidson. Basingstoke: Palgrave Macmillan, 2006. Originally presented orally as *Le pouvoir psychiatrique*, 1973–74.

———. "What Is Critique?" In *The Politics of Truth*, edited by S. Lotringer, translated by L. Hochroth, 41–81. Los Angeles: Semiotext(e), 2007. Originally presented orally as *Qu'est-ce que la critique?*, 1978.

———. *The Birth of Biopolitics: Lectures at the Collège de France, 1978–79.* Edited by M. Senellart. Translated by G. Burchell. Series edited by A. I. Davidson. Basingstoke: Palgrave Macmillan, 2008. Originally presented orally as *Naissance de la biopolitique*, 1979.

———. *Security, Territory, Population: Lectures at the Collège de France, 1977–78.* Edited by M. Senellart. Translated by G. Burchell. Series edited by A. I. Davidson. Basingstoke: Palgrave Macmillan, 2009. Originally presented orally as *Sécurité, territoire, population*, 1978.

———. *The Government of Self and Others: Lectures at the Collège de France, 1982–83.* Edited by F. Gros. Translated by G. Burchell. Series edited by A. I. Davidson. Basingstoke: Palgrave Macmillan, 2010. Originally presented orally as *Le gouvernement de soi et des autres*, 1983.

———. *The Courage of Truth: Lectures at the Collège de France, 1983–84.* Edited by F. Gros. Translated by G. Burchell. Series edited by A. I. Davidson. Basingstoke: Palgrave Macmillan, 2011. Originally presented orally as *Le courage de la vérité*, 1984.

———. *Lectures on the Will to Know: Lectures at the Collège de France, 1970–71.* Edited by D. Defert. Translated by G. Burchell. Series edited by A. I. Davidson. Basingstoke: Palgrave Macmillan, 2013. Originally presented orally as *La volonté de savoir*, 1970–71.

———. *On the Government of the Living: Lectures at the Collège de France, 1979–80.* Edited by M. Senellart. Translated by G. Burchell. Series edited by A. I. Davidson. Basingstoke: Palgrave Macmillan, 2014. Originally presented orally as *Du gouvernement des vivants*, 1980.

———. *Wrong-Doing, Truth-Telling: The Function of Avowal in Justice.* Edited by F. Brion and B. E. Harcourt. Translated by S. W. Sawyer. Chicago: University of Chicago Press, 2014. Originally presented orally as *Mal faire, dire vrai: Fonction de l'aveu en justice*, 1981.

———. *About the Beginning of the Hermeneutics of the Self: Lectures at Dartmouth College, 1980.* Edited by H.-P. Fruchaud and D. Lorenzini. Chicago: University of Chicago Press, 2015. Originally presented orally in 1980.

———. "Débat au Département de Français de l'Université de Californie à Berkeley." In *Qu'est-ce que la critique?* suivi de *La culture de soi*, edited by H.-P. Fruchaud and D. Lorenzini, 153–87. Paris: Vrin, 2015. Originally presented orally in 1983.

———. *The Punitive Society: Lectures at the Collège de France, 1972–73.* Edited by B. E. Harcourt. Translated by G. Burchell. Series edited by A. I. Davidson. Basingstoke: Palgrave Macmillan, 2015. Originally presented orally as *La société punitive*, 1973.

———. *Subjectivity and Truth: Lectures at the Collège de France, 1980–81.* Edited by F. Gros. Translated by G. Burchell. Series edited by A. I. Davidson. Basingstoke:

Palgrave Macmillan, 2017. Originally presented orally as *Subjectivité et vérité*, 1981.

———. *La sexualité: Cours donné à l'université de Clermont-Ferrand (1964)* suivi de *Le discours de la sexualité: Cours donné à l'université de Vincennes (1969)*. Edited by C.-O. Doron. Paris: EHESS-Gallimard-Seuil, 2018. Originally presented orally in 1964 and 1969.

———. *Discourse and Truth*. Edited by H.-P. Fruchaud and D. Lorenzini. English edition by N. Luxon. Chicago: University of Chicago Press, 2019. Originally presented orally in 1983.

———. *Penal Theories and Institutions: Lectures at the Collège de France, 1971–72*. Edited by B. E. Harcourt. Translated by G. Burchell. Series edited by A. I. Davidson. Basingstoke: Palgrave Macmillan, 2019. Originally presented orally as *Théories et institutions pénales, 1971–72*.

———. "Structuralism and Literary Analysis." Translated by S. Taylor and J. Schroeder. *Critical Inquiry* 45(2) (2019): 531–44. Originally presented orally in 1967.

———. "Political Spirituality as the Will for Alterity: An Interview with the *Nouvel Observateur*." Edited and translated by S. Vaccarino Bremner. *Critical Inquiry* 47(1) (2020): 121–34. Originally presented orally in 1979.

———. *The History of Sexuality*, vol. 4, *Confessions of the Flesh*. Edited by F. Gros. Translated by R. Hurley. New York: Pantheon Books, 2021. Originally published posthumously as *Histoire de la sexualité IV: Les aveux de la chair*, 2018.

———. *Speaking the Truth about Oneself: Lectures at Victoria University, Toronto, 1982*. Edited by H.-P. Fruchaud and D. Lorenzini. English edition by D. L. Wyche. Chicago: University of Chicago Press, 2021. Originally presented orally as *The Discourse of Self-Disclosure*, 1982.

Fraser, Nancy. "Foucault on Modern Power: Empirical Insights and Normative Confusions." *Praxis International* 3 (1981): 272–87.

———. "Michel Foucault: A 'Young Conservative'?" *Ethics* 96(1) (1985): 165–84.

Fricker, Miranda. "Feminism in Epistemology: Pluralism without Postmodernism." In *The Cambridge Companion to Feminism in Philosophy*, edited by M. Fricker and J. Hornsby, 146–65. Cambridge: Cambridge University Press, 2000.

———. *Epistemic Injustice: Power and the Ethics of Knowing*. Oxford: Oxford University Press, 2007.

———. "Scepticism and the Genealogy of Knowledge: Situating Epistemology in Time." *Philosophical Papers* 37(1) (2008): 27–50.

Friedlander, Eli. *Walter Benjamin: A Philosophical Portrait*. Cambridge, MA: Harvard University Press, 2012.

Fritz, James. "Pragmatic Encroachment and Moral Encroachment." *Pacific Philosophical Quarterly* 98(S1) (2017): 643–61.

Gehrke, Pat J., et al. "Forum on Arthur Walzer's 'Parrēsia, Foucault, and the Classical Rhetorical Tradition.'" *Rhetoric Society Quarterly* 43(4) (2013): 355–81.

Geuss, Raymond. "Nietzsche and Genealogy." *European Journal of Philosophy* 2(3) (1994): 274–92.

———. "Genealogy as Critique." *European Journal of Philosophy* 10(2) (2002): 209–15.

Gillot, Pascale, and Daniele Lorenzini, eds. *Foucault/Wittgenstein: Subjectivité, politique, éthique*. Paris: CNRS Éditions, 2016.

Gordon, Colin. "The Christian Art of Being Governed." *Foucault Studies* 20 (2015): 243–65.

Goulet-Cazé, Marie-Odile. "Michel Foucault et sa vision du cynisme dans *Le courage de la vérité*." In Lorenzini, Revel, and Sforzini, *Michel Foucault*, 105–24.

Gros, Frédéric. "Verità, soggettività, filosofia nell'ultimo Foucault." In *Foucault, oggi*, edited by M. Galzigna, 293–302. Milan: Feltrinelli, 2008.

———. "Vérités et contre-vérités." *Revue Internationale de Philosophie* 292 (2020): 9–15.

Gros, Frédéric, and Arnold I. Davidson, eds. *Foucault, Wittgenstein: De possibles rencontres*. Paris: Kimé, 2011.

Guay, Robert. "Genealogy as Immanent Critique: Working from the Inside." In *The Edinburgh Critical History of Nineteenth-Century Philosophy*, edited by A. Stone, 168–86. Edinburgh: Edinburgh University Press, 2011.

Gutting, Gary. *Michel Foucault's Archaeology of Scientific Reason*. Cambridge: Cambridge University Press, 1989.

Habermas, Jürgen. "Modernity versus Postmodernity." Translated by S. Benhabib. *New German Critique* 22 (1981): 3–14.

———. *The Theory of Communicative Action*. Vol. 1, *Reason and the Rationalization to Society*. Translated by T. McCarthy. Boston: Beacon Press, 1984. Originally published in 1981.

———. "Taking Aim at the Heart of the Present." In Hoy, *Foucault*, 103–8.

———. *The Philosophical Discourse of Modernity: Twelve Lectures*. Translated by F. Lawrence. Cambridge: Polity Press, 1990. Originally published in 1985.

Hadot, Pierre. "Spiritual Exercises" (1977). In *Philosophy as a Way of Life: Spiritual Exercises from Socrates to Foucault*, edited by A. I. Davidson, translated by M. Chase, 81–125. Oxford: Blackwell, 1995.

———. *Wittgenstein et les limites du langage*. Paris: Vrin, 2004.

Han-Pile, Béatrice. "Foucault, Normativity, and Critique as a Practice of the Self." *Continental Philosophy Review* 49(1) (2016): 85–101.

Harcourt, Bernard E. "Introducing *On the Government of the Living*." *Foucault 13/13*, 2016. http://blogs.law.columbia.edu/foucault1313/2016/02/07/introducing-on-the-government-of-the-living/.

———. *Critique and Praxis: A Radical Critical Philosophy of Illusions, Values, and Action*. New York: Columbia University Press, 2020.

Honneth, Axel. *The Critique of Power: Reflective Stages in a Critical Social Theory*. Translated by K. Baynes. Cambridge, MA: MIT Press, 1991. Originally published in 1985.

———. "Reconstructive Social Critique with a Genealogical Reservation: On the Idea of Critique in the Frankfurt School." *Graduate Faculty Philosophy Journal* 22(2) (2001): 3–12.

Hornsby, Jennifer. "Illocution and Its Significance." In *Foundations of Speech Act Theory: Philosophical and Linguistic Perspectives*, edited by S. L. Tsohatzidis, 187–207. New York: Routledge, 1994.

Horwich, Paul. *Truth*. Oxford: Oxford University Press, 1998.

Hoy, David Couzens, ed. *Foucault: A Critical Reader*. Malden, MA: Blackwell, 1986.

———. "Genealogy, Phenomenology, Critical Theory." *Journal of the Philosophy of History* 2(3) (2008): 276–94.

Irrera, Orazio. "Foucault e la questione dell'ideologia." *materiali foucaultiani* 7–8 (2015): 149–72.

———. "Foucault and the Refusal of Ideology." In *Foucault and the Making of Subjects*, edited by L. Cremonesi et al., 111–27. London: Rowman & Littlefield, 2016.

Irrera, Orazio, and Pierre Macherey. "Michel Foucault et les critiques de l'idéologie." *Methodos: Savoirs et textes* 16 (2016). https://doi.org/10.4000/methodos .4667.

Jaeggi, Rahel. 2009. "Rethinking Ideology." In *New Waves in Political Philosophy*, edited by B. de Bruin and C. F. Zurn, 63–86. Basingstoke: Palgrave Macmillan, 2009.

Janaway, Christopher. *Beyond Selflessness: Reading Nietzsche's "Genealogy."* Oxford: Oxford University Press, 2007.

Jankélévitch, Vladimir. *Traité des vertus* II: *Les vertus et l'amour*, vol. 1. Paris: Flammarion, 1986.

Jenkins, Mark P. *Bernard Williams*. New York: Routledge, 2014.

Jordan, Mark D. *Convulsing Bodies: Religion and Resistance in Foucault*. Stanford, CA: Stanford University Press, 2014.

Kaufmann, David. "A Plea for Perlocutions." *Conversations: The Journal of Cavellian Studies* 4 (2016): 43–60.

Kelly, Mark G. E. "Michel Foucault: Political Thought." *Internet Encyclopedia of Philosophy*, 2013. https://www.iep.utm.edu/fouc-pol/.

———. *For Foucault: Against Normative Political Theory*. New York: SUNY Press, 2018.

Kelly, Michael, ed. *Critique and Power: Recasting the Foucault/Habermas Debate*. Cambridge, MA: MIT Press, 1994.

———. "Foucault, Habermas, and the Self-Referentiality of Critique." In Kelly, *Critique and Power*, 365–400.

Kennedy, Kristen. "Cynic Rhetoric: The Ethics and Tactics of Resistance." *Rhetoric Review* 18(1) (1999): 26–45.

King, Matthew. "Clarifying the Foucault-Habermas Debate: Morality, Ethics, and 'Normative Foundations.'" *Philosophy & Social Criticism* 35(3) (2009): 287–314.

Kitcher, Philip. *Science, Truth, and Democracy*. Oxford: Oxford University Press, 2001.

Koopman, Colin. "Genealogical Pragmatism: How History Matters for Foucault and Dewey." *Journal of the Philosophy of History* 5(3) (2011): 533–61.

———. *Genealogy as Critique: Foucault and the Problems of Modernity*. Bloomington: Indiana University Press, 2013.

———. "Two Uses of Michel Foucault in Political Theory: Concepts and Methods in Giorgio Agamben and Ian Hacking." *Constellations* 22(4) (2015): 571–85.

———. "Conceptual Analysis for Genealogical Philosophy: How to Study the History of Practices after Foucault and Wittgenstein." *Southern Journal of Philosophy* 55(S1) (2017): 103–21.

———. "Critique without Judgment in Political Theory: Politicization in Foucault's Historical Genealogy of Herculine Barbin." *Contemporary Political Theory* 18(4) (2018): 477–97.

———. "Critique in Truth: Bernard Harcourt's *Critique & Practice*." *Foucault Studies* 30 (2021): 106–12.

Kusch, Martin, and Robin McKenna. "The Genealogical Method in Epistemology." *Synthese* 197(3) (2020): 1057–76.

Landry, Jean-Michel. "Confession, Obedience, and Subjectivity: Michel Foucault's Unpublished Lectures *On the Government of the Living*." *Telos* 146 (2009): 111–23.

Laugier, Sandra. *Wittgenstein: Les sens de l'usage*. Paris: Vrin, 2009.

———. "Stanley Cavell: Les voix du langage ordinaire." In *Lectures de Wittgenstein*, edited by C. Chauviré and S. Plaud, 375–412. Paris: Ellipses, 2012.

Laugier, Sandra, and Daniele Lorenzini, eds. *Perlocutoire: Normativités et performativités du langage ordinaire*. Paris: Mare & Martin, 2021.

———, eds. "The Perlocutionary and the Illocutionary." Special issue, *Inquiry: An Interdisciplinary Journal of Philosophy*. Forthcoming.

Legg, Stephen. "Subjects of Truth: Resisting Governmentality in Foucault's 1980s." *Environment and Planning D: Society and Space* 37(1) (2019): 27–45.

Lhomme, Alain. "Les métamorphoses d'une vertu." In *La sincérité: L'insolence du cœur*, edited by C. Baron and C. Doroszczuk, 18–42. Paris: Autrement, 1995.

Lorenzini, Daniele. "'El cinismo hace de la vida una *alethurgie*': Apuntes para una relectura del recorrido filosófico del último Michel Foucault." *Laguna: Revista de Filosofía* 23 (2008): 63–90.

———. "Must We Do What We Say? Truth, Responsibility, and the Ordinary in Ancient and Modern Perfectionism." *European Journal of Pragmatism and American Philosophy* 2 (2010): 16–34.

———. "Para acabar con la verdad-demostración: Bachelard, Canguilhem, Foucault y la historia de los 'regímenes de verdad.'" *Laguna: Revista de Filosofía* 26 (2010): 9–34.

———. "Éthique et politique de nous-mêmes: À partir de Michel Foucault et Stanley Cavell." In Lorenzini, Revel, and Sforzini, *Michel Foucault*, 239–54.

———. "Genealogia della verità e politica di noi stessi." In *Foucault e le genealogie del dir-vero*, edited by L. Cremonesi et al., 145–62. Naples: Cronopio, 2014.

———. *Éthique et politique de soi: Foucault, Hadot, Cavell et les techniques de l'ordinaire*. Paris: Vrin, 2015.

———. "Performative, Passionate, and Parrhesiastic Utterance: On Cavell, Foucault, and Truth as an Ethical Force." *Critical Inquiry* 41(2) (2015): 254–68.

———. "What Is a 'Regime of Truth'?" *Le Foucaldien* 1(1) (2015). http://doi.org/10.16995/lefou.2.

———. "Foucault, Regimes of Truth, and the Making of the Subject." In *Foucault and the Making of Subjects*, edited by L. Cremonesi et al., 63–75. London: Rowman & Littlefield, 2016.

———. "From Counter-Conduct to Critical Attitude: Michel Foucault and the Art of Not Being Governed Quite So Much." *Foucault Studies* 21 (2016): 7–21.

———. "Benjamin/Foucault: Histoire, discontinuité, événement." *Phantasia* 7 (2018). https://popups.uliege.be/0774-7136/index.php?id=903.

———. "The Emergence of Desire: Notes toward a Political History of the Will." *Critical Inquiry* 45(2) (2019): 448–70.

———. "Alèthurgie oculaire et littérature de témoignage: De Sophocle à Soljenitsyne." *Revue Internationale de Philosophie* 292 (2020): 17–28.

———. "Anarcheology and the Emergence of the Alethurgic Subject in Foucault's *On the Government of the Living*." *Foucault Studies* ("Foucault Lectures" series) 3(1) (2020): 53–70.

———. "From Recognition to Acknowledgment: Rethinking the Perlocutionary." *Inquiry: An Interdisciplinary Journal of Philosophy*, 2020. https://doi.org/10.1080 /0020174X.2020.1712231.

———. "Philosophical Discourse and Ascetic Practice: On Foucault's Readings of Descartes' *Meditations.*" *Theory, Culture & Society*, 2021. https://doi.org/10.1177 %2F0263276420980510.

———. "Reason versus Power: Genealogy, Critique, and Epistemic Injustice." *The Monist* 105(4) (2022): 541–57.

Lorenzini, Daniele, Ariane Revel, and Arianna Sforzini, eds. *Michel Foucault: Éthique et vérité (1980–1984)*. Paris: Vrin, 2013.

Lorenzini, Daniele, and Martina Tazzioli. "Confessional Subjects and Conducts of Non-Truth: Foucault, Fanon, and the Making of the Subject." *Theory, Culture & Society* 35(1) (2018): 71–90.

———. "Critique without Ontology: Genealogy, Collective Subjects, and the Deadlocks of Evidence." *Radical Philosophy* 207 (2020): 27–39.

Löwy, Michael. 2018. *Walter Benjamin, avertissement d'incendie: Une lecture des thèses "Sur le concept d'histoire."* Paris: Éditions de l'éclat, 2018. Originally published in 2001.

Luxon, Nancy. "Truthfulness, Risk, and Trust in the Late Lectures of Michel Foucault." *Inquiry: An Interdisciplinary Journal of Philosophy* 47(5) (2004): 464–89.

———. "Ethics and Subjectivity: Practices of Self-Governance in the Late Lectures of Michel Foucault." *Political Theory* 36(3) (2008): 377–402.

———. *Crisis of Authority: Politics, Trust, and Truth-Telling in Freud and Foucault.* Cambridge: Cambridge University Press, 2013.

———. "Authority, Interpretation, and the Space of the Parrhesiastic Encounter." *materiali foucaultiani* 5–6 (2014): 71–90.

Macherey, Pierre. *Le sujet des normes.* Paris: Éditions Amsterdam, 2014.

MacKenzie, Iain. *Resistance and the Politics of Truth: Foucault, Deleuze, Badiou.* Bielefeld: Transcript, 2018.

Mascaretti, Giovanni. "Foucault, Normativity, and Freedom: A Reappraisal." *Foucault Studies* 27 (2019): 23–47.

Maxwell, Lida. "The Politics and Gender of Truth-Telling in Foucault's Lectures on *Parrhesia.*" *Contemporary Political Theory* 18 (2019): 22–42.

May, Todd. *Between Genealogy and Epistemology: Psychology, Politics, and Knowledge in the Thought of Michel Foucault.* University Park: Penn State University Press, 1993.

McCarthy, Thomas. "The Critique of Impure Reason: Foucault and the Frankfurt School." In Kelly, *Critique and Power*, 243–82.

McGushin, Edward F. *Foucault's Askēsis: An Introduction to the Philosophical Life.* Evanston, IL: Northwestern University Press, 2007.

McIntyre, Lee. *Post-Truth.* Cambridge, MA: MIT Press, 2018.

McWhorter, Ladelle. *Bodies and Pleasures: Foucault and the Politics of Sexual Normalization.* Bloomington: Indiana University Press, 1999.

Medina, José. "Toward a Foucauldian Epistemology of Resistance: Counter-Memory, Epistemic Friction, and *Guerrilla* Pluralism." *Foucault Studies* 12 (2011): 9–35.

———. *The Epistemology of Resistance: Gender and Racial Oppression, Epistemic Injustice, and Resistant Imaginations.* Oxford: Oxford University Press, 2013.

Miller, Paul Allen. *Foucault's Seminars on Antiquity: Learning to Speak the Truth*. New York: Bloomsbury, 2021.

Moati, Raoul. *Derrida/Searle: Deconstruction and Ordinary Language*. Translated by T. Attanucci and M. Chun. New York: Columbia University Press, 2014. Originally published in 2009.

Moss, Sarah. "Moral Encroachment." *Proceedings of the Aristotelian Society* 118(2) (2018): 177–205.

Nietzsche, Friedrich. *Daybreak: Thoughts on the Prejudices of Morality*. Edited by M. Clark and B. Leiter. Translated by R. J. Hollingdale. Cambridge: Cambridge University Press, 1997. Originally published in 1881.

———. *On the Genealogy of Morality*. Edited by K. Ansell-Pearson. Translated by C. Diethe. Cambridge: Cambridge University Press, 1997. Originally published in 1887.

———. *Beyond Good and Evil*. Edited by R.-P. Horstmann and J. Norman. Translated by J. Norman. Cambridge: Cambridge University Press, 2002. Originally published in 1886.

Norval, Aletta J. "Moral Perfectionism and Democratic Responsiveness: Reading Cavell with Foucault." *Ethics & Global Politics* 4(4) (2011): 207–29.

Oksala, Johanna. *Foucault on Freedom*. Cambridge: Cambridge University Press, 2005.

———. "What Is Political Philosophy?" *materiali foucaultiani* 5–6 (2014): 91–112.

Owen, David. "Orientation and Enlightenment: An Essay on Critique and Genealogy." In Ashenden and Owen, *Foucault contra Habermas*, 21–44.

———. "Criticism and Captivity: On Genealogy and Critical Theory." *European Journal of Philosophy* 10(2) (2002): 216–30.

———. "Perfectionism, Parrhesia, and the Care of the Self: Foucault and Cavell on Ethics and Politics." In *The Claim to Community: Essays on Stanley Cavell and Political Philosophy*, edited by A. Norris, 128–55. Stanford, CA: Stanford University Press, 2006.

———. *Nietzsche's Genealogy of Morality*. Stocksfield: Acumen, 2007.

Owen, David, and Clare Woodford. "Foucault, Cavell, and the Government of Self and Others: On Truth-Telling, Friendship, and an Ethics of Democracy." *Iride: Filosofia e Discussione Pubblica* 66 (2012): 299–316.

Patton, Paul. "Foucault's Subject of Power." *Political Theory Newsletter* 6(1) (1994): 60–71.

Peters, Michael A. "Truth-Telling as an Educational Practice of the Self: Foucault, Parrhesia, and the Ethics of Subjectivity." *Oxford Review of Education* 29 (2003): 207–24.

Pinker, Steven. *Enlightenment Now: The Case for Reason, Science, Humanism, and Progress*. New York: Viking, 2018.

Plutarch. *Lives*. Vol. 6. Translated by B. Perrin. Cambridge, MA: Harvard University Press, 1961.

Porter, James I. "Living on the Edge: Self and World *in extremis* in Roman Philosophy." *Classical Antiquity* 39(2) (2020): 225–83.

Prado, Carlos G. *Starting with Foucault: An Introduction to Genealogy*. Boulder: Westview Press, 2000.

Prinz, Jesse J. *The Emotional Construction of Morals*. Oxford: Oxford University Press, 2007.

———. "History as Genealogy: Interrogating Liberalism through Philosophy's Past." Unpublished manuscript, 2018.

Prozorov, Sergei. "Why Is There Truth? Foucault in the Age of Post-Truth Politics." *Constellations* 26(1) (2019): 18–30.

Putnam, Hilary. "Literature, Science, and Reflection." *New Literary History* 7(3) (1976): 483–91.

———. *Reason, Truth, and History.* Cambridge: Cambridge University Press, 1981.

Queloz, Matthieu. *The Practical Origins of Ideas: Genealogy as Conceptual Reverse-Engineering.* Oxford: Oxford University Press, 2021.

Rabinow, Paul. *The Accompaniment: Assembling the Contemporary.* Chicago: University of Chicago Press, 2011.

Rabinow, Paul, and Anthony Stavrianakis. *Designs on the Contemporary: Anthropological Tests.* Chicago: University of Chicago Press, 2014.

Raïd, Layla. "Énoncés passionnés et performatifs selon Stanley Cavell." *Revue Internationale de Philosophie* 256 (2011): 151–65.

Reginster, Bernard. "What Is Nietzsche's Genealogical Critique of Morality?" *Inquiry: An Interdisciplinary Journal of Philosophy,* 2020. https://doi.org/10.1080/0020174X.2020.1762727.

Revel, Judith. *Foucault avec Merleau-Ponty: Ontologie politique, présentisme et histoire.* Paris: Vrin, 2015.

Rorty, Richard. *Contingency, Irony, and Solidarity.* Cambridge: Cambridge University Press, 1989.

Ross, Alison. "Why Is 'Speaking the Truth' Fearless? 'Danger' and 'Truth' in Foucault's Discussion of *Parrhesia.*" *Parrhesia* 4 (2008): 62–75.

Saar, Martin. "Genealogy and Subjectivity." *European Journal of Philosophy* 10(2) (2002): 231–45.

———. *Genealogie als Kritik: Geschichte und Theorie des Subjekts nach Nietzsche und Foucault.* Frankfurt am Main: Campus, 2007.

———. "Understanding Genealogy: History, Power, and the Self." *Journal of the Philosophy of History* 2(3) (2008): 295–314.

Saxonhouse, Arlene W. *Free Speech and Democracy in Ancient Athens.* Cambridge: Cambridge University Press, 2006.

Scarpat, Giuseppe. *Parrhesia: Storia del termine e delle sue traduzioni in latino.* Brescia: Paideia, 1964.

Schmidt, James. "Foucault, Habermas, and the Debate That Never Was." *Persistent Enlightenment,* 2013. https://persistentenlightenment.com/2013/07/17/debate1/.

Schmidt, James, and Thomas E. Wartenberg. "Foucault's Enlightenment: Critique, Revolution, and the Fashioning of the Self." In Kelly, *Critique and Power,* 283–314.

Scott, Joan Wallach. *On the Judgment of History.* New York: Columbia University Press, 2020.

Searle, John R. "Austin on Locutionary and Illocutionary Acts." *Philosophical Review* 77(4) (1968): 405–24.

Seneca. *Epistles.* Vol. 2. Translated by R. M. Gummere. Cambridge, MA: Harvard University Press, 1989.

Sharpe, Matthew. "A Question of Two Truths? Remarks on *Parrhesia* and the 'Political-Philosophical' Difference." *Parrhesia* 2 (2007): 89–108.

Sheehey, Bonnie. "Reparative Critique, Care, and the Normativity of Foucauldian Genealogy." *Angelaki: Journal of Theoretical Humanities* 25(5) (2020): 67–82.

Shelby, Tommie. "Ideology, Racism, and Critical Social Theory." *The Philosophical Forum* 34(2) (2003): 153–88.

Simpson, Zachary. "The Truths We Tell Ourselves: Foucault on *Parrhesia*." *Foucault Studies* 13 (2012): 99–115.

Sluiter, Ineke, and Ralph M. Rosen. "General Introduction." In *Free Speech in Classical Antiquity*, edited by I. Sluiter and R. M. Rosen, 1–19. Leiden and Boston: Brill, 2004.

Spinoza, Baruch. *The Correspondence of Spinoza*. New York: Lincoln MacVeagh / The Dial Press, 1928.

Srinivasan, Amia. "Genealogy, Epistemology, and Worldmaking." *Proceedings of the Aristotelian Society* 119(2) (2019): 127–56.

Stoler, Ann Laura. *Race and the Education of Desire: Foucault's "History of Sexuality" and the Colonial Order of Things*. Durham, NC: Duke University Press, 1996.

Strawson, Peter Frederick. "Intention and Convention in Speech Acts." *Philosophical Review* 73(4) (1964): 439–60.

Tagliapietra, Andrea. *La virtù crudele: Filosofia e storia della sincerità*. Turin: Einaudi, 2003.

Taylor, Charles. "Foucault on Freedom and Truth." *Political Theory* 12(2) (1984): 152–83.

———. *The Ethics of Authenticity*. Cambridge, MA: Harvard University Press, 1991.

Taylor, Chloë. *The Culture of Confession from Augustine to Foucault: A Genealogy of the "Confessing Animal."* New York: Routledge, 2009.

Taylor, Dianna. *Sexual Violence and Humiliation: A Foucauldian-Feminist Perspective*. New York: Routledge, 2020.

Thompson, Kevin, and Perry Zurn, eds. *Intolerable: Writings from Michel Foucault and the Prisons Information Group (1970–80)*. Translated by P. Zurn and E. Beranek. Minneapolis: University of Minnesota Press, 2021.

Tiisala, Tuomo. "Overcoming 'the Present Limits of the Necessary': Foucault's Conception of a Critique." *Southern Journal of Philosophy* 55 (2017): 7–24.

Trilling, Lionel. *Sincerity and Authenticity*. Cambridge, MA: Harvard University Press, 1972.

Tully, James H. "To Think and Act Differently: Foucault's Four Reciprocal Objections to Habermas' Theory." In Ashenden and Owen, *Foucault contra Habermas*, 90–142.

Turton, Stephen. "The Confessional Sciences: Scientific Lexicography and Sexology in the *Oxford English Dictionary*." *Language & History*, 2020. https://doi.org/10.1080/17597536.2020.1755204.

Vaccarino Bremner, Sabina. "Anthropology as Critique: Foucault, Kant, and the Metacritical Tradition." *British Journal for the History of Philosophy* 28(2) (2020): 336–58.

———. "On Moral Unintelligibility: Beauvoir's Genealogy of Morality in *The Second Sex*." *The Monist* 105(4) (2022): 521–40.

Visker, Rudi. *Michel Foucault: Genealogy as Critique*. Translated by C. Turner. London: Verso, 1995. Originally published in 1991.

Vogelmann, Frieder. "Lonely and Beyond Truth? Two Objections to Bernard Harcourt's *Critique & Praxis*." *British Journal of Sociology* 72(3) (2021): 852–59.

Walzer, Arthur E. "*Parrēsia*, Foucault, and the Classical Rhetorical Tradition." *Rhetoric Society Quarterly* 43(1) (2013): 1–21.

Westacott, Emrys. "Cognitive Relativism." *Internet Encyclopedia of Philosophy*, 2006. https://www.iep.utm.edu/cog-rel/.

Williams, Bernard. *Truth and Truthfulness: An Essay in Genealogy*. Princeton, NJ: Princeton University Press, 2002.

Wittgenstein, Ludwig. *On Certainty*. Edited by G. E. M. Anscombe and G. H. von Wright. Translated by D. Paul and G. E. M. Anscombe. Oxford: Basil Blackwell, 1969.

———. *Tractatus Logico-Philosophicus*. Translated by D. F. Pears and B. F. McGuinness. New York: Routledge, 2001. Originally published in 1921.

———. *Philosophical Investigations*. Edited by P. M. S. Hacker and J. Schulte. Translated by G. E. M. Anscombe, P. M. S. Hacker, and J. Schulte. Oxford: Wiley-Blackwell, 2009. Originally published posthumously in 1953.

Wylie, Kevan, et al. "Good Practice Guidelines for the Assessment and Treatment of Adults with Gender Dysphoria." *Sexual and Relationship Therapy* 29(2) (2014): 154–214.

Zerilli, Linda M. G. "Fact-Checking and Truth-Telling in an Age of Alternative Facts." *Le Foucaldien* 6(1) (2020). http://doi.org/10.16995/lefou.68.

Zurn, Perry, and Andrew Dilts, eds. *Active Intolerance: Michel Foucault, the Prisons Information Group, and the Future of Abolition*. Basingstoke: Palgrave Macmillan, 2016.

Index

truth: -demonstration, 8, 15, 18–21, 23–25, 31, 34, 41, 53, 70–71, 81–82, 102, 137n21; -event, 8, 16, 18–23, 25, 30–31, 53, 71, 87, 137n18, 137n21; as force, 53, 55, 59, 85, 88–89; history of, 2–10, 14–21, 23–25, 27, 29–31, 39, 41, 43, 49, 52–53, 61, 71, 78, 81–82, 101, 103, 106, 111–12, 115–22, 124, 129n2, 133nn42–43, 134n54, 136n4; manifestation of, 4, 15, 23–25, 27–29, 31, 33–36, 42–44, 53, 81–82, 86–89, 91–92, 94–95, 97, 100, 121, 139n47, 140n55, 143n20; theory of, 3, 7–8, 134n54; value of, 5–6, 14, 35, 49, 119–20, 121–22, 124, 131n30, 147n86; will to, 5, 37, 120–21, 123, 143n24. *See also* alethurgy; force: of truth; game of truth; politics: of truth; regime of truth
truthfulness, 58–59, 78, 90–91, 104, 116, 132n40, 139n47, 159n50, 159n53
truth-telling: as critique, 9, 53, 55, 60, 92–94, 96, 110, 120, 123; ethics and politics of, 8–10, 14, 94, 119–20, 123–24; ethnology of, 92; about oneself,

30, 92, 161n70. *See also parrhesia*; veridiction

unpredictability, 65, 89, 97, 123
utterance: parrhesiastic, 10, 53, 55, 59–60, 64–71, 73–74, 77, 80–84, 86–90, 92–94, 97, 99, 123; passionate, 9, 12, 55–57, 59, 64–68, 73, 84, 88, 94, 98, 123, 158n35; performative, 9, 11–12, 14, 55, 58–59, 63–67, 83, 85, 123, 150n26, 152nn60–61

Verginelli Galantin, Daniel, 158n30
veridiction, 6, 51, 71, 94, 102, 140n52, 148n99. *See also* truth-telling
Vogelmann, Frieder, 172n3

Walzer, Arthur E., 74–75, 154n106
we-making, 105, 115, 120, 124, 171n79
Williams, Bernard, 2–3, 7, 130n12, 132n38, 164n6, 172n5
Wittgenstein, Ludwig, 1, 8, 46–49, 88, 144n29, 146nn63–64, 146n69, 146n73, 147n78, 151n46, 153n72